I0111488

CONSOLAMINI COMMENTARY SERIES:

THE *GLOSSA ORDINARIA* ON REVELATION

THE *GLOSSA ORDINARIA* ON REVELATION

Translated by: Sarah Van Der Pas

Introduction by John Litteral

Consolamini Publications

© 2015 Consolamini Publications, West Monroe, La.

Contents

Abbreviations

Latin 588   *Bibliothèque nationale de France, Département des manuscrits, Latin 588*

Codex 24   *Langkatalogisat: Köln, Dombibliothek, Codex 24*

Rusch   *Strasbourg, Adolf Rusch pro Antonio Koberger, 1480/1481*

ACKNOWLEGEMENTS

I want to thank Sarah Van Der Pas, who translated this work into English after countless hours meticulously sorting through the Gloss manuscripts and facsimile. I also want to thank Guy Lobrichon for taking the time to answer questions and providing me with very helpful information concerning the Gloss on Revelation. I also want to thank Lee James Williams and Francis "Frank" Gumerlock for very kindly taking the time to provide me with information and suggestions.

INTRODUCTION

(By John LItteral)

The Glossa Ordinaria is a glossed Bible that took form in the twelfth century, starting perhaps late eleventh century, originating in Laon. "It contained," as stated by Lesley Smith,[1] "a digest of the opinions of all the important patristic commentators, as well as some selected 'moderns' on any given text, and apparently functioned as a reference work for teachers and students of biblical commentary." In many ways the Glossa Ordinaria shares similarities to a modern study Bible that provides the Scripture text with explanatory footnotes to assist and help a reader to understand the meaning of passages of Scripture that are doctrinally important and/or have a deeper level of meaning. Whereas study Bibles today usually follow and focus on a particular pattern of systematic exegesis, the Glossa Ordinaria often provides interpretations that vary in senses and meaning, and was, as Frans van Liere said, "not a very systematic or planned process."[2] It's not uncommon to find glosses for a passage of Scripture in which the glossator provides seemingly contradictory interpretations.

The Glossa Ordinaria manuscripts (in many cases) provide the Scripture text in the middle column of the page while providing glosses around the Scripture text, most commonly on the left and right-side margins, and concise glosses between the lines of the Scripture text above specific words and phrases in Scripture. The glosses in between the lines of Scripture (*interlinear glosses*) can provide anything from short explanations, paraphrases, to single words, which act as assisting comments. The glosses in the margins (*marginal glosses*) provide comments on the Scripture passages that provide lengthy explanations and can consist of a paragraph or more. Below is an example of how the Scripture text, marginal and interlinear glosses of Gloss manuscripts is typically arraigned.

MARGINAL GLOSS	SCRIPTURE TEXT AND INTERLINEAR GLOSS	MARGINAL GLOSS
Praeparat auditores benivolos et attentos, sicut ibi, iohannes septem ecclesiis quae sunt in asia.	*id est revelatio* *a patre data christo, secundum humanitatem.* **Apocalypsis Iesu Christi, quam dedit** *ut nihil debens ad propalandam.* *verbo et exemplo, non iudaeis non philosophis.* **illi Deus palam facere servis suis,**	Littera sic ac si ita commoneret, Attendite hanc visionem, quia visio revelata est in christo iesu Materia status asiae, et totius praesentis ecclesiae Qualitas tribulationes, intus et exterius, e contrario consolationes. Locus brevis labor, certa praemia. Intentio, patienter omnia ferre.
Deus filio suo, filius iohanni, sub sigillo, ne locus sit furibus pervertendi, et gratius sit fidelibus si cum exercitio, id est studio consequentur, sicut per signa ostendit.	*de his.* *inevitabile vel utile, ut patiantur tribulationes* *Brevis labor, festinata gloria.* **quae oportet fieri cito et** *id est per signa ostendit.* *scilicet personam christi habentem.* **significavit, mittens per angelum suum** *humili non superbo* **servo suo Ioanni,**	

Ann Matter says,[3] "The relationship of the marginal and interlinear glosses to one another seem to differ from book to book, and needs to be considered separately in the case of each book of the Bible." In the Gloss manuscripts it is not uncommon to see manuscripts with some interlinear glosses swapped with marginal glosses and vice-versa, while each manuscript usually has its own select exchanges of glosses and various arrangements. For a good example in this translation, see the interlinear glosses (i), (j), (k), (l) for Rev. 9:17, in which those interlinear glosses are found in Latin 588, but Codex 24 and Rusch have all these interlinear glosses in the form of one marginal gloss.

Anselm, the master of the school of Laon, was the author of some of the glossed books. Lesley Smith says,[4] "*Anselm's* death left the work of the Gloss barely begun, by the mid-twelfth century the Gloss covered much of the Bible... Although the book of Revelation was one of the earliest to appear, its textual history has been shown by *Guy* Lobrichon[5] to be particularly convoluted, and it may be that there was never a single agreed Revelation Gloss.... Lobrichon, the scholar most familiar with the Gloss on Revelation, thinks that it is attributed, if not to Anselm, then to his close circle." According to Lobrichon (personal communication Jun. 9, 2015) "there were five stages between c. 1090 and c. 1220, maybe more." And:

"in the case of Revelation: after the gloss and side-commentary of Anselm, which fixed for centuries the new principles of orthodox interpretation, several glosses appeared here and there. But their authors shrank back in front of Anselm's great plans: they kept the new structure imposed by him, but discarded his reformist audacities, such as his criticism of feodo-vassalic society, and substituted excerpts from another commentator for those of the master of Laon. And as early as the middle of the 12th century, another generation of glosses on Revelation spread; it still reproduced the Anselmian structure, but transmitted a deeply reworked corpus of interpretation. It is upon this new dress that within half a century and more others were to slowly polish the Gloss on Revelation, all the way to the final and "ordinary" text."[6]

That being said, it seems apparent that the stages of the Gloss on Revelation varied according to the sources the translator and I used. The oldest manuscript we used was *Bibliothèque nationale de France, Département des manuscrits, Latin 588*, which is a mid-12th century copy written in Southern France, and was, according to Lobrichon (personal communication Jun. 9, 2015) was stage four of at least five stages of the Gloss on Revelation; it varied significantly with the 13th century manuscript we used, *Langkatalogisat: Köln, Dombibliothek, Codex 24*. We also chose to use the facsimile *Strasbourg: Rusch, 1400/81*. Codex 24 shares many of the same readings with Rusch, yet Rusch has more total glosses, while Latin 588 has many glosses that vary or were not found in either Codex 24 or Rusch. Here is a comparison between all 3 witnesses…

> **Latin 588** has 370 interlinear glosses and 42 marginal glosses that are unique to itself, and shares only 54 glosses with Rusch that are not found in Codex 24, and only shares 24 glosses with Codex 24 that are not found in Rusch.

> **Codex 24** has 30 interlinear glosses and 5 marginal glosses that are unique to itself, but Rusch and Codex 24 share 259 glosses that differ from Latin 588.

> **Rusch** has 263 interlinear glosses and 17 marginal glosses that are unique to itself.

At this point in time there is neither a critical edition nor a collection of attributions of the sources to the glosses for the Gloss on Revelation. The sources of the glosses will be a challenge for a scholar to develop, and would be most helpful, since there are very little actual attributions made in the manuscripts other than a vague reference to Augustine, Gregory, and Ambrose in a gloss for Revelation chapter 4 verse 8 found in Rusch (Codex 24 only has 'Augustine' for that verse); and there are attributions to Jerome and Gilbert of Poiters (only found in Rusch). A gloss for Revelation chapter 2 verse 5 is attributed to Jerome (only in Codex 24). Otherwise there are many sources used by the glossator that provide no references to who they are attributed to. According to Guy Lobrichon (personal communication Jun. 9, 2015) "there are some glosses from the anonymous commentator published in Migne, PL 162 (not Anselmus Laudunensis). The other sources are Jerome-Victorinus, Bede, and, sometimes, Haimo of Auxerre. But there are many XIIth-century glosses...." The glossator, while compiling the glosses, rarely gave direct quotes from various sources but took the liberty of drawing from those sources by either condensing them, expanding them further with the glossator's own words, taking the ideas of a source and rewording it, or blending multiple sources into a single gloss.

The Gloss on Revelation, like various other Latin commentaries of the early Middle Ages, is divided into "seven visions". These visions indicate various chains of events concerning the state of the Church throughout its history, future tribulations, end of time, and eternal glory. Prior to the first vision (Rev. 1:1-6), "John writes a prologue and a salutation, where he makes the listeners favorable and attentive."[7] "The first vision (Rev. 1:7-3:22) is about the reproof of the churches."[8] In the second vision (Rev. 4:1-8:1), "he speaks of the one sitting in the throne and his attire, of the Lamb opening the book… and of the Lamb loosing the seven seals."[9] In the third vision (Rev. 8:2-11:18), "the subject is seven angels sounding with trumpets for the destruction of the enemies."[10] In the fourth vision (Rev. 11:19-14:20), his topic is a woman well adorned, i.e. the Church having good works, who is attacked by the Devil both openly and secretly."[11] In the fifth vision (Rev. 15:1-17:18) "he dwells on the last times… the subject is seven angels holding vials in which are contained plagues, i.e. the destructions of the wicked who shall be there in the time of the Antichrist."[12] In the sixth vision (Rev. 18:1-20:15), "he treats the subject of the last punishments the wicked shall suffer in hell for every one of their sins; and he first shows what happens concerning Babylon, then concerning the beast and the false prophets, and finally concerning the Devil himself, in which the end is manifest."[13] In the seventh vision (Rev. 18:1-20:15), "he treats the subject of the renewing of the elements and of the glorification of the saints, describing the merits by which the saints have been thus glorified."[14] These same divisions found in the Gloss on Revelation concerning the seven visions are also found in the commentaries of Stephen Langton, Richard of St. Victor, Peter the Cantor, Troyes, BM (757), BnF lat. 8865, etc.

This translation is dependent on three Gloss witnesses, that being Latin 588, Codex 24, and Rusch.[15] All three of these witnesses each have glosses that the others don't. The aim was not to provide a critical Gloss text but to provide this translation with all the glosses unique to each witness. But the age of the manuscripts and the most reliable readings did play a part when deciding between 2 or 3 witnesses that share the same readings but have variant readings among them; so when there was a reading found in one witness alone, those are provided and footnotes are provided to indicate which of the three witnesses it came from. The footnotes for each gloss are often plentiful because there are many variant readings provided. Not every single minor variant is given, but the translator went above and beyond to provide an exhaustive system of variant readings. The reader is able to read the translation of the glosses as provided for the Gloss text, and is able to quickly glance below and see the variant readings for quick comparison. The translator's preface below gives a thorough description of this aspect of the work.

Finally, as for the details and layout of this translation: The Scripture text, glosses, and footnotes are all divided for each Scripture verse, with the Scripture text in bold, the interlinear glosses underneath, the marginal glosses on the right-hand side, and each set of footnotes are placed underneath each verse they represent. The translation of the Scripture text is highly dependent upon the Douay Rheims Bible of 1609[16], while adjustments were made for those places where the Vulgate readings in the Gloss differ from the Vulgate used by the Douay Rheims. Footnotes also provide the variant readings found in the Scripture texts of the Gloss witnesses. The glosses are also translated in a manner where they are standardized with the translation of the Scripture text.

---

1 Smith, Lesley, 'Medieval Exegesis in Translation: Commentaries on the Book of Ruth,' TEAMS (the Consortium for the Teaching of the Middle Ages), 1996, p. xiv.

2 Frans van Liere, 'An Introduction to the Medieval Bible,' Cambridge University Press, Mar 31, 2014 p. 155.

3 Matter, Ann, 'The Reception of the Church Fathers in the West, From the Carolingians to the Maurists; Article: The Church Fathers and the Glossa Ordinaria,' BRILL, Nov 30, 1996. p. 85

4 Smith, Lesley, 'The Glossa Ordinaria: The Making of a Medieval Bible Commentary'. BRILL, 2009. p.26, 32.

5 Lobrichon, Guy (as referenced by Lesley Smith), "Une nouveaute: les gloses de la Bible", in Le Moyen Age et la Bible, ed. P. Riche and G. Lobrichon, Bible de tous les temps 4 (Paris 1984), p. 11.

6 "le cas de l'Apocalypse : après la glose et le commentaire annexe d'Anselme, qui fixe pour des siècles les nouveaux principes de l'interprétation orthodoxe, plusieurs gloses apparaissent ici et là. Or leurs rédacteurs font retrait devant les grands desseins d'Anselme : ils conservent la nouvelle structure imposée par lui, mais écartent ses audaces réformatrices, telle sa critique de la société féodo-vassalique, substituent des extraits d'un autre commentateur à ceux du maître de Laon. Et dès le milieu du xiie siècle, se répand une autre génération de gloses de l'Apocalypse ; elle reproduit toujours la structure anselmienne, mais transmet un corps d'interprétation profondément remanié. C'est sur cet habit neuf qu'en l'espace d'un demi-siècle et plus d'autres vont polir lentement la Glose de l'Apocalypse, jusqu'au texte définitif et « ordinaire »." Lobrichon, Guy, "Une nouveaute: les gloses de la Bible", in Le Moyen Age et la Bible, ed. P. Riche and G. Lobrichon, Bible de tous les temps 4 (Paris 1984), p. 109.

7 Preface 'a' Gilbert of Poitiers, Rusch

8 First marginal gloss on Rev. 2:1

9 First marginal gloss on Rev. 4:1

10 First marginal gloss on Rev. 8:1

11 Second marginal gloss on Rev. 11:19

12 First marginal gloss on Rev. 15:1

13 First marginal gloss on Rev. 18:1

14 First marginal gloss on Rev. 21:1

15 Bibliothèque nationale de France, Département des manuscrits, Latin 588, Langkatalogisat: Köln, Dombibliothek, Codex 24, Strasbourg: Rusch, 1400/81.

16 Allen, William, "Holy Bible faithfvlly translated into English: out of the authentical Latin, diligently conferred with the Hebrew, Greek, and other editions in divers languages: Vol. 2 Rheims New Testament (1582), Printed by Iohn Cousturier, 1635.

TRANSLATOR'S PREFACE

I have worked from three sources: two manuscripts and one incunable. The manuscripts are: Latin 588, which is 12th century, and Codex 24, which is 13th century; the incunable is Rusch (1480/81). When a gloss was found in each of the three sources but the wording of the glosses differed, I have usually favored Latin 588's reading, as being the oldest source, and mentioned the variants of the other sources in footnotes, except when the reading of one of the other sources seemed much more likely to me. In cases where a gloss is found in only one or two of the sources I have included it in the main text no matter which source it was from, but have mentioned in a footnote its absence from one or both of the other sources.

Some glosses are relatively short and written between the lines of the Bible text above the word(s) concerned; these are called "interlinear" glosses, and are those that in the present work you will find marked by letters repeated before the relevant parts of the verses.

Longer glosses are written in the margins, and so are called "marginal" glosses. The different sources have different ways of indicating what part of the text the glosses refer to: in Latin 588, usually a small sign is drawn both above the relevant part of the text and above the gloss. Rusch's method is to write the relevant word(s) (or the first few words of the relevant part of the verse when the whole of the relevant part would be too long) as a tag before each gloss. Codex 24 very often fails to indicate in any clear manner what a gloss refers to. In my translation I have not strictly followed the method employed by any one of the sources but have adopted a system that seemed to me more convenient for this modern edition and put a tag (often the same that was found in Rusch or in one of the other sources when there was one there) when I judged it to be useful. Since, unlike in the sources, the verses here are given one by one, it did not always seem necessary to put a tag when the gloss referred to the whole verse.

In Latin 588, a few glosses and parts of glosses are found written in a different ink from the rest. These may be things that were forgotten and added later. The ink is a lighter hue. It is difficult for me, not being a paleographer, to tell for sure whether the hand also is different or not, because there are both similarities and differences in the script, and my relatively inexperienced eye cannot tell whether these glosses were written by a different person or by the same person with a different pen - something that can affect the way one writes. Where this happens, I have mentioned it in a footnote, simply referring to this ink as "the other ink". There are a few other things found in yet other inks and hands, but these are very few and I have mentioned each one case by case in the notes.

Codex 24 contains, beside the Glossa Ordinaria, many notes that are clearly in both a different ink and a different hand from the rest; I have not translated them, except in a few cases where they are somehow more closely related to the glosses (e.g. when one of them is saying the same thing as a gloss found in one of the other sources). I have mentioned these cases in the footnotes as well, calling this ink also "the other ink".

I have not mentioned in the footnotes every difference, however small, between the sources, my reason being not to overload the book with footnotes, which may already seem to some readers to be too numerous. Things I have routinely omitted to mention are the most obvious mistranscriptions (though I have mentioned some things that are probably mistranscriptions; but I have omitted the cases where there was no doubt at all, as when the variant reading obviously could not make any sense) and certain small differences in phrasing that I judged to be of negligible significance. I have also not necessarily indicated when a gloss is found interlinearly in one source and marginally in another, or when one of the sources marks a gloss as referring to a different verse part from the others but clearly does so mistakenly.

With regards to which glosses are interlinear or marginal, I have usually followed Latin 588, with a few exceptions for practical reasons (e.g. if a gloss that is interlinear in Latin 588 is marginal in Rusch, and is followed in Rusch by a second marginal gloss that is not present in Latin 588 and would be less easily understood if it were not placed directly after the first gloss because it refers to it, I have presented the first gloss as marginal despite its being interlinear in Latin 588). I have not mentioned this in the footnotes.

A preface is found in the three sources before the beginning of Revelation and the glosses, but it is not identical in all. I have presented it as follows: I have first given it as it is found in Latin 588, and I have assigned a number to every paragraph. Then I have given the numbers of those of these paragraphs that are also found in Codex 24 in the order in which they are found in Codex 24 (when what were several paragraphs in Latin 588 were fused into one in Codex 24, I have put them together in brackets). Between these, in the right order, I have given the paragraphs that are in Codex 24 and not in Latin 588, and have assigned letters to them alphabetically. Finally, I have done the same with Rusch, giving the numbers and letters of the paragraphs in the order in which they are found in it, and adding the paragraphs that are unique to Rusch.

When a biblical passage is quoted in the glosses or in the preface, I have added the reference in parentheses for the reader's convenience, although the sources do not give the references.

I would like to add a note concerning some of the terms I have used in my translation:

"The superiors": this is my translation of *praelati*, which means more or less literally "those who are carried in front (of others)", "those who are given precedence". The word can sometimes mean specifically "prelates" (it is the origin of the English word), but, not being sure that it was used here in this restricted sense, I preferred to translate it with a more general term.

"The inferiors": I have used this to translate *subditi*, which means more or less literally "those who are placed under", i.e. under the authority of someone else. It probably designates the simple faithful under the authority of the clergy or spiritual masters; possibly also members of the lower clergy under the authority of the upper clergy.

I would like to thank Cristalle Watson and the other members of LatinDiscussion.com who gave me help and advice concerning some passages. This help and advice concerned only a few specific points and the final decision was always taken by me, so others are not of course responsible for any mistakes the book may contain. I would also like to thank John Litteral for giving me the opportunity to undertake this work and publish it. Finally, I would like to thank Cristalle Watson a second time for her delightful poem on precious stones that she kindly let us reproduce in this book.

Sarah Van Der Pas

THE GLOSSA ORDINARIA ON REVELATION

AN ENGLISH TRANSLATION

PREFACES

(LATIN 588)

(1) In the same way as concerning secular books, three things are asked: namely the intention, the utility, and which part of humanity's philosophy it pertains to.[1] There is indeed a voluptuous life, a practical life, and a theoretical, i.e. contemplative, life, which this book pertains to. The intention of the author of this book is to give signs through which he may recommend us patience, i.e. make us patient for the name of Christ, so that, by going from patience to the contemplation of heavenly glory, we may be able to reach the utility, i.e. the reward of our patience, i.e. the double robe, happiness of the soul and body. And it should be noted in what manner he recommends patience: namely by showing, through various similes, like the horses and similar things, the persecutions of the present and future Church in the time of the Antichrist, i.e. by reporting the various tribulations of various statuses of the Church, he prepares us so that we may be stronger to endure them, for *whatever we have seen in advance hurts us less*[2]. That is because it is the foundation of all virtues[3], as Prudentius testifies: *Widowed (i.e. weak) is the virtue which patience does not strengthen*[4]

> (1) 1 Codex 24 and Rusch: "In the same way as three things are asked concerning secular books, namely the intention, the utility, and which part of philosophy it belongs to, so concerning this divine book too, three things are asked: the topic, the intention, the utility, and which part of humanity, i.e. of life, it pertains to."] 2 Distichs of Cato, book 2, 24.] 3 Codex 24 and Rusch: "One should also know that he rather recommends patience because it is the foundation of all virtues".] 4 Prudentius, Psychomachia.

(2) The name of the author is also asked, which means "grace of God", that is "John", which tallies well with the intention, for all those who endure for Christ endure by the grace of God, i.e. by the help of God, for otherwise they would succumb[1]. As the apostle Paul says, "By the grace of God, I am what I am" (1 Corint. 15:10).

> (2) 1 "For otherwise they would succumb" is Codex 24's and Rusch's reading. Latin 588 has "for they define it otherwise", which, in my opinion, is probably a mistranscription.

(3) The place in which he composed it is also noted: namely the island of Patmos, where[1] he had been exiled by the emperor Domitian because of the Word of God that he preached. By this island, the Church is signified, which suffers every day the attacks of this world, standing however immovable. Indeed "Patmos" is interpreted as "ebullition" or "heat". We should also see by what sort of vision John saw such things. For there are three sorts of vision: one when we see the sky and the earth and similar things with our physical eyes; another when, sleeping or even awake, we see something through which we represent something else, as Pharaoh saw the fat cows and the meager ones (Gen. 41); another sort is intellectual, when we conceive something in our minds, not through images, but as it is, like David in the Psalms[2]. John saw images[3], and understood the truth in them.

> (3) 1 Codex 24: "The place also in which he composed it is called Patmos, namely the island where...".] 2 Codex 24 and Rusch go on: "... saying, "I will hear what the Lord God will speak in me" (Ps. 84:9)".] 3 Codex 24 and Rusch add "in his mind".

(4) This Apocalypse, among the other books of the New Testament, is called prophetic[1], but more outstanding than other prophecies, because it announces, concerning Christ and the Church, sacraments that have for a great part already been fulfilled.[2] And just as the Gospel surpasses the observances of the Law, so does this prophecy surpass the old prophecies which foresaw events to come a long time in advance[3]. And the authority of the one who sent it, of the one who brought it, and of the one who received it, as well as that of the place itself where the vision took place[4], also present themselves to confirm its reliability. For it is God, i.e. the whole Trinity, who sent it; for about the Father it is said, "sending by his angel" (1:1), and the Son says, "I Jesus have sent my angel" (22:16); but about the Holy Spirit too it is written, "Lord God Omnipotent" (4:8).

> (4) 1 Codex 24 and Rusch: "is called a prophecy".] 2 Rusch has one more sentence here: "Or even because, while to others a one fold prophecy was given, to this one a threefold one was given, that is, concerning at the same time the past, the present, and the future".] 3 This is Rusch's reading. Latin 588 and Codex 24 have: "... so does this prophecy surpass the old ones which foresaw prophecies to come a long time in advance".] 4 "As well as that of the place itself where the vision took place" only in Latin 588.

1

(5) Therefore one should know that when "spirit" is said without addition, the whole Trinity is usually understood; whence "God is a spirit" (John, 4:24) and "He that has an ear, let him hear what the Spirit says to the churches" (Ap. 2:7, 2:11, 2:17, 2:29, 3:6, 3:13, 3:22). And although the angel only wore the mask of the Word incarnate, yet the whole Trinity was at work in the angel. As to the fact that John saw these things in exile, it indicates that Christ's faith claims heaven as its own in earthly afflictions.

(6) One should also know that when he says "The Apocalypse", one should understand "This is..."; but this kind of expression which is done with the removal of a verb, we often find in the divine Scriptures; whence Solomon says, without the support of a verb, "The parables of Solomon" (Proverbs, 1:1), and Isaiah, "The vision of Isaiah" (Isaiah, 1:1).

(7) Alpha is the beginning of the Greek letters, and Omega the end, which is well suited to the one about whom Isaiah says, "Before me there was no God formed, and after me there shall be none" (Isaiah, 43:10). The reason that prompted the blessed John to write was that while he was kept in exile by Domitian, meanwhile, many villainies developed in the churches that he was in charge of. He is urged to correct them by an angel in a vision, either while sleeping or seized spiritually. By the fact that John was visited by the divinity when he was destitute of all human conversation and help[1], it is hinted to us too[2] that the more we withdraw from this fuss, the more we shall be judged worthy of and suitable for[3] divine visitation.

(7) 1 Latin 588: "by the fact that John is destitute of all human conversation and is visited by the help of the divinity".] 2 "Too" not in Rusch.] "And suitable for" only in Latin 588.

(8) And this is the topic in this book: the Church, concerning which are all the visions. And whatever is introduced concerning the Antichrist and demons, is done for the confirmation of the integrity of the Church. He treats this topic in this way: by showing the condition of the Church according to its present and future status. According to its present status, he shows that the Church must suffer many persecutions here, and that on the other hand there are many honors in the present, like the remission of sins, the illumination of souls, and such things, while in the future it must obtain life and endless joy.

(9) His purpose is to encourage[1] those who are placed under his authority, to whom he is principally writing, and then the others, to endure tribulations with patience without doubting[2] the reward[3].

(9) 1 Codex 24 and Rusch: "to prompt".] 2 Rusch: "unless they are doubting".] 3 Codex 24 and Rusch: "the great reward". In Latin 588, the end of the line is actually faded, so that even the last word, "reward", is not entirely visible, so it is not entirely impossible for the word "great" to have been there too and no longer be visible, but it seems that there would have been little room left at the end of the line to add it.

(10) God the Father, foreseeing the tribulations that the holy Church was about to go through after it was founded by the apostles, decided with the Son and the Holy Spirit to reveal those tribulations and their rewards. For the darts that are seen in advance hurt less. So he disclosed them to Christ according to his humanity, Christ disclosed them to John, and John revealed them to the Church. And Christ revealed them to John deservedly[1], who surpassed all thanks to his chastity, and whose name is interpreted as "grace of God"; who ascribed to divine grace all good things that he did, and endured all monstrous torments with equanimity. But since it is well-known that this revelation was made in a vision, we must see what kind of vision it belongs to. There is a physical vision, with which we see the sky and the earth and all other things of the kind. There is a spiritual vision, when something else is shown in that which is seen, as was the case for Moses, who saw a bush that was not burning burn (Ex. 3), which was signifying something else. Finally, there is an intellectual vision, when, as the Holy Spirit intimates it to them, someone conceives something mystical[2], as Saint John did in this book. For he did not see these things materially[3], but, by a divine breath of inspiration, he shaped in his intellect consistent signs designative of the sufferings[4].

(10) 1 "And Christ revealed them to John deservedly" not in Rusch.] 2 Latin 588 has "something else mystical".] 3 The negation is missing in Latin 588, so that it has, "For he saw these things materially".] 4 Codex 24: "... but, as a divine breath was inspiring him consistent signs of the passions, he shaped the signs designated to his intellect".] 5 Codex 24: "... but, as a divine breath was inspiring him consistent signs of the passions, he shaped the signs designated to his intellect".

(11) Now let us see what the topic is. The topic is seven signs, i.e. kinds of tribulations. The intention is to invite us to patience, so that through it we may come to contemplation, through contemplation to revelation, and thence to happiness, in which we have the purpose of this work. And since in the divine there is no question of philosophy, but of life, and since there are two lives, the practical one and the theoretical one, let us see which one it belongs to: to the theoretical one.[1][2] It should moreover be noted that a certain part of this book is taken as a preface or prologue, namely the part to the verse[3] "I John, your brother, etc.". In this part he invites us to read,[4] and to keep: because if we do this well[5] we shall obtain happiness. And thus does he first[6] recommend his work: this book ought to be read, because it is the Apocalypse, that is the Revelation, not of anyone, but of Jesus Christ. Or this book ought to be read because *blessed is he that reads and hears the words of this prophecy*[7] (1:3), i.e. of the Apocalypse, i.e. of the Revelation of Jesus Christ, etc[8].

(11) 1 Codex 24: "And since in the divine there is no question of philosophy, but of life, let us see which life it belongs to. There is a theoretical life, a contemplative life, and a practical life, but it is agreed that it is referred to the theoretical one"; Rusch: "And since in the divine there is no question of philosophy, but of life, let us see which life it belongs to. There is a theoretical, i.e. contemplative, life, and a practical, i.e. active, life. But it is agreed that the practical one is referred to the theoretical one".] 2 Codex 24 and Rusch have something more here: "And it is to be noted why he invites us to patience more than to other virtues. To this it should be replied that just as faith is the foundation of all virtues, so is patience somehow their support. Whence Prudentius: "Widowed is the virtue which patience does not strengthen".".] 3 "Or prologue, namely the part to the verse" not in Latin 588, but I chose to include it for clarity's sake.] 4 Codex 24 and Rusch add also "to hear".] 5 "Well" only in Latin 588.] 6 "First" not in Rusch.] 7 Rusch: "of the prophecy of this reading".] 8 "Etc" not in Rusch.

(12) Asia Minor is a part of greater Asia. It contains seven cities, of which Ephesus is the metropolis. Paul first preached the Gospel in this region. But afterwards, with the dispersion of the apostles, the apostle John was put in charge of this same region[1], and, having ordained bishops in every city with an archbishop, he himself gave his time to preaching. When he heard of his preaching, Domitian had him brought to Rome and thrown into a vat of boiling oil *(See Tertullian, De praescript., 36).*[2] As he had come out of it unharmed, he ordered him to be sent in exile to the island of Patmos with the criminals who cut marble there[3]. And while he was kept in exile[4] there, some vices sprang forth in the churches of Asia through negligence of the bishops[5]. A vision was revealed to John by the Lord concerning those vices and their correction, as well as concerning the present and future status of the Church; he wrote an account of this vision and sent it to his churches for them to read. After Domitian was murdered by the senate for his wickedness, and when all his decrees were annulled by *senatus consultum* out of hatred for him[6], John, freed from exile together with the other captives, returned to Ephesus with great joy. And after some time, as various heresies concerning faith in the Trinity were arising in the same province, he wrote at his brethren's' request his Gospel in order to give shape to[7] the faith that he had taught.[8]

(12) 1 Codex 24: "This Asia is Asia Minor, not the big one (i.e. the one that is said to be the third part of the world), but some province in which there were seven cities, and seven churches with seven bishops. The metropolis of these cities is Ephesus. But afterwards, with the dispersion of the apostles, Paul first preached the Gospel in this Asia Minor. John was put in charge of it...".] 2 Codex 24: "When he heard of his preaching, the emperor Domitian put him into a vat of boiling oil".] 3 Codex 24, shorter: "... he sent him in exile to the island of Patmos".] 4 "In exile" not in Codex 24.] 5 Codex 24: "through their negligence".] 6 Codex 24, shorter: "After Domitian was murdered by the senate, and as they had ordered all his decrees to be annulled..."] 7 Codex 24: "in order to strengthen". The difference is only in one letter in Latin.] 8 This paragraph is not in Rusch, but it has part of it in the fifth and sixth marginal glosses to 1:4.

(13) This revelation was shown to the blessed John through some images while he was in an ecstasy of mind, and in some places the meaning of those images was explained to him, so that he might write it in the same way as it had been revealed to him; for God wanted his mysteries to be revealed to the faithful through images, so that they might not be understood without effort, because what is acquired with effort is possessed more pleasurably and more securely. He also wanted images to be explained in a few places, so as to hint that an explanation for the images had to be sought in all places, and so that the faithful might find it when seeking, and that the unfaithful or the heretics who strive to corrupt and tread holy mysteries underfoot might not understand at all. When John is being taught by the angel, he wears the mask of the universal Church, for he is being taught in the way in which the Church had to be taught; when he is teaching those who are placed under his authority, he bears a resemblance to the teaching angel, writing down the images and explaining in some places what is meant by them.[1]

(13) 1 Only in Latin 588.

(14) "Ephesus" is interpreted as "my will", "advice", or "deep fall".
"Smyrna" as "canticle", or as it were "myrrh", from the bitterness of sufferings.
"Pergamus" as "division of the horns" or "when beauty is added to the prince".
"Laodicea" as "vomit" or "lovely tribe".

"Thyatira" as "infamed".[1]
"Sardis" as "the beginning of beauty".
"Philadelphia" as "brotherly love" or "dividing the inheritance".
"John" is interpreted as "grace" or "he in whom there is grace", and this name is suited to all the faithful who have grace and are not overconfident in themselves.[2]

(14) 1 Cf. interlinear gloss (b) to 2:18. The Latin words for "infamed" and "kindled" look similar (much like "infamed" and "inflamed").] 2 (14) is only in Latin 588, though some of these interpretations are found later in the glosses in the other books as well, as you will see.

(10), (11), [(4), (5), (6)], [(7), (8), (9)], [(2), (3)]

(a) John the apostle and evangelist, chosen and loved by the Lord Christ, was held in such great affectionate love by him, that he leaned on Christ's chest at the Last Supper, and that, while he was standing alone by the cross[1], Jesus entrusted him his own mother, so that to him whom he had made embrace virginity while he wished to get married, he also gave the Virgin to guard. So, when exile in the island of Patmos befell him on account of the Word of God and of the testimony of Jesus Christ, the Apocalypse was foreshown to him and written down by him there, so that in the same way as in the beginning of the canon, i.e. of the book of Genesis, the incorruptible beginning is written out, so was the incorruptible end also rendered by the virgin in the Apocalypse of the one who says, "I am Alpha and Omega, the beginning and the end". This is the John who, knowing that the day of his going out of his body had come, after having summoned together his disciples in Ephesus, went down into the place dug for his grave, and, when he had finished saying a prayer, passed away, having been made as free from pain[2] as he is known to be free from decay of the flesh *(See Apocryphal Acts of John, 111)*. The disposition of this scripture or the arrangement of the book, however, is not explained here by us in detail so that those who do not know may be given a desire to investigate, and that the fruit of their effort may be kept for those who seek, and the teaching of mastership for God[3].

(a) 1 Codex 24 has only "while he was standing by alone"; I followed Rusch in including "the cross" for clarity's sake.] 2 Rusch: "from the pain of death".] 3 This last sentence is Rusch's reading, which seemed the more likely to me. Depending on how the Latin sentence is punctuated (I have found printed versions that differed in this respect), it could also be: "so that those who do not know may be given a desire to investigate, that those who seek may be given the fruit of their effort, and that the teaching of mastership may be kept for God". Codex 24 has something that could be interpreted as either "so that those who do not know may be given a desire to investigate and that those who seek may be given the fruit of their effort, and that therefore the teaching of mastership may be kept" or "so that those who do not know may be given a desire to investigate and that those who seek may be given the fruit of their effort, and therefore let the teaching of mastership be kept".

(1), (12)

(b) It should be noted that a vision that indicates future events can be physical, imaginary, or intellectual. The physical vision is like the one in which Balthasar saw, with his physical eyes, a physical hand writing on the wall (ref. Dan. 5:5). The imaginary vision is like when images of seen bodies are impressed in the mind, as when the blessed Peter saw the dish, and he was in an imaginary vision, in the passage "kill and eat" (Acts, 10:13). The intellectual vision is when, bodies and images of bodies being removed, the superior power of the soul is lifted up to the understanding of divine things, as was the case of Paul's vision. Whence he is also said to have been taken to heaven, because he ascended to this third sort of vision (2 Corint. 12:-16). Note, however, that an imaginary vision happens sometimes without understanding on the part of the person who sees it, as was the case of Pharaoh's vision, which he himself did not understand and Joseph explained to him (Gen. 41); sometimes with understanding, like the vision of the blessed John. Note also that such a vision sometimes happens when one is sleeping, as it happened to Peter or Pharaoh; sometimes when one is awake, as it happened to Ezekiel, who was seized into an ecstasy while he was sitting among the ancients of Israel (Ezekiel 8), and to the blessed John, whence he says later, "I was in spirit on the Dominical day" (1:10).[1]

(b) 1 Only in Codex 24.

Prologue to the Apocalypse of John

(a)

Preface of Gilbert of Poitiers to the Apocalypse of John

"All that will live godly in Christ Jesus", as the apostle says, "shall suffer persecution" (2 Timothy, 3:12). According to that: "Son, when you come to the service of God, stand in justice and in fear, and prepare your soul for temptation" (Ecclesiasticus, 2:1). For the life of man on earth is temptation. But so that the faithful may not succumb in these things, the Lord comforts and encourages them, saying, "I am with you even to the consummation of the world" (Matt. 28:20), and "Fear not, little flock" (Luke, 12:32). Therefore God the Father, seeing the tribulations that the Church founded by the apostles on the stone which is Christ was about to suffer, decided, so that they might be feared less, to reveal those tribulations together with the Son and the Holy Spirit. And the whole Trinity revealed them to Christ according to his humanity, Christ revealed them to John through an angel, and John to the Church, and he composed this book concerning this revelation. Whence this book is also called Apocalypse, that is Revelation, because here are contained the things that God revealed to John, and John to the Church, namely how great trouble the Church went through in its first time, is now going through, and shall go through in the last times of the Antichrist — which tribulation will be so great that it is possible even for the elect to get perturbed (see Matthew 24:24) — and what rewards it shall receive for these things both now and in the future, so that those whom the announced torments frighten, the promised rewards may gladden. Therefore this book is distinguished among the rest of the Scriptures of the New Testament by the name of prophecy; and it is more outstanding than other prophecies, for just as the New Testament is superior to the Old, the Gospel superior to the Law, so is this prophecy superior to the prophecies of the Old Testament, because it announces, concerning Christ and the Church, sacraments that have for a great part already been fulfilled. Or even because, while to others a one fold prophecy was given, to this one a threefold one was given, namely, concerning at the same time the past, the present, and the future. And the authority of the one who sent it, of the one who brought it, and of the one who received it also come together to strengthen its authority. The one who sent it: namely the Trinity; the one who brought it: an angel; the one who received it: namely John. However, since these things were revealed to John in a vision, and since there are three kinds of visions, we must see which kind it belongs to. There is indeed one vision that is physical, that is when we see something with our physical eyes; there is another that is spiritual or imaginary, that is when, asleep or even awake, we perceive images of things by which something else is signified; that is, in the same way as Pharaoh saw ears of corn (Gen. 41) and Moses saw the bush on fire (Ex. 3), the former asleep, the latter awake. There is another vision that is intellectual, that is when, as the Holy Spirit reveals it to us, we grasp by mental understanding the truth of mysteries as it is. This is the way in which John saw the things that are related in this book. For he did not only see shapes in spirit, but he understood their meanings with his mind. John saw and wrote these things on the island of Patmos, where he had been exiled by Domitian, the very wicked ruler. The reason that urged him to write was that while he was kept in exile by Domitian on the island of Patmos, many vices and various heresies sprang forth and developed in the churches of which he was in charge. There were indeed some heretics there who said that Christ did not exist before Mary because he was born of her temporally *(See Irenaeus on the Ebionites. Adversus Haereses 1.26)*; whom John refutes in the beginning of his Gospel, saying, "In the beginning was the Word" (John, 1:1), and in this book when he says, "Alpha and Omega", that is, "the beginning and the end". Some also said that the Church would come to an end before the end of the world because of the weight of tribulations, and would receive no eternal reward for its labor. Wishing therefore to demolish the errors of these people, John showed that Christ was the beginning and the end — whence Isaiah: "Before me there was no God formed, and after me there shall be none" (43:10) — and that through the exercise of tribulations the Church was not coming to an end, but progressing, and that it received an eternal prize for these. John writes to the seven churches of Asia and their seven bishops, instructing them about the aforementioned things, and teaching in these the whole Church in general through those seven churches. So John's topic in this work is especially the status of the Asiatic church, but also that of the whole Church, that is, the things that it is suffering in the present, and shall receive in the future. His intention is to advise patience, which should be kept both because the labor will be short and because the reward will be great. His way of treating the subject is such: first, he writes a prologue and a salutation, where he makes the listeners favorable and attentive, after which he comes to the narration. But before the narration, he shows that Christ has been from eternity without beginning or end, representing him himself speaking and saying, "I am Alpha and Omega", that is, "the beginning and the end". After this, coming to the narration, he distinguishes seven visions; these being delimited, the division of this book is made. He first writes the prologue saying, "The Apocalypse of Jesus Christ" — you understand "This is...", as in other places: "The vision of Isaiah": "This is...", and "The parables of Solomon": "These are..."

(1), [(10), (11)], [(4), (5), (6)], [(7), (8), (9)], [(2), (3)], (the second marginal gloss to 1:1)

i

Another Prologue by Jerome (Letter 53.9 (NPNF, 2nd series 6:102) as it is found in some Bibles

The Apocalypse of Jesus Christ of John has as many mysteries as words, and all praise is too small for the book's merit. Manifold meanings lie hidden in its every word.

CHAPTER 1

1:1 (a)*The* (b)*Apocalypse* (c)*of* (d)*Jesus* (e)*Christ which* (f)*God gave* (g)*to him,* (h)*to make manifest* (i)*to his servants* (j)*the things which* (k)(l)*must be done* (m)*quickly: and* (n)*signified, sending by* (o)*his* (p)(q)(r)*angel to* (s)*his servant John,*

a.	This is.
b.	I.e. revelation.*
c.	Given by the Father to Christ according to his humanity.*
d.	I.e. savior.*
e.	I.e. king.*
f.	God the Father*, as he who owes nothing.
g.	To Christ.*
h.	To make it known by word and by example
i.	Not to the Jews, not to philosophers, but to the brethren.*
j.	Concerning these things.
k.	It is inevitable or useful that they should suffer tribulations.*
l.	In the person of the Church.*
m.	Short labor, hastened glory.
n.	I.e. showed through signs.
o.	Consubstantial with him.*
p.	Sc. having the role of Christ.
q.	Of the great plan.*
r.	He says some things on Christ's behalf, as when he says "I am Alpha and Omega", and some on his own behalf, as when he forbids himself to be adored.*
s.	Humble, not proud.

The Apocalypse of Jesus Christ. He prepares the listeners to be favorable and attentive, as he does also in that place "John to the seven churches which are in Asia". (1:4)

The letter is as if he were thus warning: Pay attention to this vision, because it is a vision revealed in Jesus Christ. The topic is the state of the church of Asia and of the whole present Church. The pattern is tribulations inside and outside and consolations on the other hand. The point is: short labor, sure rewards. The intention: to endure everything patiently.

Which God gave, etc. He received it as a man from the Father, the Word united to himself, and the Holy Spirit.[1]

Quickly. He says this so that they may prepare themselves, so that it may not be heavy to suffer. Labors must end quickly, and rewards be given. [2]

And signified. God the Father showed them to the Son, and the Son to John, as it were through signs, under seal, so that there might be no occasion given to thieves to corrupt them, and so that it might be more pleasurable for the faithful if they understood them with effort.

1:1 (a) and (b): In Rusch, these are one gloss saying "This is the revelation". Latin 588 has only (b).] (c) *Only in Latin 588.] (d) *Only in Codex 24.] (e) *Only in Codex 24.] (f) *"God the Father" not in Latin 588. Codex 24 has a second gloss right above this one saying "The Son"; maybe this is a mistake and it should have been "To the Son" above "to him".] (g) *Only in Rusch.] (i) *"But to the brethren" only in Codex 24.] (k) *Codex 24 has here an interlinear saying "As if we were saying: It is inevitable that they be done and useful that they be done", and a marginal gloss to "servants" saying "They must suffer tribulations". Rusch has one marginal gloss reading "As if he were saying: It is both inevitable that they be done and useful that they be done. They must suffer tribulations quickly".] (l) *Only in Codex 24.] (o) *Only in Codex 24.] (q) *Only in Codex 24. English "angel" and Latin angelus come from Greek ἄγγελος (angelos) meaning "messenger". Maybe the glossator was having this in mind.] (r) *Only in Codex 24.] 1 Not in Latin 588.] 2 Not in Latin 588.

1:2 (a)*who has given testimony* (b)*to the word of God, and the testimony of Jesus Christ,* (c)(d)*what things soever he has seen.*

a.	Who bears witness to the words of Christ himself, both those he spoke concerning the Word, i.e. the divinity, and those he spoke concerning the humanity*.I.e. to the Son. The Son is called the Word because through him the Father was manifested and signified in the world.
b.	In these are things that he has seen physically, as, for example, that Jesus suffered, or that he has seen only in mind, as, for example, that he was with the Father before everything.
c.	To this, "Do not seal the words of the book" (ref. 22:10).*

1:2 (a) *Codex 24: "concerning the nativity of Jesus Christ"; Rusch: "concerning the humanity of Jesus Christ".] (b) *"I.e. to the Son" only in Latin 588.] (d) *Only in Codex 24.

1:3 (a)*Blessed is he* (b)*that reads and* (c)*hears the words* (d)*of this prophecy and* (e)(f)*keeps those things which are written in it,* (g)*for the time is near.*

a.	Christ gave this to me, and blessed is he who receives it from me.
b.	Like the educated.
c.	Like laymen who are learning*. By this he means listeners, who

Blessed is he that reads and hears, etc. Because this is *the Apocalypse of Jesus Christ*, etc. [1]

He that reads, i.e. tells others what he has heard, because from one person who has read, more people can hear.

They alone are blessed who hear them to keep them in mind, who keep

are more numerous**.

d. Of this book.*
e. Reader and listener.*
f. i.e. he who does not profane the faith of Christ and of the Church, and fears the things threatened and seeks the things promised.
g. He is really blessed, because the labor shall not last long, because the rewards are near.

them in mind to fulfill them in deed, and fulfill them in deed to possess eternal life. [2]

Keeps those things. So do I say "if he keeps them". For not those who hear the law, but those who act according to it are just. [3]

1:3 (c) *Codex 24 and Rusch: "Like laymen and those who are learning". **Instead of having this sentence here, Codex 24 and Rusch have "by this he means listeners, because they are more" at the end of the gloss "He that reads, i.e. tells, etc.".] (d) *Only in Rusch.] (e) *Not in Latin 588.] 1 Not in Latin 588.] 2 Not in Latin 588.] 3 Not in Latin 588.

1:4 John to the seven churches which are in (a)Asia. (b)Grace to you and (c)peace from (d)him (e)that is, and (f)that was, and (g)that shall come, and from (h)the seven spirits which are (i)in the sight of his throne,

a. I.e. pride.*
b. I.e. remission of sins.
c. I.e. rest from vices.
d. I.e. Christ.
e. Sc. incorruptible according to his divinity.
f. Sc. once born eternally.
g. Such, even if he does not appear such now.*
h. I.e. the sevenfold Spirit, which is one in nature, but manifold in the distribution of graces.
i. Angels and holy men are thrones, in whom he now sits and judges, not to judge in the future; in whom God sits, illuminating them.

To the seven churches. God gave it to Christ, Christ to John, and John to the churches; principally to those to which he had been appointed as a master, and to the others through a simile.

Or by seven all the churches are meant, because seven signifies universality, or because they are illumined by a sevenfold spirit.

Ephesus was the metropolitan city or capital of all Asia, where John was exercising superintendence.

In Asia. Asia means pride. So the Church is now in the pride of virtues, and[1] was formerly in the pride of vices.

This Asia is not the big one (i.e. the one that is said to be the third part of the world), but some province in which there were seven cities, and seven churches with seven bishops.[2]

Asia Minor is a part of greater Asia; it contains seven cities of which Ephesus is the metropolis. Paul preached the Gospel in this Asia Minor (Acts 16), but afterwards, with the division of the apostles, John was put in charge of it.[3]

Grace and peace. He prepares the listeners to be favorable and attentive, as he did also in the prologue.

And from the seven spirits. "Spirit" denotes the same as "love"; whence the remission of sins and other gifts, which are gifts of the whole Trinity, are attributed to the Spirit, so that we may understand that the Trinity works out of love alone.

He passes over in silence the person of the Father, because no one had misunderstood what concerns God the Creator; he mentions the person of the Son and of the Holy Spirit, concerning whom the heresies of Marcion and Terebinthus arise in the churches.[4]

1:4 (a) *Only in Latin 588.] (e), (f), (g) *Instead of (e), Codex 24 has "Eternally, even though he was born in his time"; it does not have (f), but does have (g); it also has an additional marginal gloss saying "Incorruptible since long ago, now also immutable according to his humanity". Rusch has one marginal gloss combining different elements of all this with some variations: "Eternally, even though he was born in his time; now immutable through his humanity, and once corruptible; he shall come such, even if he does not appear such now".] 1 Codex 24 and Rusch: "or".] 2 Only in Rusch.] 3 Only in Rusch.] 4 Instead of "the heresies of Marcion and Terebinthus", Codex 24 and Rusch have "all heresies".

1:5 and from (a)Jesus Christ who is the faithful witness, the first-born of (b)the dead, and (c)the prince of (d)the kings of the earth, who (e)(f)has loved us, and (g)washed us from (h)our (i)sins in (j)his blood.

a. As he is about to say more, he speaks again about Christ.*
b. I.e. those who, despairing concerning the death of Christ, said, "But we hoped that it was he that should have redeemed Israel" (Lk.24:21).*
c. Let this not frighten us, because he has risen again and is impassible. Or the prince of those who mortify themselves, because he has committed no sin.
d. I.e. those who control earthliness.*
e. Especially the preachers*.
f. I.e. deemed it worthy to die.*
g. Sc. with love alone.
h. Not his, because he has not sinned.
i. Sc. original and actual.
j. Not that of a calf or of a ram as in the old law.

1:5 (a) *Codex 24 and Rusch: ".... about Christ according to his humanity".] (b) *Codex 24 and Rusch have, as a marginal gloss: "He says this for those who despair concerning the death of Christ, like those who said, ..."] (d) *Not in Codex 24.] (e) *Not in Latin 588.] (f) *Only in Latin 588.] 1 Codex 24 and Rusch: "... believe this revelation and obvious exhortation...".] 2 This gloss is not in Latin 588. The words "or of the saints" are only in Rusch. Maybe "of his people" and "of the saints" are two different readings mentioned by the editor of Rusch. Abbreviations for these resemble each other, so a misreading and/or mistranscription of whichever was the original one would have easily happened. Or one may think that they added "or of the saints" as an explanation, to clarify who "his people" were.

He commends the person of the Son, who had made this revelation to John through an angel, as if he were saying: believe this revelation[1] which Christ has made manifest, he who suffered for us and rose again, who did not deny that he was God even when death was imminent. Or the witness of our works in the day of the judgment, when he says "You saw me hungry and thirsty" (See Matt. 25:35) and "Come, you blessed of my Father, etc." (Matt. 25:34).

Prince of the kings of the earth. The prince of earthly powers, having the power to remove them, and permitting the wicked to serve the interests of his people, or of the saints[2].

1:6 And has made us (a)(b)a kingdom and (c)(d)priests to God and (e)his Father, (f)to him be (g)(h)glory and (i)(j)empire forever and ever. Amen.

a. I.e. capable of resisting vices.
b. According to the fact that he is a man.
c. According to the fact that he is God.*
d. I.e. offering ourselves to God for ourselves and for our brethren.
e. I.e. Creator.*
f. And therefore.
g. Sc. for what concerns himself.*
h. For him to be praised.*
i. For what concerns other benevolent men.*
j. So that you should obey him.

1:6 (b) and (c) *Only in Rusch. In the book, (b) is in fact placed right above "priests" and (c) above "his father", but this does not quite make sense to me (although I may, of course, be missing something that someone else may see), and the placement of glosses is not always absolutely precise. Two interpretations came to my mind: either that (b) was meant to refer to "kingdom" - he made us a kingdom according to the fact that he is a man, with the image of an earthly kingdom belonging to a man - and (c) to "priests" - he made us priests according to the fact that he is God, because a God has priests - , or that (b) was meant to refer to "God " - he made us a kingdom and priests to him whom he regards as God according to the fact that he himself is a man - and (c) to "his Father" - he made us a kingdom and priests to him whom he regards as his Father according to the fact that he himself is God.] (e) * Only in Latin 588.] (g) *Only in Latin 588.] (h) *Not in Latin 588.] (i) *Only in Latin 588.] (j) *Not in Latin 588.

1:7 (a)Behold he comes with (b)the clouds, and (c)every eye shall see him, and (d)they that pricked him. And (e)all the tribes of the earth (f)shall bewail themselves upon him. (g)Yes. Amen.

a. He speaks in the manner of prophets, who saw things to come as if they were present, as "Behold a virgin shall conceive" (Isaiah 7:14).*
b. I.e. the saints.*
c. The good to be rejoiced, the wicked to be confounded.*
d. So that they be tormented more. Like the Jews and Pilate.*
e. I.e. all the earthly people and those who are given over to vices.*
f. I.e. they shall grieve when seeing those who are founded above them*, and they shall not grieve as much because of their torment itself as because they are rejected from such a community.

Behold he comes. You really ought to preach him and praise him[1], because it is he who will come to give rewards with the clouds, i.e. the saints, who were clouds by raining[2] upon others, and by doing miracles. Or, just as he ascended in a cloud, he will come in a cloud, by which we understand God's mercy, which is a consolation and an illumination to the good, and a terror and a blinding to the wicked. This is what was signified by the cloud by which the sons of Israel were led out of Egypt: to them it was an illumination, to Pharaoh a terror and a blinding. So in the day of the Judgment will God look like an illumination to the good, and like a terror and a blinding to the wicked[3].

And every eye shall see him. Another translation has "all the earth[4] shall see him such", as if saying "they shall see him such as the impious did not believe he would come".

8

g.   As if he were saying: Surely, this is true.*

They shall bewail themselves, or dash[5] themselves upon him, incapable of resisting his power, after the likeness of a stone and earthen vessels[6].

Yes. Amen (In the Latin: *Etiam. Amen.*). By these two adverbs, one of which is Greek - namely *etiam*[7] - the nations are signified; by *amen*, which is Hebrew, the Jews: all these shall see God in the judgment. [8]

The first vision gives a correction; through correction one comes to happiness, through happiness to contemplation, through contemplation to eternal life. [9]

1:7 (a) *Only in Latin 588.] (b) *Not in Rusch. In Codex 24 in the other ink.] (c) *Codex 24 has "The good to be rejoiced, the wicked to be confounded. The good shall see as well as the wicked", while Rusch has "The good one as well as the wicked one" here as an interlinear, and a marginal gloss with "The good shall see to be rejoiced, the wicked to be confounded.] (d) *"So that they be tormented more" not in Latin 588; "Like the Jews and Pilate" only in Latin 588.] (e) *"And those who are given over to vices" not in Codex 24.] (f) *Codex 24 and Rusch: "upon him". The same Latin word can mean "upon" or "above".] (g) *Instead of this, Codex 24 has "As if because it must be confirmed in every language" and Rusch "Because it must be confirmed in every language" followed by another short gloss saying "Also amen".] 1 Instead of "preach and praise", Codex 24 and Rusch have "glorify".] 2 Rusch: "by raining teaching".] 3 The part from "to them it was an illumination, to Pharaoh a terror..." to the end is unique to Latin 588.] 4 Codex 24 has "the flesh" instead of "all the earth".] 5 To understand how they came to this interpretation, one has to know that the Latin verb *plangere*, which is used here and translated as "bewail", originally meant "to beat" or "strike", then more specifically "to beat one's breast as a sign of mourning", and finally "to bewail". The verb used in the original Greek shares the same meanings.] 6 Instead of "and earthen vessels", Latin 588 has an abbreviation consisting of four letters, which must be the four first letters of four words of a Bible passage referred to, as this is the usual way used in Latin 588 to refer to a passage of the scriptures (writing one or two words in full and then only the first letter of each following word), but I have been unable to find which one it is.] 7 *Etiam* ("yet, still, also, even, yes"), though cognate with Greek ἔτι (eti, "yet, still, besides"), is an altogether Latin word and was not borrowed from Greek. But it would be more logical if the glossator meant not *etiam* itself, but its equivalent in the original Greek text; ναι.] 8 This gloss is only in Rusch.] 9 Only in Latin 588.

1:8 I am (a)Alpha and Omega, the beginning and (b)end, says our (c)Lord God, (d)which is, and which was, and which (e)shall come, the Omnipotent.

He will really come, because he himself promised he would come. Or, after writing a salutation first, he makes readers attentive, as if he were saying: do not believe that this is said by me, but by Christ himself.

a.   Before whom there was no one, or from whom everything started.
b.   After whom there is no one, or in whom everything shall end.
c.   Of the prophets who say that everything shall end in him.*
d.   I, the Lord, say this.*
e.   Sc. in Judgment Day.*

1:8 (c) *Only in Latin 588. Codex 24 has "He says this by the voice of the prophets" after (d); Rusch has "He says this in the manner of the prophets".] (d) *Maybe another interpretation is possible: "I say (= mean) the Lord", as if the glossator meant that "the Lord" was implied after "is" and "was"; "which is (the Lord), and which was (the Lord)".] (e) *Only in Latin 588.

1:9 (a)I John (b)(c)your brother and partaker in tribulation, and (d)the kingdom, and (e)patience in (f)Christ Jesus, was in (g)the island, which is called (h)(i)Patmos, (j)for the word of God and (k)the testimony of Jesus.

I John. As if he were saying: I know that you are afflicted, but that you endure patiently following the example of Christ, so that you may be sharers of his kingdom. And the salutation being finished, he moves on to the narration by mentioning four things: the protagonist, the place, the reason for the place, and the time; things which are useful for the recommendation[1] of the revelation itself.

The Church is compared to an island because as an island is beaten by marine storms, so is the Church afflicted by the persecutions of marine, i.e. worldly people.

a.   From the protagonist.*
b.   The master's humility.*
c.   I.e. in the unity of faith, and having been afflicted for that faith, like others I have patiently endured that through which one can attain the kingdom, by holding Christ as an example in all things.
d.   I.e. in paradise.*
e.   I.e. patient in God.*
f.   I.e. Christ's example.
g.   I.e. the Church.*
h.   I.e. "heat" or "tribulation", in which heavenly things are better revealed to the faithful.
i.   The place.*
j.   The reason.*
k.   Sc. given to his divinity and to his humanity.

1:9 (a) *Only in Rusch.] (b) *Not in Latin 588.] (d) *Only in Latin 588.] (e) *Only in Latin 588.] (g) *Only in Latin 588.] (i) *Only in Rusch.] (j) *Not in Latin 588.] 1 Codex 24: "confirmation".

1:10 I was ⁽ᵃ⁾in spirit ⁽ᵇ⁾⁽ᶜ⁾on the Dominical day, and ⁽ᵈ⁾heard behind me a ⁽ᵉ⁾great ⁽ᶠ⁾voice as it were of a ⁽ᵍ⁾trumpet,

a. I.e. in an ecstasy of mind.
b. The time.*
c. I.e. placed in hope of resurrection through the resurrection of Christ.
d. I.e. recognized.*
e. Because he was about to talk about future things and about great things.
f. I.e. manifestation.
g. Sc. by which one is roused to war.

On the Dominical day. The quality of things is often marked by the time at which they happen, as Abraham, in the fervor of his faith, saw the angels at midday (Gen. 18); Adam [heard the voice of the Lord] after midday (Gen. 3); Lot, in the destruction of Sodom (Gen. 19), in the evening[1]; Solomon received at night the wisdom he would not keep (2 Chron. 1).

Heard behind me a great voice. He heard it behind him because while, led out of the present matters, he was stretching his power of contemplation to the past[2], he was reminded to look back at others as well. Or he heard it behind him because he understood that this same thing had been foretold by the law and the prophets.[3]

1:10 (b) *Not in Latin 588.] (d) *Or "became aware of". The Latin can mean either and I cannot make up my mind as to which interpretation is more likely.] 1 Codex 24: "... Abraham, in the fervor of his faith, saw the angels at midday; Lot, in the destruction of Sodom, in the evening; Adam heard the voice of the Lord after midday..."; Rusch: "... Abraham, in the fervor of his faith, saw the angels at midday; Lot, in the destruction of Sodom, in the evening; Adam after midday...".] 2 Rusch has something like "he was stretching himself to the past/anterior things of true contemplation", which does not make a lot of sense to me. Codex 24 has something which does not look better, but one thing that might be of some significance is that it has "inner things/matters" instead of "past/anterior" ones. If you replaced "the past" with "inner things/matters" in Latin 588's version, it would make some sense, as if contemplating personal inner thoughts, he was reminded to look back at, think of, other people too. So I think that either "past" or "inner" could have been the original reading, even more so seeing that only one letter differs between these two words in Latin (anteriora/interiora), so a mistranscription could easily have happened at some point.] 3 This last sentence "Or he heard it behind him because he understood that, etc." is not in Codex 24.

1:11 saying: That ⁽ᵃ⁾which you see, ⁽ᵇ⁾write in a book, and send to ⁽ᶜ⁾the seven churches which are in Asia, to ⁽ᵈ⁾Ephesus, and ⁽ᵉ⁾Smyrna, and ⁽ᶠ⁾Pergamus, and ⁽ᵍ⁾Thyatira, and ⁽ʰ⁾Sardis, and ⁽ⁱ⁾Philadelphia, and ⁽ʲ⁾Laodicea.

a. Sc. which you already see or are about to see.
b. I.e. keep it in your mind, or literally.
c. By the seven, we can signify all churches, or literally.*
d. I.e. it translates to "my will", "deep fall" or "advice*".
e. I.e. "canticle".
f. I.e. "division of the horns".
g. I.e. "illuminated".
h. "The beginning of beauty".
i. "Preserving" or "saving".
j. I.e. "lovely tribe".

That which you see, write, etc. A common warning is given to John, which advises him to send it in common to the churches of Asia, and by these, all other churches must be understood. This common warning is done to the angel of Ephesus and to all the others. John saw this vision either at the same time and in one look or through various times; the angel could have bestowed either on him[1].

1:11 (c) *Only in Latin 588.] (d) *This is only one of the meanings of the Latin word *consilium*, the principal meanings of which are "advice", "plan", "decision".] 1 In Codex 24, this last sentence, in a slightly different version, is put as a separate gloss to "on the Dominical day" in the previous verse: "I saw this vision either at the same time in one look or through various times on the same Dominical day. The angel could have bestowed either on him".

1:12 ⁽ᵃ⁾And I ⁽ᵇ⁾turned, ⁽ᶜ⁾to see the voice that spoke with me. ⁽ᵈ⁾And being turned I saw seven ⁽ᵉ⁾candlesticks of gold:

a. And therefore, because I heard a voice, I turned, etc.*
b. I.e. I remembered those who were placed under my authority.
c. I.e. to understand.
d. And because I turned.
e. I.e. churches illumined by the wisdom of the divine word.*

It is the churches that are signified because as candlesticks bear light and give it to others, so does the Church bear the true light, i.e. Christ, and show it to others by preaching his brightness. The Church is said to be of gold because it is founded on love and wisdom.[1]

Of gold. As gold tested by fire and stretched by beatings becomes a candlestick, so does the Church stretched by tribulations and by the beatings of temptations get completed.[2]

If it has the voice in mouth and not in work, it is a candlestick indeed, but not one of gold.[3]

1:12 (a) *The part "because I heard a voice I turned, etc." not in Latin 588.] (b) *Codex 24 and Rusch: "I.e. seven churches burning and illumined by the wisdom of the divine word".] 1 Only in Latin 588.] 2 Codex 24 and Rusch: "As gold tested by fire and stretched by beatings becomes a candlestick, so does the Church, cleansed by tribulations and stretched into forbearance by the beatings of temptations, get completed.] 3 Not in Latin 588.

1:13 and (a)in the middle of the seven candlesticks of gold, (b)one like the Son of man, vested in a priestly garment to the feet, and (c)(d)girded about near to the paps with a (e)girdle of gold.

a. I.e. in public, because God offers himself to all, i.e. he is ready to come to help all.
b. An angel in the role of Christ, who is no longer the son of man, but like the son of man, because he no longer dies.
c. This is a sign given to us that we too should keep the thoughts of our hearts under control.*
d. The head shows in himself what he requires from his people.
e. The belt of love.*

Like the son of man because he appeared not with sin, but in a likeness of the flesh of sin.

A priestly garment, i.e. the flesh in which he offered himself, and offers himself every day, presenting himself to God the Father. Or the priestly garment is the Church in which God is clothed as in a tunic, which is long to the ankles because it will last until the end of the world.

Girded about near to the paps. Daniel saw the same angel in the role of Christ girded[1] around the loins in the Old Testament (Dan. 7), because there fleshly works are kept under control; here he is girded near to the paps because in the New Testament the thoughts of the heart are also judged.

1:13 (c) *Only in Latin 588.] (e) *Codex 24 and Rusch go on saying "because he keeps love".] 1 Codex 24 and Rusch do not have "the same angel in the person of Christ girded..." but only "(one/him) girded...".

1:14 And his (a)head and hairs were white, as (b)white (c)wool, and as (d)(e)snow, and his (f)eyes as the flame of fire,

a. I.e. Christ in whom is all that is necessary for the management of the Church.
b. Shining with simplicity and innocence.*
c. I.e. garment against cold, i.e. vices.
d. Snow is whiter than any creature; by it the purity of immortality is meant.
e. Immortality with glory is more glorious than any creature.*
f. I.e. the spiritual ones* in the Church, who** must see on either side.

Hairs. I.e. the saints[1] made smaller[2] and sticking to the head, or his thoughts.

As white wool. Or as white wool is able to take any colors, so are the saints able to take any tribulations. [3]

Eyes. I.e. the gifts of the Holy Spirit which belong to Christ who has them and gives them, and to the Church which receives them; eyes that illumine and make one burn. Or the eyes are the very spiritual ones in the Church, or the divine commandments[4].

1:14 (b) *Only in Codex 24.] (e) *Only in Rusch.] (f) *Codex 24 and Rusch: "the faithful". **I am not entirely sure whether this should be "who", "the spiritual ones" meaning spiritual people, or "which", "the spiritual ones" meaning spiritual eyes. The Latin could mean either.] 1 "The saints" only in Rusch. I have included it because I do not really see what sense the gloss makes without it.] 2 Latin 588: "made smaller and soft".] 3 Not in Latin 588.] 4 Second sentence "Or the eyes..." not in Latin 588, except that it has interlinear (f) whose beginning only is similar.

1:15 (a)and his feet like to latten, (b)as in a burning furnace. And (c)his voice as of many waters.

a. In another translation there is "latten of Lebanon", by which it is shown that that tribulation will have the most force* in that region where the Lord was crucified.
b. Not any latten, but...*
c. I.e. his preaching possesses the force of water because it cleanses. Or the voice which has already been received by many people, which are compared to water because of their abundance. You ought to stand firm all the more. Or the voice giver of many waters, i.e. graces, whence the voice follows.

The feet are the last faithful who are to come in the last times, similar to heated latten because as latten is changed into the color of gold by heating, so will those faithful too by the excessive tribulation in the time of Antichrist be changed for the better. Or otherwise: feet, i.e. the last faithful who with many shocks will not retain their first nature, as latten that is often heated and takes a better color.[1]

Latten is a kind of metal that becomes more precious the more it is heated, and is said to be seven times as precious as gold. Some, however, say that it is amber.[2]

1:15 (a) *Codex 24: "... that the greatest tribulation will arise..."] (b) *Not in Latin 588.] 1 Codex 24 and Rusch have only the part starting from "feet, i.e. the last faithful who with many shocks..."] 2 Only in Latin 588.

1:16 And he had in his right hand seven stars. And (a)(b)(c)from his mouth proceeded a sharp two-edged sword:

Stars. I.e. bishops, who ought to shine upon others by word and by example; who are called stars even if they have sinned, given that they have been ordained; whom he has in his right hand, i.e. in the greater

and (d)**his face, as the sun shines in his virtue.**

a. Through the preachers or the Scriptures.*
b. I.e. from his teaching proceeds preaching, which cuts both fleshly works in the Old Testament and concupiscences in the New.
c. Whence "it is not you that speak, but the Spirit of your Father that speaks in you" (Matt. 10:20).*
d. I.e. Those* who are like him will shine, i.e. they will become like him.

and better gifts, which are signified by the right hand.

As the sun shines in his virtue. I.e. at midday[1], or when it shall be fixed forever. Or as Christ himself in his resurrection, who is interpreted as the sun[2].

1:16 (a) *Only in Rusch.] (c) *Not in Latin 588.] (d) *Rusch: "the just". This gloss looks a little contradictory at first sight, because if they are already like him, how will they become like him? But on the other hand, "his face" symbolizing "those who are like him" makes sense. So perhaps they meant first those who are like him only to some extent.] 1 Codex 24 and Rusch have "at midday without clouds".] 2 "Who is interpreted as the sun" not in Codex 24 and Rusch.

1:17 And (a)**when I had seen him, I** (b)**fell** (c)**at his feet as** (d)**dead. And he put** (e)**his right hand** (f)**upon me,** (g)**saying,** (h) (i)**Fear not.** (j)**I am the First and the Last,**

a. Because.*
b. I.e. I threw away the care for humanity.
c. I.e. to* the likeness of the last faithful.**
d. Sc. to the world; alive to God. Desiring nothing belonging to the earth.
e. I.e. his help, the comforting Spirit.
f. I.e. upon* the strength of humanity**.
g. Through the preachers or the Scriptures.*
h. For this reason.*
i. Sc. to suffer tribulations and even death, because I did not need death for myself since I am the First and the Last.*
j. Sc. because I am... *

At his feet. So that I was ready to suffer as much as the last faithful shall suffer, or ready to imitate his footsteps.[1]

And when I had seen. Behold, John who seemed to stand while seeing the Lord fell as dead, because the higher every holy man lifts himself to contemplate the divinity, the lower he falls within himself, because, compared to God, his greatness that he has attained is easily disdained. It is because of this that Abraham recognized that he was dust and ashes when he saw the Lord. Similarly Job "With the hearing of the ear, I have heard you, etc." (Job 42:5).[2]

1:17 (a) *Not in Latin 588.] (c) *"To " and "at" are the same word in Latin in this context.] (b) and (c) **Rusch has these two combined in one marginal gloss. Codex24 has a marginal gloss with nothing indicating clearly what it refers to; perhaps it refers to the same words but just contains mistranscriptions, because I cannot make full sense of it. It goes something like: "That is, the previous care for humanity to the likeness of the last faithful; or I looked back at Christ's humanity, which is a human example", although I am not completely sure I am reading "human" correctly.] (f) *Or "above". It is the same word in Latin. **Rusch: "my humanity".] (g) *Not in Rusch.] (h) *Only in Rusch.] (i) *Codex 24 and Rusch: "Fear not to suffer tribulations and even death for me, because I, who did not need to for myself since I am the first and the last, was dead and alive".] (j) *Only in Latin 588.] 1 Only in Latin 588.] 2 Only in Rusch.

1:18 and (a)**alive, and was** (b)(c)**dead,** (d)**and behold I am** (e)**living forever and ever,** (f)**and have the keys of death and of hell.**

a. Sc. eternally.
b. According to the flesh.*
c. Sc. for you.*
d. But do not be frightened, because I have manifestly risen, and I shall not die any more.
e. Sc. eternally alive.*
f. And I will not let you be tempted above what you can sustain, because I have power over the Devil and over his members. The Devil is death, because he is the cause of death*; his ministers are hell, in whom he has his place.

He who has the key of a house lets anyone he wishes in and keeps anyone he wishes from entering the house. Therefore he possesses the keys of death and of hell because he frees those he wishes from the damnation of eternal death, and on the other hand he justly lets those he wishes stay in the same danger of damnation.[1]

1:18 (b) *Only in Rusch.] (c) *Codex 24 has this same gloss twice, the other one of which could refer to "alive".] (e) *Only in Latin 588.] (f) *Codex 24 and Rusch: "the cause of sin, i.e. of death".] 1 Only in Rusch.

1:19 Write therefore the things (a)which you have seen, and (b)that are, and (c)that must be done (d)after these.

    a.   Like in the passion and in the resurrection.*
    b.   The present tribulations and the present help.
    c.   Among the last faithful, by whose example the present faithful
        should be much encouraged.
    d.   Sc. write.*

1:19 (a) *Codex 24 and Rusch: "Like the passion and the resurrection".] (d) *Only in Latin 588.

1:20 (a)The (b)(c)sacrament of the seven stars, which you have seen in my right hand, and the seven candlesticks of gold: (d)the seven stars are the angels of the seven churches, and the seven candlesticks are the seven churches.

    a.   You understand "I shall teach you".*
    b.   Or "mystery".*
    c.   Where one thing is seen and another is understood.
    d.   The angel explains and partly reveals the allegory in order to
        inform us that an explanation must be sought everywhere.

As John plays here the role of the learner, so should we too play the role of John, so that we may learn from him as he learnt from the angel.[1]

1:20 *(a) Only in Codex 24.] (b) *Mentioning a variant reading in the Latin Vulgate text, as it will happen regularly. Not mentioned in Latin 588.] 1 Only in Latin 588.

CHAPTER 2

2:1 ^{(a)(b)(c)}*And to the angel of the church of Ephesus write: Thus says he which ^(d)holds the ^(e)seven stars ^(f)in his right hand, which ^{(g)(h)}walks ⁽ⁱ⁾in the middle of the seven candlesticks of gold,*

- a. John.*
- b. Note that in all these things he talks not only to the bishop, but also to those who are in his charge.*
- c. I.e. write* to the bishop; of whose hand Christ** asks the sins of those placed under his authority, and without whose assent he*** does not dare to judge those placed under his authority.
- d. Although they have sinned, he does not forsake them yet if they will repent.*
- e. I.e. seven bishops.*
- f. I.e. in his power.*
- g. Sc. as one distributing gifts, or not at rest yet.
- h. Because they are not such as he could rest in.*
- i. I.e. in the middle of the seven churches.*

The first vision is about the reproof[1] of the churches.

He starts giving individual warnings, which can be individual and universal, for the various members of any church.

"Ephesus" translates to "will", "advice" or "deep fall".[2]

"Ephesus", for the part of those who persevere well, translates to "will", because the will of God is in them[3], by whose works God is delighted. Concerning these he then says[4] that those who had fallen into error should be corrected by their example; for them[5], "Ephesus" translates to "advice", i.e. "needing advice", or "deep fall", or "my will".

John writes to the bishop of each church, to him who asks.[6]

2:1 (a) *Only in Rusch.] (b) *Only in Rusch.] (c) *Rusch: "he writes". **Codex 24 and Rusch: "he". ***Codex 24 and Rusch: "John himself".] (d) *"If they will repent" only in Latin 588.] (e) *Only in Latin 588, in a different ink from the rest.] (f) *Only in Latin 588, in the same ink as (e).] (h) *Not in Latin 588.] (i) *Only in Latin 588, in the same ink as (e) and (f).] 1 Codex 24: "correction". Only one letter differs between the two words in Latin.] 2 Not in Rusch.] 3 "Because the will of God is in them" missing in Codex 24 and Rusch.] 4 Codex 24 and Rusch: "he proposes". The two phrasings differ but by a couple of words in Latin, whence mistranscription would have easily happened.] 5 Rusch has "since" instead of "for them". Again, both resemble each other in Latin.] 6 Only in Codex 24.

2:2 ^(a)*I know your works and ^(b)labor, and your ^(c)patience, and that ^(d)you cannot bear ^(e)evil men, and ^(f)have tried them which say themselves to be ^(g)apostles, and are not, and ^(h)have found them liars:*

- a. I.e. I approve.
- b. I.e. tribulation.
- c. I.e. that you do not grumble about the delayed reward.
- d. I.e. you cannot help expelling or correcting evil men.*
- e. Acting inhumanly against you.*
- f. I.e. you have tested their doctrine, because only those who are inside, i.e. in the Church, are tried.
- g. I.e. sent by God, so that they may deceive you more easily.
- h. By their evil preaching and their evil life.

2:2 (d) *Codex 24 has "With the strength of humanity, because you cannot help correcting or expelling evil men" and Rusch "With the strength of humanity, or you cannot help correcting or expelling evil men".] (e) *Only in Rusch.

2:3 And you ^(a)have patience, ^(b)and have borne ^(c)for my name, and have not fainted.

- a. In the evils that they bring upon you and inflict upon you through earthly powers.*
- b. I.e. not for human praise, but to glorify my name, so that others may take example from it.*
- c. I.e. through.*

And have not fainted. It indicates that there would have been a reason for human failing if help had not come to prevent it.

2:3 (a) *Codex 24 and Rusch: "In the evils that they, united together, inflict upon you through earthly powers".] (b) *The part "so that others etc." is only in Latin 588.] (c) *Not in Latin 588.

2:4 (a)*But I have* (b)*against you a few things,* (c)*because you have left your first charity.*

a. This concerns the advice.*
b. I.e. the reverse of the crown.
c. Either the bishop in his person, affected by weariness over the vices in those under his authority, or those under his authority out of love for earthly things.

Heli was a good priest and yet he was condemned because of his sons whom he did not want to correct (1 Kings 3).[1]

2:4 (a) *Codex 24 has this gloss above "out of its place" in the next verse.] 1 Not in Latin 588.

2:5 *Be mindful* (a)*therefore* (b)*from where you are fallen: and do* (c)*penance, and do* (d)*the* (e)*first works. But if not,* (f)*I come to you, and* (g)*will move* (h)*your candlestick* (i)*out of its place,* (j)*unless you do penance.*

a. Since it is against you.
b. From the community of the saints*.
c. I.e. worthy fruits of penance.
d. Your.*
e. I.e. as you first started well, continue so.*
f. Sc. to kill you in the soul and in the body.
g. I will take away the virtues and the gifts of the Holy Spirit by which the candlesticks were set up.
h. I.e. own.*
i. I.e. in what is interpreted as "will".*
j. Here again the will.*

[JEROME] I will not let you fall into such sins from which you could acquire neither humility nor some virtues, i.e. that which is good according to the will of God.[1]

Here he speaks for that part for which "Ephesus" is interpreted as "advice".[2]

2:5 (b) *Codex 24 and Rusch: "of the faithful".] (d) *Only in Codex 24.] (e) *Codex 24 and Rusch: "Works similar to the first ones".] (h) *Only in Latin 588, in the other ink met before.] (i) *Not in Latin 588.] (j) *Not in Latin 588.] 1 Only found in Codex 24. The reading "that which is good" is somewhat doubtful.] 2 Only in Codex 24.

2:6 (a)*But* (b)*this you have,* (c)*that you hate* (d)*the facts of the Nicolaites,* (e)*which I also hate.*

a. Although this is against you, do not however despair, because this you have good.
b. Here again the will.*
c. Namely.*
d. Namely, the common use of women and the consuming of sacrifices made to idols.
e. Which you hate because you see that I hate them.*

Nicolas was one of the seven deacons mentioned in the Acts of Apostles (6:5), who, after having been disapproved for proclaiming that others could come to his wife[1], preached that all wives[2] should be shared, and preached the consuming of sacrifices made to idols.[3]

"Nicolas" is interpreted as "foolish people", i.e. the gentiles who did not know God and used their wives publicly; who ate sacrifices made to idols and believed that Jupiter was reigning[4]. The heretics who are imputed the error of the cult of idols and commit fornication, serving the impurity of the flesh, are also foolish for God. Foolish are the Jews also, foolish also the false Christians who, devoted to earthly things, worship the world.

2:6 (b) *Only in Codex 24.] (c) *Only in Rusch. Perhaps it is merely the beginning of the next gloss that was taken as a separate gloss?] (e) *Codex 24 has only "which you see that I hate".] 1 Codex 24: "disapproved for coming back to his wife".] 2 Codex 24: "women".] 3 This gloss is not in Rusch.] 4 Codex 24 and Rusch have all this in present tense, "do not know... eat... etc.".

2:7 (a)*He that has an* (b)*ear, let him hear what* (c)*the Spirit says to the churches. To him* (d)*that overcomes, I will give to eat of the tree of life, which is* (e)*in the Paradise of* (f)*my God.*

a. What I say to one, I say to all.
b. I.e. divine understanding.*
c. I.e. the Trinity.
d. I.e. that perseveres.*
e. I.e. in the garden of delights, i.e. in the Church.

To him that overcomes. Why should he hear? Because to him that overcomes, i.e. that perseveres, Christ is the tree of life, because he is a source of strength and shade, giving fruit, i.e. his body and blood, here and mostly in the future.

The tree of life. Christ is called the tree of life because he does the same thing in the Church as the tree of life in the paradise. Indeed the function of that tree was to preserve those who enjoyed its fruit from death and the decline of old age. Christ fulfills this same function in

f.   According to my humanity.*

the Church, for he protects his people both from the true death and from all failure. But Adam, eating of the forbidden fruit, lost that which the tree of life bestowed upon him, and obtained in the experience knowledge of good and evil. Before, when placed in delights, he did not know what was good and evil. He eventually came to know both, since he had now experienced both.[1]

When "Spirit" is said without addition, the whole Trinity is more often understood, as here and "God is a spirit" (Jn. 4:24).[2]

2:7 (b) *The Vulgate text of all three books actually has "he that has ears to hear", and this gloss is above "to hear".] (d) *Only in Latin 588.] (f) *Not in Codex 24.] 1 Only in Latin 588.] 2 Only in Codex 24.

2:8 And to the (a)angel of the church of (b)Smyrna write: (c)Thus says the first and the last, who was (d)dead, and (e)lives:

a.   I.e. bishop.*
b.   "Smyrna" is interpreted as "canticle" or as it were "myrrh" from the bitterness of sufferings.*
c.   Which is to say, do not succumb, because I who am so great suffered death for you and rose from it, and you too should expect the same.
d.   Sc. for you.*
e.   Eternally.*

Smyrna. "Smyrna" is interpreted as "canticle" or as it were "myrrh". The canticle is those by whom he is delighted. Myrrh is so bitter that it preserves corpses from rotting.[1]

Write. That is, describe[2] a Christ who is such that he may do something for the consolation of those upon whom tribulations are inflicted.

2:8 (a) *Only in Latin 588.] (b) *Only in Latin 588, although the beginning is found in a marginal gloss in the other books, as you will see.] (d) *Only in Latin 588.] (e) *Only in Latin 588.] 1 Not in Latin 588.] In Codex 24 and Rusch, this gloss starts with "He describes" and is referred to the part "thus says the first and the last, etc.".

2:9 I know your (a)tribulation and your (b)poverty, but you are (c)rich: and you are (d)blasphemed (e)of them that say themselves to be (f)Jews and (g)are not, but are the (h)synagogue (i)of Satan.

a.   I.e. persecution.*
b.   Literally.
b.   Sc. in hope of reward.
c.   I.e. defamed. It is an increase of misery to him that suffers tribulation if he is defamed.*
d.   No pest is more effective than a domestic enemy.
e.   I.e. confessing.
f.   Because if they were the children of Abraham, they would do the works of Abraham (Ref. Jn. 8:39).
g.   Sc. congregation.
h.   I.e. of the adversary.

The synagogue is a congregation that seems to pertain to that which is devoid of reason, as if it were a congregation of cattle. But the Church is called a convocation, because it is manifestly said of that which has reason.[1]

2:9 (a) *Only in Latin 588.] (d) *"I.e. defamed" only in Latin 588.] 1 Only in Latin 588. It is difficult to render exactly the nuances of this gloss in English, because the glossator seems to have been playing on the root meaning of the words *congregatio* (which I have imperfectly translated as "congregation") and *convocatio* (which I have imperfectly translated as "convocation"). *Congregatio* means literally an assembling/crowding/flocking together, and hence an association, assembly, congregation; but it is related to the word *grex* whose first meaning is a group of animals, flock or herd, though it can also mean a group of people. Whence the comparison with cattle. *Convocatio* means literally a calling together, hence also an assembling together. I apologize for the obvious smell of anti-Semitism this (as well as a few other glosses) has; I am of course merely translating and not expressing my own opinions.

2:10 (a)Fear none of these things which you shall suffer. (b)Behold the Devil will send some of you into (c)prison (d)that you may be tried, and you shall have tribulation (e)ten days. (f)You be faithful until death, and I will give you (g)the crown of life.

Some of you. Here it is clear that it refers not to one person only but to several people.[1]

Ten days. The life of the just man is symbolized by the number ten, because it is under the control of the ten commandments of the law, while secular life is well symbolized by the number seven, because it

a. Sc. but yet.*
b. Or should I say "I will permit"?*
c. He says "prison" for any tribulation.
d. I.e. that you may be an object of contempt for the Devil and his limbs.*
e. I.e. the time of the war, for, when God sends his people to war, he arms them with the Decalogue. Or ten days, i.e. all the time during which the Church fights for seven days against the three principal vices: avarice, vainglory and cupidity.
f. But whatever they inflict upon you, you be faithful.
g. I.e. eternal life will be your crown.*

is completed in seven days.[2]

2:10 (a) *Codex 24: "You are blasphemed of them that say themselves to be Jews, but yet".] (b) *The Latin of this gloss is extremely ambiguous and I am at a loss as to how to interpret it. And to complicate matters still a bit more, it is not altogether clear in all books what part of the verse it is referring to. Latin 588 and Rusch have it above "behold the Devil will send etc.", whereas Codex 24 has it above "you shall suffer", but the placement of glosses is not always precise. My theories are the following: if it refers to "behold etc." the translation might be "Or should I say "I will permit"?", i.e. the Devil will do that only because I will permit it. If it refers to "you shall suffer?", the translation might be "or shall I suffer?" or "or should I say "I shall suffer"?", the idea perhaps being that he will suffer because his faithful suffer. I have chosen the first interpretation to put in the main text because the majority of books (two against one), including Latin 588, have it in that place, and the interpretation also looked slightly more likely to me. But I repeat that I am not sure, of neither translation or interpretation, and the people whose opinion I asked on the matter were not any more sure than I. The Latin could also possibly translate to one of the following "or perhaps I shall permit", "or perhaps I shall suffer", "shall I permit?". If the majority of books is right and if it is indeed meant to comment on "behold the Devil will send etc.", I cannot figure what the point the glossator wished to make would have been with any of those. In the Bible text, the angel seems to be speaking of this as of something absolutely sure to happen, and I am a bit hard put to it to understand how the glossator could have interpreted it as a mere possibility like "or perhaps..." or "shall I...?".] (d) *Codex 24 and Rusch start with "I.e. that you may be tested, or..." and continues with the same thing as in Latin 588.] (g) *Only in Latin 588.] 1 Only in Rusch.] 2 Only in Latin 588.

2:11 *He that has an ear, let him hear what [(a)]the Spirit says to the churches. [(b)]He [(c)]that shall overcome, shall not be hurt by the [(d)]second death.*

a. The Trinity.*
b. Because...*
c. I.e. that shall persevere until the end.*
d. Which is in* the Gehenna.

The second death. There are two lives of the soul, and two deaths, and similarly of the body. The first life of the soul is perseverance in virtues[1]; its second life is to be granted eternal life. The first death of the soul is to persist in sins, the second one is to be punished forever[2]. The first life of the body is to be joined to a soul, the second one is to be brought back to life. The first death of the body is to be detached from the soul, the second one is to be damned in the judgment.[3]

The first death of the soul is in sin, the second in the penalties.[4]

The first death of the body is when it is dissolved, the second when it is damned in the future judgment.[5]

2:11 (a) *Only in Codex 24.] (b) *Not in Codex 24.] (c) *Only in Latin 588, in a different ink from the other glosses.] (d) *"In" missing in Rusch.] 1 Latin 588 has "in strength", but it is doubtless a mistranscription (*in viribus* = "in strength"; *in virtutibus* = "in virtues", and the latter would resemble the former even more if abbreviated).] 2 Codex 24: "the first death of the soul is in sins, the second one is to be punished for its sins".] 3 This gloss is not in Rusch.] 4 Not in Codex 24.] 5 Not in Codex 24.

2:12 *And to the [(a)]angel of the church of [(b)(c)(d)]Pergamus write: Thus [(e)]says he that has [(f)]the sharp two-edged sword,*

a. I.e. bishop.*
b. "Pergamus" is interpreted as "division of the horns".
c. So that those who are preserving the unity of the Church be divided from the wicked.*
d. By the horns some battle is signified, as in this Church the bad part was attacking the good one.*
e. I.e. he requires them* to have this sword in the choosing of the good and the reprobation of the wicked.
f. The sharp two-edged sword is the sentence of the Lord with which he will condemn the wicked in their bodies and souls.*

Pergamus. Because it has the discernment between the horns of the good and of the wicked, that is, it discerns what virtues are true and what virtues are fake, because the horns of the good shall be exalted and those of the wicked brought down (Ref. Psalm 74:11 and possibly also 111:7-9).[1]

2:12 (a) *Only in Latin 588.] (c) *Not in Latin 588.] (d) *Not in Latin 588.] (e) *Codex 24 has "the just" with "or them" written above in the ink I mentioned in the preface. The two differ only in one letter in Latin.] (f) *Only in Rusch.] 1 Only in Latin 588.

2:13 I know where you dwell, (a)(b)where (c)the seat of Satan is: (d)and you hold (e)my name, and (f)have not denied my faith. And (g)in those days (h)(i)Antipas (j)(k)my (l)faithful (m)witness, (n)who was slain among you, where Satan dwells.

a.	Namely, where the seat of Satan is, that is, in the middle of perverse action*.
b.	Among others who are the seat of Satan.*
c.	I.e. the congregation of Satan, i.e. the adversary.*
d.	Sc. yet.*
e.	Sc. against those who dispute it.
f.	Sc. because of any tribulation. Tribulation is an illumination to the just.
g.	Sc. you also did this.*
h.	Sc. there was.*
i.	Bishop.*
j.	Was.* Work following his example.
k.	Who is.*
l.	Who is my witness because faithful.*
m.	I.e. he was a martyr.
n.	Conclusion because they killed him.*

Have not denied my faith. Tribulation is an illumination to the just, a rebuke to the defiant, a blinding to the stubborn.[1]

They slew him because Satan dwelled there, or he dwelled there because they slew him. It is for this that he says "like a conclusion, etc."[2]

2:13 (a) Codex 24 and Rusch: "in the middle of a perverse nation", which is perhaps likely to be the right reading.] (b) *Only in Codex 24.] (c) *Only in Rusch.] (d) *Not in Rusch.] (g) *Codex 24 and Rusch: "In which you did this".] (h) *Only in Codex 24.] (i) *Only in Latin 588.] (j) *"Was" not here in Codex 24 and Rusch.] (k) *Not in Latin 588.] (l) *Only in Codex 24.] (m) *Only in Rusch. Note that the word "martyr" comes from Greek μάρτυρ which means "witness".] (n) *Codex 24 and Rusch have "Like a conclusion because they killed him" above "where Satan dwells".] 1 Only in Rusch.] 2 Only in Codex 24. This gloss in fact explains interlinear (n).

2:14 (a)But I have against you (b)a few things: because (c)you have there them that hold the doctrine of (d)Balaam, who taught (e)Balac to cast a scandal before the children of Israel, (f)to eat and (g)(h)commit fornication:

a.	Although you are constant in this...
b.	If you do not correct yourself.*
c.	I.e. you tolerate them and do not expel them.
d.	"Vain people".
e.	"Knocking out".
f.	I.e. to take pleasure in vain* things.
g.	With the Devil.
h.	Either carnally or spiritually.*

Balaam. It refers to the story from the Old Testament (Num. 31), how Balaam taught Balac the king of the Midianites to corrupt the sons of Israel so that they might sin in the sight of God, sc. so that he might entice them into fornication and idolatry through beautiful women. Some people of this church are reproached with these sins. This may also be applied to the present Church through an allegory. "Balaam" is interpreted as "vain people", "Balac" as "knocking out". The vain people is the heretics who teach earthly princes, who are knocking out a way to deceive, i.e. to deceive the men who see God. Or the vain people means demons who teach the human body to knock out, i.e. destroy, every virtue in itself.[1]

Balaam. I.e. the heretics who teach earthly princes how to cause the ruin of those who see God[2]. Or Balaam, i.e. the demons who teach the flesh to deceive the souls that see God.

2:14 (b) *Codex 24 and Rusch go on with something that could mean either "even in a few things" or "or in a few things", the latter of which could be simply mentioning a variant reading of the Vulgate, but I have not myself found it - which does not mean much, since I am far from being able to check every version of the Vulgate that ever existed, of course!] (f) *Rusch: "various". The Vulgates of Latin 588 and Codex 24 have "to eat of the sacrifices of idols" instead of just "to eat", and Codex 24 has a gloss above it saying "carnally", unless it be an accidental duplication of part of (h).] (h) *Not in Latin 588.] 1 Only in Latin 588.] 2 Codex 24: "of the lovers of God".

2:15 (a)so you have also (b)them that hold (c)(d)the doctrine of the Nicolaites.

a.	I.e. similarly.*
b.	I.e. them that attack us.
c.	He mentions the Nicolaites again in order to invite to penance, which he did not do above.
d.	In most versions, "which I hate" is added.*

2:15 (a) *Not in Codex 24.] (d) *Only in Rusch, but Codex 24 has those words in the verse.

2:16 [a]*In like manner do penance:* [b][c]*if not, I will come to* [d]*you quickly, and* [e]*will fight against them with the sword of my mouth.*

    a.   For this as for the other thing.
    b.   Because.
    c.   I.e. if you do less than I say.*
    d.   Sc. who are not correcting.
    e.   I.e. I will convict those adulterers of having sinned, by saying "Go, you cursed, into everlasting fire" (Matt. 25:41).*

2:16 (c) *Only in Latin 588, in the other ink already met earlier. Instead of this, Codex 24 and Rusch have "if you do less than you ought to in anything". This gloss seems to be an interpretation of the very literal meaning of the Latin, which is not seen in its English translation. The Latin *si quominus*, translated by "if not", means here very literally "if by anything less". The original Greek, translated literally, does not have this meaning. It might also be worth noting that this is an unusual meaning for *quominus*; its usual meaning is "so that not" (literally "by which less"); the *quo* part in itself can mean "by which" or "by anything", or other things in different contexts that are not relevant here, but the former meaning is the one it usually has in this word); so the unusualness of its use here is probably what prompted the glossator to explain it.] (e) *Codex 24 has, divided into two glosses: "I.e. and I will convict those fornicators of having sinned by teaching" and "Saying "Go, you cursed, into everlasting fire"". In Latin only one letter differs from "by saying" (dicendo) to "by teaching" (docendo). So this is again one of those places where a scribal error could easily happen.

2:17 *He that has an* [a]*ear, let him hear what the spirit says to the churches. To him that overcomes I will give* [b]*the* [c]*hidden* [d][e]*manna, and* [f]*will give him* [g]*a* [h]*white counter: and* [i]*in the counter,* [j]*a new name written,* [k]*which no man* [l]*knows, but he* [m]*that receives it.*

    a.   Of the heart.*
    b.   Or myself who was hidden in the manna.*
    c.   *Which eye has not seen, nor ear heard* (1 Corint. 2:9).
    d.   I.e. eternal glory.*
    e.   Another translation has "pearl".*
    f.   Meanwhile.
    g.   I.e. a solid body.*
    h.   I.e. bright with virtues.*
    i.   I.e. in such a body.
    j.   Christian, in which there is nothing old.*
    k.   I.e. the meaning of which.*
    l.   To which he is invited by this name.*
    m.   I.e. who fulfills it in deed, because he who says that he knows Christ*, and keeps not his commandments, is a liar (1 John 2:4).

A counter is a solid and bright stone, by which the divine speech is symbolized, which is said to be bright with regards to the truth, and solid because it cannot be broken. Therefore by the counter is symbolized a human body solid against vices and bright by the manifoldness of virtues. Some other translations have

"carbuncle", but they always symbolize the same thing. [1]

A white counter. In Daniel, "A stone was cut out without hands" (Daniel, 2:34). In the proverbs, "The expectation of him that expects, is a most acceptable jewel" (Prov. 17:8).[2]

And in the counter a new name written which no man, etc. Or on top of baptism I add martyrdom, which a hypocrite who suffers in order to be praised does not understand the meaning[3] of.

Written. It was with five letters, that is, with five wounds, that it was shown on his body on the cross that he was a martyr.[4]

2:17 (a) *Not in Latin 588.] (b) *Not in Latin 588.] (c) and (d) *Instead of having these two glosses here, Codex 24 and Rusch have a marginal gloss saying: "*Manna.* I.e. eternal glory, of which everyone will say "What is this?"; *which eye has not seen, nor ear heard, (neither has it entered into the heart of man)*", the part in parentheses being only in Codex 24.] (c) *Not in Latin 588. In Codex 24, it could refer to "counter", whereas Rusch clearly refers it to "manna".] (g) *Codex 24: "I.e. a human body solid against vices, or himself"; Rusch: "That is, a solid body, or himself".] (h) *Codex 24: "Bright with virtues and immortal in hope"; Rusch has "Bright, white with virtues and hope of immortality", and it has "bright" in the verse instead of "white", with an interlinear gloss mentioning the latter as a variant.] (j) *Not in Rusch. Latin 588's Vulgate text has "my new name", with "I.e. Christian" as a gloss to "my" and "in which there is nothing old" to "new".] (k) *Not in Rusch. What I have translated as "meaning" can also mean "force".] (l) *Codex 24 has "Which one reaches through this name". Rusch has "What for? For him to be invited by this name".] (m) *Codex24 and Rusch: "God".] 1 Only in Latin 588.] 2 Only in Rusch.] 3 Or "force".] 4 Only in Rusch.

2:18 *And to the* [a]*angel of the church of* [b]*Thyatira write, thus says the Son of God, which has* [c]*eyes as a flame of fire, and his* [d]*feet like to latten.*

    a.   I.e. bishop.*
    b.   "Thyatira" means "illuminated" or "kindled".*
    c.   I.e. the gifts of the Holy Spirit. And he gives them to or takes them away from whom he wants. And therefore let those who have already received those gifts see to it that they do not lose them by sympathizing with the wicked.
    d.   Which must be imitated.*

Thyatira is interpreted as "illuminated" or "living victim", or "kindled", because in this church there are some kindled ones, and also some wicked ones.[1]

2:18 (a) *Only in Latin 588.] (b) *Codex 24 and Rusch: "Thyatira is interpreted as "illumined" or "living victim".] (d) *Codex 24 has "Which must be imitated, i.e. Christ's humility, or the last faithful"; Rusch has two glosses: "Which must be imitated" and "I.e. the last faithful".] 1 Only in Latin 588.

2:19 [a]*I know your works,* [b]*and faith, and your charity, and* [c]*ministry, and your* [d][e]*patience, and* [f]*your last works more than the former.*

a. I.e. I have accepted.
b. First comes faith; from faith, charity; from charity, good works.
c. In almsgivings.
d. Because from these things comes tribulation.*
e. In every adversity.
f. Because the unpolished Church has come from lesser things to more perfect ones*.

I know your works, and faith, and your charity. Or charity and faith; reversed order - not because charity comes before faith.[1]

2:19 (d) *Not in Latin 588. Codex 24 has it in a mistranscribed form.] (f) *Rusch: "to perfection". I have followed Codex 24 in the main text, because Latin 588 seems here to have a mistranscription.] 1 Only in Rusch.

2:20 But I have against you a few things: because you [a]*permit the* [b]*woman* [c]*Jezebel, who* [d]*calls herself a prophetess, to teach, and* [e]*to seduce* [f]*my servants,* [g]*to fornicate, and to eat of things sacrificed to idols.*

a. Sc. you do not excommunicate her, but you permit.
b. I.e. voluptuous and lustful.
c. "Flow of blood" or "dung-pit".*
d. According to what is said.*
e. Sc. in fact.
f. Who imitate her.*
g. With women or with the Devil.

Jezebel is interpreted as "flow of blood", "flowing" or "dung-pit". As women suffer a flow of menstrual blood in due time, so does a reprobate soon achieve when it is time the bad plan he conceives. And then, when he is filled with a flame, he is said to be all flowing; and when he turns it into a habit, he scatters a foul smell widely[1]. These are the three dead resurrected, one in the house, the other one outside the gate, the third one in the grave[2].

Jezebel. Ahab's wife or that of this bishop. Through her you understand the heretics who pretend to be good but entice people[3] into licentiousness and lust.[4]

Fornication is said to be fourfold: in the mind if you look on a woman to lust after her (ref. Matt. 5:28), in the act itself, in the love of earthly things, and in the cult of idols.

2:20 (c) *Only in Latin 588.] (d) *Only in Rusch.] (f) *Only in Rusch. Considering Codex 24's version of the marginal gloss on Jezebel (see note 3), it is possible that this be a mistranscription for "who invite her", or even that some exchange between the glosses happened one way around or the other. "Her" or "them" is the same word in Latin in this context, so only the "who invite" or "imitate" part changes, and these words look fairly similar.] 1 Codex 24 adds "like a dung-pit".] 2 The last sentence concerning the dead resurrected is not in Latin 588.] 3 Codex 24 has "people who invite them".] 4 Latin 588 does not have this gloss except "Ahab's wife or that of this bishop" as an interlinear.

2:21 And I gave her a time that she might do penance: and she will not repent from her fornication. 2:22 [a]*Behold I will* [b]*cast her* [c]*into a bed: and* [d][e]*they that commit adultery with her, shall be in very great tribulation, unless they do penance from their works:*

a. And because she will not.
b. By blinding her.
c. Into confidence to sin, or a bed of pain.
d. I.e. I will send her with her works into perdition.*
e. I.e. those who are like her, or the works for which they shall be punished.*

Into a bed. Another translation has "mourning" instead of "bed", by which it designates eternal misery.

2:22 (d) *Only in Rusch.] (e) *Codex 24: "Those who become like her through the works for which they shall be punished"; Rusch: "I.e. they become like her though the works for which they shall be punished".

2:23 and [a]*her children* [b]*I will kill unto death, and* [c]*all the churches shall know that I am* [d]*he that searches the reins and* [e]*hearts,* [f]*and I will give* [g]*to everyone of you according to his works.*

a. I.e. all her followers.

b.   Sc. condemning them to eternal punishment.*
c.   I.e. they shall know in the future by the facts that which here they know only by faith.
d.   I.e. he that punishes carnal concupiscences.
e.   I.e. bad thoughts.*
f.   And they shall know that I will give...*
g.   Good things to the good, bad things to the bad.

2:23 (b) *Not in Latin 588.] (d) and (e) *Codex 24 and Rusch have assembled these two into one gloss: "He that punishes carnal concupiscences and bad thoughts". Latin 588's meaning is undoubtedly the same.] (f) *Not in Latin 588.

2:24 *(a)***But I say to you the rest** *(b)***which are at Thyatira,** *(c)(d)***whosoever** *(e)***have not this doctrine, which have not** *(f)***known the** *(g)***depth of Satan, as** *(h)***they** *(i)***say, I will not cast upon you** *(j)***another weight.**

I will not cast. Some pseudo-prophets were frightening them by saying that the Lord was still about to send greater tribulations than those they had suffered; he contradicts this by saying that he will not cast a greater weight or legal observances.[1]

a.   This I do to them.
b.   I.e. illuminated or kindled ones.*
c.   Change of person, parenthesis in the sentence.
d.   Of you.*
e.   That there is no salvation without the law.*
f.   I.e. approved.
g.   I.e. pride.
h.   Some people who came from Judea.
i.   That I will cast.*
j.   Sc. that of the old law.

2:24 (b) *Only in Latin 588.] (d) *Only in Rusch.] (e) *Only in Rusch.] (i) *Not in Latin 588.] 1 Only in Rusch.

2:25 *(a)***Yet** *(b)***that which you have, hold till I** *(c)***come.**

a.   Although they say this.
b.   As if he were saying: Work so as not to lose what he has already given, but strive for greater things.*
c.   Sc. to repay.

2:25 (b) *Only in Rusch here, but Latin 588 and Codex 24 have it to 3:1.

2:26 And he *(a)***that shall overcome,** *(b)***and keep my works** *(c)***unto the end, I will give him** *(d)***power over** *(e)***the nations,**

a.   I.e. that does not yield to them.*
b.   And with this.
c.   Of his life, or unto perfection of the works.
d.   Sc. in this world.
e.   Those who live heathenishly.

2:26 (a) *Codex 24: "Not believing them".

2:27 and he shall rule them (a)**with a rod of iron, and** (b)**as the vessel of a potter they shall be broken,**

    a.   I.e. with an inflexible justice.
    b.   Some so that they will perish completely*, some so that they will be changed for the better.

2:27 (b) *Codex 24 has "so that they will sin immediately", with "or so that they will perish completely" written above in the other ink I mentioned in the preface.

2:28 (a)**As I also** (b)**have received of my Father: and** (c)**I will give him** (d)**the morning star.**

    a.   So will I give him power.*
    b.   Sc. through my humanity.*
    c.   Sc. in the future.*
    d.   I.e. myself or the first resurrection.*

The morning star is Lucifer[1] which announces the day by its rising, i.e. Christ who brought the light of faith and immortality[2] to the world when he rose again. Therefore he will give the morning star, i.e. himself and the glory of resurrection, or the morning star, i.e. the first resurrection.

2:28 (a) *Only in Latin 588.] (b) *Codex 24 has one gloss saying "unity" and a second one "through unity". Rusch has "according to my humanity".] (c) *Not in Codex 24.] (d) *Only in Latin 588.] 1 "Lucifer" = in Latin literally "light-bringing" or "light-bringer".] 2 Latin 588 says that he "brought the light of faith and immortality" in the sense "brought the light of faith and brought immortality", whereas Codex 24 and Rusch have the sense "brought the light of faith and brought the light of immortality".

2:29 He that has an ear, let him hear what the Spirit says to the churches.

CHAPTER 3

3:1 AND to the ^(a)angel of the church of ^(b)Sardis write, ^(c)Thus says he that has the seven Spirits of God, and the seven stars, ^(d)I know your works, ^(e)that you have the name that you live, ^(f)and you are dead.

Sardis. The beginning of beauty means him who first has no or little virtue, and then becomes ugly through vices, or the hypocrites who are beautiful outside but ugly inside. Or the beginning of beauty is to have gone out of the world.[1]

a. I.e. bishop.*
b. "The beginning of beauty", or "appropriate for the beginning* of beauty".
c. As if he were saying: Work so as not to lose what he has already given, but strive for greater things.*
d. I.e. I learn about.
e. I.e. I know that you seek human praise in those works.
f. Because he who offends in one point is guilty of all (ref. James 2:10).

3:1 (a) *Only in Latin 588.] (b) *Latin 588 has "for the prince". Only one letter differs: "for the beginning" = *principio*; "for the prince" = *principi*.] (c) *Not in Rusch here, but it has it to 2:25.] 1 Only in Rusch.

3:2 ^(a)Be ^(b)vigilant, and ^(c)confirm ^(d)the rest of the things ^(e)which were ^{(f)(g)}to die. ^(h)For ⁽ⁱ⁾I find not your works full ^(j)before my God.

Be vigilant. Or be vigilant because even if you are perfect in mind[1], yet you are not perfect if you do not incite others to do good works[2]. Or it is not enough to confess Christ if you do not also do works (see James 2:14-26).

a. Therefore.*
b. I.e. concerned about salvation.
c. Sc. and through this.*
d. Of the limbs.*
e. I.e. those who were to die from sins.*
f. If you are not vigilant.*
g. Or "dead".*
h. I mean, be vigilant for I find not...
i. Sc. as they are without love, or for praise, or because he commits a criminal sin.
j. And therefore they are not in his good pleasure.

3:2 (a) *Not in Rusch.] (c) *Not in Rusch.] (d) *Only in Codex 24.] (e) *Only in Latin 588, in the other ink.] (f) *Only in Codex 24.] (g) *Only in Rusch.] 1 Codex 24 and Rusch: "even if you are undisturbed in mind, or laudable in mind".] 2 "To do good works" only in Latin 588.

3:3 ^(a)Have in mind therefore in what manner you have ^(b)received and heard: and ^(c)keep, and ^(d)do penance. ^(e)If therefore you watch not, ^(f)I will come to you as a thief, and ^(g)you shall not know what hour I will come ^(h)to you.

Heard. Sc. from the holy fathers. I.e. that he who offends in one point is guilty of all (ref. James 2:10), or "they have received their reward" (Matt. 6:2), or "... and have not charity, I am nothing" (1 Cor. 13:2).

a. And because they are not full, therefore...
b. I.e. started working.
c. I.e. fulfill in deed.
d. For having ceased.
e. Because they are not full, therefore...*
f. Sc. blinding you to rob and kill you.*
g. I.e. you shall not be able to take precautions.*
h. I.e. against you.

3:3 (e) *Not in Rusch.] (f) *Not in Codex 24, except that it has "blinding you" above the second "I will come to you".] (g) *Not in Rusch.

3:4 But you have (a)(b)(c)*a few names in Sardis, which* (d)*have not* (e)*defiled their garments:* (f)*and they shall walk with me* (g)*in whites,* (h)*because they are worthy.*

a. I.e. a few people named, i.e. good people who are worthy of naming.
b. But there are a few people that you can imitate.*
c. A good number are such.*
d. Sc. with a criminal stain, or if a stain had been made they erased it with tears.
e. Like the perverse people.*
f. Therefore they shall walk with me from virtue to virtue, just as I have led the way*.
g. Clothed in innocence and immortality.*
h. If.*

Have not defiled their garments. I.e. the dress of immortality and innocence that they received in baptism, or their good works.

3:5 (a)(b)*He that shall overcome, shall* (c)*thus be vested in white garments, and* (d)*I will not put his name out of the book of life, and I will confess his name* (e)*before my Father,* (f)*and before his angels.*

a. And similarly.
b. I am talking about their imitators*.
c. I.e. they shall similarly be vested in white garments.*
d. I.e. I will not take grace away from him. He says less and means more.
e. I.e. In the good pleasure of my Father.
f. And in the joy of holy* angels.

I will not put his name out. But he put the reprobates out according to that: "The Lord hardened Pharaoh's heart" (Ex. 10:20).

Out of the book of life. That is, out of God's prescience, in which everything is unchanging. Saying, "Come, you blessed of my Father, because you gave me to eat and to drink" (ref. Matt. 25:34-35).

3:6 He that has an ear, let him hear what the Spirit says to the churches.
3:7 And to the (a)*angel of the church of Philadelphia write, Thus says the* (b)*Holy One and the* (c)*True One, he that has* (d)*the key of David; he that* (e)*opens, and no man* (f)*shuts:* (g)*shuts,* (h)*and no man opens.*

a. I.e. bishop.*
b. Sc. in work.*
c. Sc. in his promises.*
d. I.e. the flesh of David, which is not an unreal one, thanks to which are all the good things.*
e. Sc. the hearts to faith or the Scriptures.
f. Sc. by taking grace away.
g. Sc. before the heretics.
h. Lest they trample the pearls, i.e. the divine Scriptures, under their feet like swine (ref. Matt. 7:6).*

Philadelphia means "brother's love" or "saving the inheritance", because it is through the brotherhood of love that one acquires the inheritance of the heavenly Fatherland.[1]

Thus says he. As if he were saying: Work at the conversion of brothers as you have started. Because I, who promised, "If you ask the Father anything in my name, he will give it to you" (John, 16:24), am truthful in my promises; therefore you may know that I will join many people to you if you believe.[2]

The key of David. I.e. his flesh; not an unreal one, not an imaginary one as some heretics used to invent, but a true one as the Catholic Church confesses.[3]

Or the key of David that opens the prophets is Christ, who revealed the hidden secrets of the Scriptures, and he is compared to a key because he opens to view that which is hidden and shut.[4]

Or he shuts so that we may seek, he opens so that we may find, so that the seeker may receive the fruit of his sweat, and the bestower have the gratitude for his goodness.

3:7 (a) *Only in Latin 588.] (b) *Only in Latin 588.] (c)* Only in Latin 588.] (d) Rusch has "The flesh of David, but also that of Adam, not a new one; thanks to which are all the good things". Codex 24 has "The true flesh of David, thanks to which are all the good things" with "not new" written as a correction above "true" in the other ink mentioned in the preface, as well as an explanation in the margin, "because it was from Adam".] (g) and (h) *Instead of these two glosses, Codex 24 and Rusch have one (to "shuts") saying "before the swine that would trample them/the pearls" - "them" in Rusch, "the pearls" in Codex 24.] 1 Codex 24 and Rusch only have the interpretations of the name without the explanation ("because...") that follows. Rusch has "saluting" instead of "saving".] 2 Codex 24 and Rusch have "as you desire" instead of "if you believe".] 3 Only in Latin 588.] 4 Only in Latin 588.

3:8 (a)*I know your* (b)*works.* (c)*Behold I have given* (d)*before you* (e)*a door opened which no man can shut: because you have a* (f)*little power, and have kept* (g)*my word, and* (h)*have not denied my name.*

    a.   I.e. I approve.
    b.   Good.
    c.   And.*
    d.   I.e. in your good pleasure.*
    e.   I.e. the hearts of men which were first hard, or the Scriptures which were obscure, or myself who am the true door*. Whence the disciples, after having been forbidden from speaking and scourged, said, "We cannot but speak the things which we have seen and heard" (Acts, 4:20)**.
    f.   I.e. not proud, or little compared to the future one, when there shall be no labor.
    g.   I.e. my preaching.*
    h.   In straits.

Behold I have given before you, etc., because you have a little, etc. I have given it for a good reason, because you could obviously not have it by yourself, because you have little power.[1]

3:8 (c) *Not in Codex 24.] (d) *Only in Latin 588.] (e) *Codex 24 and Rusch: "the true door to life". **Codex 24 has the part starting from "whence the disciples" to "word".] (g) *Not in Rusch.] 1 Only in Rusch.

3:9 (a)*Behold I will give of the synagogue of Satan,* (b)*which say they be Jews, and are not, but do lie.* (c)*Behold I will make them* (d)*come and* (e)*adore before your feet. And they shall know* (f)*that I have loved you.*

    a.   And because you are such.
    b.   They lost this name when they said about Christ "This man, we know not from whence he is" (John, 9:29).
    c.   Here is how I will give them.
    d.   To faith.
    e.   I.e. venerate, as Joseph's brothers adored him, ready to imitate* your footsteps**, humbled by similarity.
    f.   I.e. because the people outside did not believe that God loved the Church, which he let be afflicted. Now it will persuade them of his love, i.e. give them the certitude of his love.*

In the sixth vision, he talks about the conversion of angels.[1]

As is often the case in the sixth place in what follows, here too in the sixth angel is the last persecution indicated, in which some of the Jews must be deceived, and it is believed that some, following Elijah's advice and fulfilling the law spiritually, will overcome the enemy (ref. Rev. 11:1-14).

Lie. That is, they try to make you believe it with words and with some simulations.

3:9 (e) *Codex 24: "wonder at". **Codex 24 and Rusch: "your works".] (f) *Codex 24 and Rusch have more words here: "Do not succumb, because I come to reward you".] 1 Not in Latin 588.

3:10 *Because you have kept the word of my patience, and* (a)*I will keep you from the hour of* (b)*temptation, which shall come upon the whole world to tempt the inhabitants on the earth.*

    a.   Because you have kept.
    b.   Sc. either the general persecution of Christians right after Nero or in the last time of the Antichrist.

You have kept the word of my patience. That is, you have kept the commandment concerning patience that I showed in myself when I prayed for my persecutors, like Stephen: "Lord, lay not this sin to their charge" (Acts, 7:59).[1]

3:10 1 "Like Stephen" and the following quote only in Latin 588.

3:11 (a)*Behold I come quickly:* (b)*hold that which you have, that no man take your* (c)*crown.*

    a.   Temptation will really come, but do not succumb, because behold I come to reward you, and not slowly, but quickly.*
    b.   And therefore meanwhile hold your faith and your works.
    c.   I.e. reward.*

That no man take your crown. Since God has already determined the number of his people, if anyone falls back out of that number, another is received into it by his mercy, as the Gentiles succeeded the Jews due to the arrogance of the latter.

3:11 (a) *Codex 24 has "Temptation will come in its time, but I come", and Rusch "Temptation will really come, but do not succumb, because I come to reward you".] (c) *Only in Latin 588.

3:12 *(a)He that shall overcome, I will make him a (b)pillar in the temple of my God: and (c)he shall go out no (d)more: and I will write upon him (e)the name of my God, and the name (f)of the city of my God, (g)new Jerusalem which descends (h)out of heaven from my God, and (i)my (j)new name.*

a. Because*
b. I.e. strong in himself, and supporting others by word and example.
c. I.e. I will not let him fall or go away.*
d. I.e. more than the mind of man.*
e. In some way, he shall be God.*
f. I.e. he shall be called the city of God, i.e. a man fortified with virtues. Where there will be nothing of the ancient times, but a full vision of peace.*
g. I.e. from conformity with heavenly creatures.
h. I.e. "Christian", i.e. "anointed with grace".
i. I.e. having nothing of Adam.

He shall go out no more. The younger son, the people of the gentiles, had gone out: but after being reconciled by the death of the fatted calf, i.e. by the blood of Christ, he shall go out no more.

From my God. Because God sends virtues[1]

3:12 (a) *Not in Codex 24.] (c) *Codex 24 and Rusch: "I will not let him go away anymore".] (d) *Codex 24 and Rusch have "More than the mind of man can grasp"; in Codex 24, it is unclear what it is meant to refer to, whereas Rusch has it to "upon him". Note that the Latin word for "upon" can also mean "above".] (e) *Not in Codex 24. I have followed Rusch's reading here; Latin 588 has something like "in some way God to him", which does not make as much sense to me, and the difference stands in two letters of a word (or even rather one letter and an abbreviation sign) that are missing in Latin 588, and this may very well be a simple scribal error.] (g) *Codex24: "And there will be no necessity, but an eternal vision of peace".] 1 Rusch has "all virtues".

3:13 *He that has an ear, let him hear what the Spirit says to the churches.*
3:14 *And to the (a)angel of the church of (b)Laodicea write, Thus says (c)Amen, the faithful and (d)true (e)witness, which is the beginning (f)of the creature of God.*

a. I.e. bishop.*
b. "Vomit"* or "lovely tribe".
c. I.e. the truth.*
d. Steadfast* in all his words.
e. Of our works before the Father.
f. Of the first creation and* of the recreation.**

Thus says Amen, the faithful and true witness. As he is about to say a surprising thing - that lukewarm people, who are thought by all[1] to be true[2], should be excommunicated - he says that he is truthful in all things, so that he may be believed in this as well. And if they will return to their senses, he promises fulfillment, because he first gave an assurance.

Faithful and true. Because the promises of the Father are fulfilled through him.[3]

Witness of the works he has heard from the Father[4]; or to whom credence must be given.[5][6]

3:14 (a) *Only in Latin 588.] (b) *Codex 24: "in vomit".] (c) *Only in 588 as a separate gloss, but in Codex 24 and Rusch it seems to have been merged with another gloss, as you will see in note 3.] (d) *The word "steadfast" only in Latin 588.] (f) *Rusch: "or". **This gloss is not in Codex 24.] 1 Codex 24 and Rusch: "by men". Two versions that look rather alike, especially in abbreviated writing.] 2 Codex 24 and Rusch: "good".] 3 Codex 24 and Rusch have "He is the truth because the promises of the Father are fulfilled through him".] 4 Codex 24: "Witness of the things that he, not lukewarm, has heard from the Father"; Rusch: "... the things that he, fearless, ..."; I am almost sure that the latter is merely a scribal error (again, the Latin words are somewhat similar).] 5 Codex 24 adds here "in all words"; Rusch adds "in all things".] 6 This gloss is written in the other ink in Latin 588.

3:15 *(a)I know (b)your works, that you are (c)neither cold, (d)nor hot. I would you were (e)cold, or hot.*

a. I.e. they are not concealed from me.
b. You do not want to correct yourself from your desire.*
c. I.e. neither are you completely ignorant of faith.
d. I.e. nor do you openly deny the faith you have received.
e. Because there is more hope regarding him who is cold.

I would you were cold. He does not wish him to be simply cold, but to be such as regarding whom there is more hope.[1]

Neither cold. It is better not to know the way of truth than to turn back and leave it afterwards (See 2 Peter 2:21).[2]

3:15 (b) *This gloss is difficult. Codex 24 has "slothfulness" instead of "desire" (two words that resemble each other in Latin). Rusch has something that makes no sense at all and can only be a mistake. Another version I found has "your perverseness".] 1 Only in Rush.] 2 Only in Latin 588, in the usual other ink.

3:16 But because you are ^(a)lukewarm, and ^(b)neither cold nor hot, ^(c)I will begin to vomit you out of my mouth.

    a.   I.e. sluggish.
    b.   That is.*
    c.   I.e. by excommunicating you.

Lukewarm and neither cold nor hot. I.e. trusting too much in the good things you have, unwilling to work.[1]

Out of my mouth. He is vomited out of his mouth who throws himself down into the worse or who dies unrepentant.[2]

To vomit you out of my mouth. That is, to remove you from the community of the saints through my preachers who are my mouth[3] and through whom I speak.

3:16 (b) *Only in Latin 588.] 1 Only in Latin 588, in the other ink.] 2 Not in Latin 588.] 3 "Who are my mouth" only in Latin 588.

3:17 Because you say, I am rich, and ^(a)enriched, and ^(b)lack nothing: and ^(c)know not that you are a miser, and ^(d)miserable, and ^(e)poor, and ^(f)blind, and ^(g)naked.

    a.   I.e. filled with virtues.
    b.   But I have added this on my own part too.
    c.   Because such works do not lead to salvation.
    d.   Since you are perishing by your ignorance.
    e.   In works of virtue.
    f.   Because you do not realize your vices.
    g.   Of virtues in your mind.

I am rich. That is, cleansed in baptism, or rich in divine and[1] secular knowledge.

3:17 1 Codex 24 and Rusch: "or".

3:18 ^(a)I counsel ^(b)you* ^(c)to buy of me ^(d)gold ^(e)fire-^(f)tried, ^(g)that you may be made ^(h)rich: and may be clothed in ⁽ⁱ⁾white garments, ^(j)that the confusion of your ^(k)nakedness appear not: and with ^(l)eye-salve anoint ^(m)your eyes, that you may see,

    a.   But I do not deny mercy.
    b.   And everyone.*
    c.   Sc. with* the fruit of penance.
    d.   Myself or burning love*.
    e.   Either ignited, i.e. placed in fire, or igniting.*
    f.   By the fire of tribulation.*
    g.   Although you are such.*
    h.   Sc. in works of virtues.
    i.   I.e. the virtues themselves.
    j.   I.e. that you not give (them?*) up on account of shame.
    k.   In virtues.*
    l.   I.e. the gift of the Holy Spirit.*
    m.   I.e. your mind.*

That the confusion of your nakedness appear not. It is better to blush before a few now than in the future before all.

That the confusion of your nakedness appear not. I.e. that your sins appear not in the day of judgment.[1]

With eye-salve anoint. The eye-salve is the commandment of the Lord, enlightening the eyes (Ref. Ps. 18:9). Or: Anoint with the gift of the Holy Spirit your mind which earthly things have shut up.

Eye-salve. We anoint our eyes with eye-salve so that we may see when we help the sight of our intellect to perceive the brightness of the true light with the medicine of good work.

3:18 *In the verse: Rusch's Vulgate adds here "although you are such", with a gloss above it saying, "Absent from other versions".] (b) *Only in Codex 24.] (c) *"With" not in Codex 24 and Rusch.] (d) *Codex 24: "igniting love"; Rush: just "love".] (e) *The Latin translated by "fire-tried", *ignitum probatum*, means literally "ignited tried", this gloss referring to *ignitum*, "ignited".] (f) *Only in Rusch.] (g) *Only in Codex 24.] (j) *Uncertain reading; one small word faded in Latin 588, which is not there in the other books.] (k) *Not in Latin 588.] (l) *Only in Latin 588.] (m) *Only in Latin 588.] 1 Only in Latin 588, in the other ink.

3:19 ^(a)I, whom I love, do ^(b)rebuke and ^(c)chastise. ^(d)Be zealous therefore and ^(e)do penance.

    a.   The reason mentioned first.
    b.   That is, I make them realize their sins.

    c.   I.e. I make them virtuous.*
    d.   Emulate those you see endure adversity.*
    e.   Sc. for your lukewarmness.

3:19 (c) *This gloss is based on an etymological fact. The Latin words *castigare*, "to chastise", and *castus*, "morally pure, guiltless, virtuous, chaste", are related. The same relatedness could have appeared in the English translation if I had translated the gloss as "I make them chaste", but the glossator probably meant more than just that.] (d) *What is translated as "be zealous" in the verse, *emulare*, can (and most often does) mean "emulate"; so the gloss in fact reads only "those you see endure adversity", and I added "emulate" because given the English version of the verse it would have been incomprehensible without it.

3:20 ^(a)Behold I stand ^(b)at the door and ^(c)knock. If any man shall ^(d)hear my voice, and ^(e)open ^(f)the gate, ^(g)I will come in to ^(h)him, and ⁽ⁱ⁾will sup with him, and ^(j)he with me.

    a.   And you must do so because I stand, i.e. I wait, or inspire, or I
          call through the preachers, or through weaknesses*.
    b.   I.e. at the closed heart.
    b.   I.e. rebuke.
    c.   Sc. understanding it.
    d.   To do the work.
    e.   Through true faith. *
    f.   I.e. into the secrets of his heart.
    g.   By pouring grace into him.*
    h.   Because I am delighted by faith and work.*
    i.   Because he will be delighted by my help.*

3:20 (a) *"Or through weaknesses" only in Latin 588.] (f) *Only in Rusch.] (h) *Only in Rusch.] (i) *The scribe first wrote "I shall be delighted", which was corrected to "I am delighted". Codex 24 has "I shall be delighted by his faith and work"; Rusch has "Because I shall be delighted by his faith and work", and has another gloss next to it saying "on account of the justification of the same".] (j) *Codex 24 has "Because he will rejoice in my help", and Rusch the same but adding "sc. on account of the pleasantness of good conscience".

3:21 ^(a)He that shall overcome, I will give unto him ^(b)to sit with me ^(c)in my throne: ^{(d)(e)}as I also have overcome, and have sat with my Father in his throne.

    a.   Why say more?
    b.   I.e. to judge in those in whom I sit and judge. And this
          concerning the superiors, and, through the superiors, the
          inferiors.
    c.   I.e. in my judicial seat.*
    d.   That is, not only in a privileged dignity, but also in a uniformity
          of love and will.*
    e.   Because his victory and his sitting is the cause of their victory
          and their sitting.

3:21 (c) *Rusch has "by which judicial power is symbolized" instead. Codex 24 has nothing here.] (d) *Only in Rusch.

3:22 He that has an ear, let him hear what the Spirit says to the churches.

28

4:1 ^(a)*AFTER these things* ^(b)*I looked, and* ^(c)*behold* ^(d)*a door open in heaven, and the* ^(e)*first voice which I heard, was as it were of a trumpet* ^(f)*speaking* ^(g)*with me,* ^(h)*saying,* ⁽ⁱ⁾*Come up here, and I will show you* ^(j)*the things which must be done quickly after these*^(k).

a. Sc. not in time but in order.
b. I.e. I was able to see.*
c. He was able to see because... *
d. Sc. the Scripture, which is the way to life. Or Christ is the door; sc. also the Old Testament, which precedes the New*, and whose mysteries, which used to be shut, are now open to those who, by their faith and work, are heaven.
e. Sc. as far as the other things that he saw in this vision are concerned.*
f. I.e. exhorting me to war.*
g. I.e. not at odds with my rationality.*
h. I.e. explaining the reason why it behooves to endure.*
i. I.e. after being reproved*, extend your mind to these other things.
j. He says that things that are already passed must still be done, seeing that they must remain in the same state in which they began.*
k. Among the last faithful. Or, after the reproof*, they must see the secrets so that by them they may be encouraged for the battles.**

In this second vision, he speaks of the one sitting in the throne and his attire, of the Lamb opening the book, i.e. the divine disposition, of the renewal of mankind, and of the Lamb loosing the seven seals, i.e. uncertainties, so that when we have seen that God has granted the faithful[1] so great an understanding of the Scriptures, we should be grateful to him, and should not[2] fear to suffer for him.

The second vision concerns the revelation of mysteries. After people have been corrected, a revelation of secrets suitably follows.

This vision may be called "the revelation of mysteries that are revealed by the Spirit".[3]

This vision comes second and not first because, as he invites his people to tribulations, they cannot endure them if their negligences[4] are not corrected first, which was done in the first vision[5].

Almost all of this vision concerns the last faithful, which can do a lot for the encouragement of the present faithful. He also mentions a few things concerning those who suffered before the Lord's incarnation, which he does for the same purpose.

In this second vision he exhorts to endure tribulations for faith, and for this purpose he first gives a confirmation of faith itself, showing the renewal of mankind which was planned by God from eternity and fulfilled by the Son incarnated, and this faith confirmed by the testimony of the four beasts and of the twenty-four seniors, so that the faithful should not hesitate to suffer for a sure faith.[6] As if he were saying: I saw them preparing themselves to receive God the sitter; and so that they may not succumb, I saw help.[7]

4:1 *(b) Only in Latin 588, though (c) seems to be a variation of this. Codex 24 has a kind of conflation of (a) and (b) or (c), where "I" or "he was able" seems to have been forgotten, giving "Not in time but in order, to see because behold a door open". It is perhaps worth noting that the Latin word translated as "I looked" in the verse most basically means "I saw".] (c) *Only in Rusch as such, but see previous note.] (d) *Codex 24 and Rusch have "Sc. the Old Testament, which precedes the New" separately as another interlinear; in Codex 24 above "door open", and in Rusch above "the first voice", so that in those book (d) reads "... Or Christ is the door, whose mysteries..."] (e) *Codex 24: "The first grace by which he saw in this vision"; Rusch: "As far as the things that I saw in this vision are concerned".] (f) *Codex 24 has here a conflation of (f) and (h). Rusch has "Exhorting me to war; then, that I should endure, which means the same".] (g) *Codex 24: "Not at odds with rationality, giving reasons in it, asking for a reason"; Rusch: "Not at odds with my rationality in giving reasons".] (h) *Not in this place in Codex 24, but see the note to (f). Codex 24's Vulgate text misses the word "saying".] (i) *Codex 24 and Rusch: "corrected". You may have noticed that it is not the first time that Codex 24 and Rusch speak of "correction" where Latin 588 speaks of "reproof" (2:1 note 1); this is due to the resemblance of the words in both Latin spelling and meaning. Cf. *correptio*, "reproof"; *correptus*, "reproved"; *correctio*, "correction"; *correctus*, "corrected".] (j) *In the other ink in Latin 588.] (k) *Here again, Codex 24 and Rusch have "correction". **In Codex 24 and Rusch, the second part of this gloss, from "Or, after...", is forming one marginal gloss together with (j). As to the part "among the last faithful", it appears in Codex 24, in the same place as in Latin 588, as "Or after these, i.e. among the last faithful"; Rusch has, as a marginal gloss following the conflation of (j) and the second part of (k), "Either *the things that must be done quickly after these*, i.e. among the last faithful, or *after these I was in spirit*". Indeed the Vulgate versions differ a little in this place concerning, among other things, whether "after these" should belong to the end of this verse or to the beginning of the next. None of the three books actually reads exactly the same as the Douay-Rheims translation: Latin 588 and Codex 24 have: "... the things that must be done after these. And immediately I was in spirit..."; Rusch has: "... the things that must be done quickly. After these, immediately I was in spirit..."] 1 Codex 24 has "everyone" instead of "the faithful"; Rusch has "men".] 2 Codex 24 and Rusch: "so that we should not" instead of "and should not". The difference in Latin stands in one letter.] 3 Not in Latin 588.] 4 Codex 24 has "even the elect" instead of "their negligences".] 5 Codex 24 and Rusch: "correction".] 6 This whole preceding part of the gloss is only in Latin 588.] 7 Codex 24 and Rusch have this last part in the beginning of the gloss on "rainbow" in verse 3.

4:2 ^(a)*Immediately I was in spirit:* ^(b)*and behold there was* ^(c)*a seat set in heaven, and* ^(d)*upon the seat one sitting.*

a. I.e. I did not resist, but I threw away care for all earthliness.
b. Because I so desired.
c. I.e. the greater ones in whom God sits and judges, as well as among others who are placed under. Or some were so fitted that God could suitably sit and rest in them.
d. As overtopping.*

One sitting. Above, Christ was walking among the candlesticks, and not sitting; but now he is sitting, i.e. judging the merits of each one; of this he appropriately reminds those whom he exhorted to battle.

4:2 (d) *The Latin word used in the verse for "upon", *supra*, can also mean "above".

4:3 And he that (a)sat, was (b)like in sight, to (c)the jasper (d)stone, and (e)the sardine: and there was (f)a rainbow (g)round about the seat, like to the sight of an (h)emerald.

a. Sc. ready to judge.
b. Previously unknown, now like, i.e.* he appeared to the world** through the flesh.
c. The jasper stone is green.* The divinity is green** and gives pasture to its people.
d. Sc. breaking his enemies in pieces, and a source of strength for his people.*
e. The sardine is black, white and red.* The flesh is red in the passion.
f. I.e. peace.*
g. I.e. in protection.*
h. Emerald is green and red.

He that sat. Where there are only good people, there is no need to judge, i.e. to make a distinction; where there are good ones and bad ones, there is need for distinction.[1]

The jasper stone and the sardine. By the colors of the two stones he symbolizes God and man.

A rainbow. I.e. peace, i.e. God's mercy, which is round about, as protecting, and which both baptism, which is the green color, and the blood of Christ, which is the red color, make. And[2] by these colors are symbolized the past judgment through water, and the future one through fire, by which colors he will save his people.[3]

Emerald. By the green color of the emerald, which is an aquatic color, baptism is meant; by the redness of the same stone, the gifts of the Holy Spirit received in baptism, by which sins are burned up.[4]

4:3 (b) *"Now like, i.e." only in Latin 588. **Codex 24: "he has now appeared" instead of "he appeared to the world". The Latin words used here for "world" and "now" look somewhat similar.] (c) *"The jasper stone is green" only in Latin 588. **Instead of "is green", Codex 24 has "glitters", and Rusch has "let the divinity enter", but the latter is most probably a mistranscription for the former.] (d) *Codex 24 has "Breaking his enemies in pieces by his strength".] (e) *"The sardine is black, white and red" only in Latin 588.] (f) *Not in Codex 24.] (g) *Only in Latin 588.] 1 Not in Latin 588.] 2 Codex 24 and Rusch: "or".] 3 In Codex 24 and Rusch, this gloss contains something more in the beginning: see 4:1 note 7. In the last sentence, Codex 24 has "us" instead of "his people".] 4 Not in Latin 588.

4:4 And (a)round about the seat, (b)four and twenty seats: and upon the thrones, (c)four and twenty seniors sitting, clothed about in (d)white garments, and (e)on (f)their heads (g)crowns of gold.

a. Sc. as depending from it*, and agreeing with his judgment.
b. I.e. the minor Church in the Old as well as in the New Testament.
c. I saw.*
d. Sc. those that are put on in baptism, and by which sins are covered, and they are white with virtues.*
e. I.e. in their minds.
f. I.e. the superiors' or the inferiors'.*
g. I.e. victories through wisdom or* love even towards enemies.

Four and twenty. The twelve prophets and the twelve apostles, although there are more in both orders[1].

The doctors are sometimes said to be twenty-four, sometimes to be twelve.[2]

Seniors. All the doctors of the old or of the new law are said to be twelve because of the faith in the Trinity which they announce to the four parts of the world, or 24 are made by 6 × 4: 6 refers to the works that he made in six days, and 4 to the Gospels, i.e. the Church, which honors[3] the works of God in the Old and in the New Testament.

4:4 (a) *Rusch: "as appendages".] (c) *Only in Rusch.] (d) *Rusch has two glosses here: a marginal ones saying "Sins are covered, and they are white with virtues", and an interlinear saying "Which they put on in baptism, those in which the elect are clothed". Codex 24's and Rusch's Vulgates have "robes" instead of "garments" in the verse, and Rusch mentions the variant "garments" in an interlinear.] (f) *Only in Latin 588.] (g) *Rusch: "and".] 1 Codex 24: "in the same order".] 2 Not in Latin 588.] 3 Codex 34: "brought together" instead of "honors".

4:5 And (a)from the throne proceeded lightnings, and (b)voices, and (c)thunders: and (d)seven lamps burning before the throne, which are the seven spirits of God.*

a. I.e. from the Church which rains lightnings, i.e. miracles that frighten and illumine.
b. Warnings.*
c. I.e. threats.
d. That is, the gifts of the Holy Spirit, which kindle and illumine, ready for all those who are God's seat*.

4:5 *In Rusch's Vulgate, this verse goes on "sent into all the earth", with a gloss above it saying "absent from most versions".] (b) *Not in Rusch.] (d) *Codex 24: "... which kindle and illumine in all those who are God's seat".

4:6 And in the sight of the seat, as it were a sea of glass like to crystal: and (a)in the middle of the seat and (b)round about the seat (c)four (d)beasts full of eyes before and behind.

    a.   Jerusalem as the sustainer of the weak.*
    b.   All around like a watch.
    c.   Because of the duty of preaching in the four parts, devoted to the contemplation of heavenly things, and receiving remembrance concerning those who are below them.
    d.   Animate and animating.*

In the sight of the seat, as it were a sea of glass. Because they understand both the sacrament and the matters of the sacrament[1], and they receive no one but those who they have seen are suitable.

A sea of glass like to crystal. Baptism, shining with the purity of faith, and after which[2] the elect are led to firmness[3] by the fire of tribulation, as hard crystal is formed from water.

In the middle. Some sort of flat surface similar to that of a judge, who has a broad and large area where he sits and passes his judgments.[4]

Full of eyes before and behind. I.e. remembering the sins of the past, and on their guard for the future. Or having knowledge of the things that God has done and will do in the end of the world, or of the Old and of the New Testament. Or pleasing to God and men.[5]

4:6 (a) *Rusch has "Jerusalem, as sustainers, as the man, as the calf, as the lion, as the eagle" as a marginal gloss. Codex 24 has "Jerusalem" and "as sustainers" as two glosses.] (c) *In Codex 24 and Rusch, this is two glosses: an interlinear above "four" with "Because of the duty of preaching in the four parts", and the rest of the gloss as a marginal gloss in Codex 24 with nothing indicating clearly what it is meant to refer to, and in Rusch as an interlinear above "as it were a sea of glass". Rusch's version also has "receiving care or remembrance" instead of just "receiving remembrance". My feeling is that the part concerning contemplation and remembrance must rather originally have been meant to refer to "full of eyes before and behind".] (d) *Codex 24 has "animate and inanimate", which is most probably a mistake. The Latin word translated as "beasts" in the verse, *animalia*, is formed from *anima* meaning "breath" or "soul/spirit" and closely related to *animus*, "spirit/soul/heart/mood" or "spirits/courage". So *animal* (singular of *animalia*) basically means that which has breath or soul/spirit, a living being, animal. Here the glossator is saying that these animals do not only have breath/soul/spirit, but also give it.] 1 Codex 24 : « because the sacrament and the matters of the sacrament are understood ».] 2 Codex 24 : « after water ».] 3 Rusch has "firmness of good works".] 4 Not in Latin 588.] 5 Latin 588 first put this gloss to « round about and within » in verse 8, but then a sign (the same sign repeated above the part of the verse concerned and above the gloss, which is the usual method in Latin 588 to indicate what a marginal gloss refers to) was made in the usual « other ink » to refer it these words.

4:7 And the first beast, like to a lion: and the second beast, like to a calf: and the third beast, having a face as it were of a man: and the fourth beast, like to an eagle (a)flying.

    a.   Not sitting.*

Christ who was born, suffered, rose again, and ascended. Also the faithful, who are rational and civilized like man[1], enduring adversity without fear like the lion, mortifying themselves like the calf, and betaking themselves to heavenly things like the eagle.

Ezekiel, because he foresaw the future, put the man first, then the lion because Christ was a lion in his preaching, then the calf because he was sacrificed, and finally the eagle because he ascended to the heavens (Ezekiel 1:10; 10:14). John, seeing things that were already accomplished, put the lion first as the foundation of all faith.

A lion is born dead, and is revived on the third day by the voice of its father. Thus did Christ rise again on the third day, and he had to rise again because he was dead, and he had to[2] die because he was a man. And he was able to rise again although he was a dead man[3] because he is the eagle, i.e. God.

4:7 (a) *Only in Latin 588.] 1 Codex 24 : « ... the faithful, rational and civilized men... ».] 2 Codex 24 and Rusch : « could ».] 3 Codex 24 : « ... and he was able to rise again although he was a man and dead... » ; Rusch : « ... and he had to rise again although he was a man and dead... »

4:8 (a)And the four beasts, every one of them has six wings (b)round about: and (c)within they are full of eyes; and (d)they had no rest (e)day and night, saying, (f)Holy, Holy, Holy, (g)Lord God Omnipotent, (h)which was, and (i)which is, and (j)which shall come.

    a.   As if he were saying: And in order to proclaim these things about Christ, they had been well instructed.
    b.   I.e. they instruct simpler people by the literal meaning.
    c.   And the more perfect ones by allegory.*
    d.   I.e. they did not stop.
    e.   I.e. in prosperity and in adversity, or every day*.

The first wing is the natural law, the second one the law of Moses, the third one the prophecies[1], the fourth one the Gospel, the fifth one the teachings of the apostles, and the sixth one those of all those, like Augustine and the others[2], through whom[3] the Church strives for what is high, and from whom preachers receive the support for all preaching[4]. Or the six wings are the knowledge of the works of God made in six days, by whose knowledge those who do good works in them are lifted up on high.

And round about and within. Or because they keep themselves clean, and instruct others by their examples. Or because they illuminate them

f. Thrice because there is Trinity in persons.	in the middle and in the far ends of the earth.
g. Once because there is unity in majesty.	
h. Without beginning.	
i. Immutable.	They are full of eyes within, i.e. they are clean in their conscience, and
j. The Son will appear corporally, because* the whole deity will manifest itself to the faithful.	round about, i.e. they are irreprehensible in the sight of men.

4:8 (b) and (c) *The Vulgates of all three books have « and round about and within they are full of eyes », instead of putting « round about » with « has six wings ».] (e) *Codex 24 and Rusch have « continuously » instead of « every day », the former perhaps making more sense.] (j) *The word « because » only in Latin 588.] 1 Codex 24 and Rusch : the prophets ».] 2 Codex 24 has only « like Augustine » ; Rusch has « like Augustine, Gregory and Ambrose ».] 3 Codex 24 and Rusch : « through which ». The following « whom » could in theory also be « which », the Latin form being the same in this case.] 4 Codex 24 and Rusch : « the foundation of all preaching ».

4:9 And (a)when (b)those beasts gave (c)glory and (d)honor and (e)benediction to him (f)that sits upon the throne, (g)that lives forever and ever:

Gave glory, i.e. proclaimed the splendor of the divine majesty; *and honor,* i.e. won him many people while serving him; *and benediction,* when they exalted his name by proclaiming it everywhere.[1]

a. I.e. because.*
b. I.e. preachers assigned those things to him, and confessed, and preached everywhere.
c. Of their faith, or of resurrection.*
d. Of their work, or in Christ's ascension.*
e. Of the reward of above, or in exaltation, that *every knee should bow, of those that are in heaven, on earth, and under earth* (Philippians, 2:10).
f. According to the fact that *the Word was made flesh* (John, 1:14).*
g. According to the fact that *the Word was with God* (John, 1:1).*

4:9 (a) *Not in Latin 588. Joined to the beginning of the next gloss in Codex 24, i.e. it has « I.e. because preachers... »] (c) *Codex 24 has "of their faith and work, either in the resurrection or in the ascension"; Rusch, "of their faith in the resurrection or in the ascension". Some mix-ups obviously happened between this gloss and the following one.] (d) *Not in Codex 24, but see note to (c).] (f) *Only in Latin 588.] (g) *Only in Latin 588.] 1 Only in Latin 588.

4:10 (a)the four and twenty seniors (b)(c)fell down (d)before him that sits in the throne, and (e)adored him that lives forever and ever, and (f)cast their crowns before the throne, (g)saying,

a. I.e. all the judges of the old and of the new law.
b. I.e. humbled themselves.*
c. While it would be fair enough to judge them superior here.*
d. I.e. in his good pleasure.
e. I.e. they sought from him by their voices and their work that which they did not have by themselves.
f. I.e. attributing to God in the secret of their hearts their victory over vices or tribulations.
g. I.e. giving example to others.

4:10 (b) *Not in Codex 24.] (c) *Codex 24 : « They who were preachers above are here fair judges » ; Rusch : « They who were preachers above are here more fairly judges ».

4:11 You are worthy O Lord our God (a)to receive glory and honor and (b)power: because you have created all things, and (c)(d)for your will they (e)(f)were and (g)have been created.

You have created all things. Therefore all things must be returned to you, because all things have their beginning from you.

Also invisible things, or angels and souls, as, when of impious people he makes pious ones created spiritually, he says that they are spiritual.[1]

a. That we should return them to you.
b. Which above was "benediction".
c. And not suddenly, but *that which was made, in him was life* (John 1:3-4).* According to.*

d. Sc. in theory, before they were formed in deed.
e. They existed in theory, i.e. in the wisdom of God.*
f. By appearing visibly, or according to some spiritual creation.*

4:11 (c) *They were dividing these verses differently from modern Bibles. What we now have as belonging to two different sentences: *3 Omnia per ipsum facta sunt et sine ipso factum est nihil quod factum est. 4 In ipso vita erat et vita erat lux hominum:* « 3 All things were made by him: and without him was made nothing that was made. 4 In him was life, and the life was the light of men », the glossator took as going together: *3 Omnia per ipsum facta sunt et sine ipso factum est nihil. 4 Quod factum est, in ipso vita erat et vita erat lux hominum:* « 3 All things were made by him: and without him was made nothing. 4 That which was made, in him was life, and the life was the light of men ». The latter English version I took from the old Douay-Rheims of 1609 (the D-R was later revised in the 1700's, and the first English version with the "current" division of the verses comes from the revised one), but it also mentions the version "nothing that was made" in the margin. Finally, I shall also add that if *quod factum est in ipso vita erat* is taken as one sentence, it is also in theory possible to interpret it as "that which was made, in it was life", although it may be unlikely given the surrounding context. I am personally in favor of the interpretation found in modern Bibles, but what is important here is to try and understand what the author of the gloss had in mind. This gloss is not in Latin 588.] (d) *Not in Latin 588.] (f) *Not in Latin 588.] (g) *Codex 24 has "By appearing visibly, or some according to a spiritual understanding", Rusch "By appearing visibly, some according to a spiritual understanding or creation".] 1 Only in Rusch.

CHAPTER 5

5:1 AND I saw (a)in the right hand of him that sat upon the throne, (b)(c)a book (d)written within and without, (e)sealed with (f)seven seals.

- a. I.e. in the Son, through whom he has done everything, and to whom the whole book's intention is turned.
- b. The divine disposition.*
- c. I.e. the two Testaments, which are the same, "without" signifying the Old one, or because it promises exterior things, "within" signifying the New Testament, or because it sometimes promises happiness.* Or within with more esoteric words for the more perfect people, without with simpler words for the less perfect.
- d. Manifest.*
- e. Secured.*
- f. I.e. all the obscurities, or it is closed by the sevenfold Spirit through which faith operates*.

A book, i.e. the divine disposition of the renewal of men, which is *written*, i.e. manifested *within*, i.e. obscurely, in the Old Testament, as when Moses said, "You shall sacrifice the lamb in the evening" (ref. Exodus, 12), showing our future renewal in the last age[1], *and without*, i.e. clearly, in the New Testament. He says "seven" because in what follows he will define those seven seals, namely the white horse, the red one, the black one, and the rest, which were evident and well-known things in the beginning of the Church, which was the white horse, upon which Christ sat and which he fortified with his teaching and his example, and which the red horse and the others[2] attacked.

Sealed. The Scriptures of the prophets were made closed and obscure, but afterwards they were made open by him.[3]

5:1 (b) *Not in Latin 588.] (c) *Codex 24 and Rusch: " I.e. the two testaments, which are the same; without is the old one, which signifies, or because it promises exterior things; within is the New Testament, which is what is signified, or because it sometimes promises happiness", with "sometimes promises happiness" struck through in Codex 24 and corrected to "promises inner happiness", in the other ink.] (d) *Only in Codex 24.] (e) *Not in Latin 588.] (f) *Rusch has "is revealed" instead of "operates". Only the first letter of the word differs in Latin.] 1 Codex 24 and Rusch add here "through Christ's sacrifice".] 2 "And the others" only in Latin 588.] 3 Not in Latin 588.

5:2 And (a)I saw (b)a strong angel, (c)preaching with a loud voice, Who is worthy (d)to open the book, and to loose the seals thereof?

- a. I heard.*
- b. I.e. any one of the first fathers.
- c. I.e. asking, announcing to others, and, for his too great desire, complaining of so long a delay.
- d. I.e. to fulfill.*

Angel. The holy fathers understood that the renewal of men had been planned by God some time, and they were longing to see when it would happen, but they did not know how it would happen until the Holy Spirit revealed it to some before it happened[1].

To open and to loose the seals. The divine disposition, or to remove all the obscurities of the Scriptures.[2]

5:2 (a) *Not in Latin 588.] (d) *Codex 24 has "to explain the mysteries or to fulfill the secrets of the Old Testament". Rusch has "to fulfill or to receive", and Latin 588's Vulgate in fact has "receive" instead of "open" in the verse.] 1 "To some before it happened" not in Codex 24.] 2 Only in Rusch, except "the divine disposition", which Codex 24 has as an interlinear to "the book".

5:3 (a)And no man was able neither (b)in heaven nor (c)in earth, nor (d)under the earth, (e)to open the book, nor (f)look on it.

- a. It is John who says this.*
- b. Sc. like an angel.
- c. Sc. like a man.
- d. Sc. like the souls stripped of bodies.
- e. I.e. to fulfill.
- f. I.e. understand it perfectly, whence "Who shall declare his generation?" (Is. 53:8).

5:3 (a) *Not in Latin 588.

5:4 And I wept much [(a)]**because no man was found worthy** [(b)]**to open the book, nor** [(c)]**to see it.**

a.   I.e. because all were impure.
b.   Sc. through incarnation.
c.   I.e. to understand it perfectly.

I wept. This he does on behalf of the fathers, who either did not understand or grieved the delayed renewal. Whence, "Many prophets and kings have desired to see the things that you see, and have not seen them" (Matt. 13:17; Luke, 10:24).

The holy fathers before the law and under the law, and even philosophers, investigated a lot, and searched with an ardent desire whence and how salvation would come to them, knowing and by no means doubting that the justice of the just shall deliver him[1], but they could not find how that salvation would be done, except if the Spirit happened to reveal it to someone, as it did to Isaiah when he said "Behold a virgin shall conceive, and bear a son" (Isaiah, 7:14).[2]

5:4 1 It is strange that a *negative* version of this is found in Ezechiel 33:12 (The justice of the just shall not deliver him, in what day soever he shall sin: and the wickedness of the wicked shall not hurt him, in what day soever he shall turn from his wickedness).] 2 Only in Latin 588.

5:5 And [(a)]**one of the seniors said to me, Weep not: behold the lion of the tribe of Judah,** [(b)]**the root of David,** [(c)]**has won,** [(d)]**to open the book, and to loose the seven seals thereof.**

a.   I.e. any prophet who comforts others by announcing Christ's coming.
b.   Descended from David or the support of David.
c.   He will overcome the Devil.*
d.   I.e. for the purpose of opening it.

When a lion is put to flight, it flees through the mountains and erases its footprints with the knob of hair it has on its tail so as not to be found: thus did Christ flee through the mountains, i.e. his divinity was hidden from the Jews, he concealed his divinity with the flesh he assumed so that he might not be recognized. A lion sleeps with open eyes: thus did Christ expire, his divinity living on.

5:5 (c) *Rusch has only "the Devil". "To win" and "to overcome" are the same word in Latin in this context.

5:6 And [(a)]**I saw, and** [(b)]**behold in the midst of the throne and of the four beasts and in the midst of the seniors,** [(c)]**a Lamb** [(d)]**standing as it were slain, having seven horns and seven eyes: which are the seven spirits of God, sent into all the earth.**

a.   Sc. as he had foretold.
b.   He describes how the lion won and where.
c.   Christ who was a victim.
d.   I.e. helping those who were fighting.*

In the midst of the throne. The Church, which by Christ is possessed like a throne, pastured like beasts, honored in having judicial authority like seniors, being itself founded, i.e.[1] built, upon Christ, is illuminated by signs and virtues in the seven horns[2].

As it were slain. Because even though he is dead, *he lives by the power of God* (2 Cor. 13:4). Or slain like a victim[3] among his people, in whom he is mortified every day.

The horns and eyes are the Holy Spirit, which gives[4] the kingdom that is denoted by the horns. The eyes, because they illuminate. Or the horns are the more eminent saints, fixed on the head which is Christ[5], and surpassing the flesh.

5:6 (d) *Not in Codex 24.] 1 Codex 24 and Rusch have only "built upon Christ".] 2 Codex 24 and Rusch: "is exhalted by the kingdom of strength in the seven horns, and illuminated by signs and virtues in the seven eyes".] 2 Codex 24 and Rusch: "Or he is as it were slain..." instead of "Or slain like a victim...".] 4 Rusch: "*Seven horns and seven eyes.* Because he gives...".] 5 Codex 24: "on Christ's head".

5:7 And [(a)]**he** [(b)]**came, and** [(c)]**received the book** [(d)]**out of the right hand of him that sat in the throne.**

a.   Sc. the lamb.*
b.   Sc. to the acquaintance of men through the flesh.
c.   As a man.*
d.   From the Word of God united to himself.

5:7 (a) *Not in Latin 588. It is here in Rusch; in Codex 24, it is above "the seven spirits of God sent into all flesh" in the previous verse — this book having "all flesh" instead of "all the earth".] (c) *Instead of this, Rusch has "Christ man" above "he came".

5:8 And (a)(b)when he had opened the book, (c)the four beasts and (d)the four and twenty seniors (e)fell before the Lamb, having every one (f)harps, and (g)(h)golden vials (i)full of (j)odors, (k)(l)which are the prayers of saints:

a. I.e. because.
b. After he fulfilled the disposition of the Father by obeying him.*
c. I.e. all the preachers.
d. I.e. all the judges.
e. I.e. they have felt humble, and they imitate him, whence it follows "having every one, etc.".
f. Sc. the mortification of vices and concupiscences.
g. I.e. large* hearts even for the love of their enemies.
h. With perfect love.*
i. I.e. overflowing.*
j. I.e. works smelling good.*
k. I.e. whatever they do in this life is prayers, and their whole life is a prayer.*
l. The vials are flasks of life.*

Harps. A harp is made of wood and strings. By the wood is symbolized the cross of Christ, and by the strings the flesh of the saints, which is stretched on the wood while, giving the same sound in different tortures, they imitate the cross of Christ.

5:8 (b) *Only in Latin 588.] (g) *Codex 24 and Rusch have "joyful" instead of "large". The two words differ only in one letter, and similar letters, "e" or "a", but, though it is very small and a little unclear in Latin 588, I think it has an "a", giving "large", though I am not sure.] (h) *Only in Latin 588.] (i) *Only in Latin 588.] (j) *Codex 24 and Rusch have only "smelling good".] (k) *Only in Latin 588.] (l) *Only in Latin 588, in the other ink.

5:9 and (a)they sang (b)a new canticle, saying, You are (c)(d)worthy O Lord to take* the book, and to open the seals thereof: because you were slain, and have redeemed us to God** in your blood out of every tribe and tongue and people and nation,

a. Sc. with exultation.*
b. I.e. the New Testament.*
c. Without sin.*
d. Because free from sin.

And they sang a new canticle. The Church professes the New Testament[1] with exultation while it is baptized in his death.

"Tribe" is said after the three orders[2], in which there are 72 tongues, in every one of which there are many peoples, and in a people nations.

Sc. in the workers, the soldiers, and the orators.[3]

The three orders of those who are to be saved: Noah, Daniel, and Job, or the three orders of nations: the Greeks, the Hebrews and the Christians.[4]

Every tribe and tongue and people and nation. Here are symbolized the three orders in the Church: namely, by Noah, who steered the ark, are symbolized the rulers of the churches; by Job, those who make use of worldly things rightfully; by Daniel, the contemplative ones, out of all of whom, as one may read elsewhere, some are taken, some are left.[5]

5:9 In the verse: *The Vulgates of all three books have "You are worthy O Lord God to open the book", and the variant "to take" (or "receive") is mentioned in an interlinear gloss in Rusch. **Codex 24 and Rusch have "and have redeemed us, O God".] (a) *Only in Latin 588.] (b) *Only in Latin 588.] (c) *Not in Latin 588. It looks like a quasi-duplication of the following gloss happened.] 1 Codex 24 and Rusch: "professes the New Testament in deed".] 2 Latin *tribus* = "tribe"; a *tribus ordinibus* = "from the three orders".] 3 This is written above the previous gloss in Latin 588, in the other ink, to explain the three orders. It is not in the other books.] 4 Not in Latin 588.] 5 Only in Latin 588.

5:10 and have made us to our God (a)a kingdom and (b)priests, and we shall reign upon (c)the earth.

a. Spiritually kings.
b. Offering ourselves and praying* for others.
c. Upon earthliness or upon the earth of the living.*

5:10 (b) *Codex 24: "dying".] (c) *Codex 24 and Rusch: "upon earthly matters or upon the earth of the living".

5:11 And (a)I looked, and heard the voice of many angels (b)round about the throne and the beasts and the seniors: and (c)the number of them was (d)(e)thousands of thousands.

 a. I did not only see the beasts and the seniors applying themselves to the same thing by virtue of their duty, but also angels.*

 b. Sc. appearing.

 c. The finite for the infinite; that which is finite for God is infinite here for men.*

 d. I.e. many thousands.*

 e. The more numerous they are, the greater is the testimony and the greater the joy.

Angels. I.e. the spirits of above who defend and protect the Church, rejoice at the renewal of the community of the saints[1], give testimony to Christ, and declared in the nativity[2], in the passion, in the resurrection, and in the ascension that the judge would come.

Or the angels are the lesser inferiors in the Church who lead an angelic life, who surround and honor their preachers and their judges, agreeing with their testimony and confirming[3] it.

5:11 (a) *Codex 24 and Rusch: "I did not only see the beasts and the seniors bearing witness to the same thing by virtue of their duty, but I also heard...".] (c) *Codex 24 and Rusch: "Because that which is infinite for men is finite for God".] (d) *Not in Latin 588.] 1 Codex 24: "community of many".] 2 Codex 24 and Rusch: "in the nativity when they appeared to the shepherds".] 3 Rusch: "conforming to".

5:12 saying with a loud voice, The lamb that was slain, is (a)worthy to receive (b)power, and (c)divinity, and (d)wisdom, and (e)strength, and (f)honor, and (g)glory, and (h)benediction.

 a. As if saying: We are not ashamed to preach about you, because you are worthy.

 b. I.e. immunity from sin.

 c. Because he was God even if he was alive and dead*.

 d. I.e. knowledge of all things like the Word united to him has.

 e. Because he overcame the Devil when he remained firm in the Passion.

 f. In the Resurrection.

 g. Impassibility and immortality.

 h. In exaltation.

5:12 (c) *Codex 24 and Rusch: "even if he was seen dead".

5:13 (a)(b)And every creature (c)that is (d)in heaven, and (e)upon the earth, and (f)under the earth, and that are in (g)the sea*, and (h)that are therein: (i)all did I hear saying, To (j)him that sits (k)in the throne, and to (l)the Lamb, (m)benediction and (n)honor and (o)glory and (p)power (q)forever and ever.

 a. And to receive...*

 b. That in the name of Jesus every knee should bow,

 c. He describes the creatures.*

 d. of those that are in heaven,

 e. on earth,

 f. under the earth.*

 g. Literally or the world.

 h. And all things.*

 i. I.e. the beasts and the seniors declare their agreement with the testimony of the angels all at the same time.*

 j. I.e. the Trinity.

 k. The order is changed.*

 l. According to his humanity.

 m. I.e. exaltation.

 n. I.e. impassibility.

 o. In the resurrection.

 p. Because he is omnipotent.

 q. To our Lord.*

Let *benediction,* i.e the amelioration we have in good works, the *honor* that ensues from that, the *glory* of the virtues that we received in baptism, and the *power* with which we resist concupiscences be attributed not to us, but to you.

5:13 In the verse: *Codex 24 and Rusch have "and the sea" instead of "and that are in the sea".] (a) *Not in Latin 588.] (c) *Only in Latin 588.] (b), (d), (e), (f) * = Philippians, 2:10. I must say that it looks less repetitive in Latin than it is in English, because more different (in this context synonymous) words are used in Phil. 2:10 and here in Rev. 5:13 than in the English version.] (h) *Not in Latin 588.] (i) *In Rusch, this gloss is to the beginning of the next verse.] (k) *Only in Latin 588. Should this not have been above "benediction and honor, etc.", where we indeed find a changed word order compared to the previous verse...?] (q) *Only in Codex 24.

5:14 [a]*And the four beasts said,* [b][c]*Amen. And the four and twenty seniors* [d]*fell* [e]*on their faces: and* [f]*adored him that lives forever and ever.*

a. It behooves the preachers, by virtue of their duty, to confirm the testimony of the others.
b. Sign of confirmation.*
c. Because you have a judge in the heavens.*
d. They did not get haughty because they punish* others, but they fell, i.e. humbled themselves.
e. I.e. into their hearts.
f. With their minds, their mouths, and their deeds.

On their faces. Not backwards like Heli (1 Samuel, 4:18), but forwards in their minds, because he who falls forwards sees where he falls; he who falls backwards does not know.[1]

5:14 (b) *Only in Rusch.] (c) *Only in Codex 24. It is actually unclear which word(s) it refers to.] (d) *Codex 24 and Rusch: "judge". The words resemble each other.] 1 Only in Latin 588.

CHAPTER 6

6:1 AND I saw that the Lamb had opened one of the seven seals, and I heard ^(a)one of the four beasts, saying, as it were the voice of ^(b)thunder, ^(c)Come, and see.

    a.   The beasts invite John*, i.e. the first ones invite the Church that comes after them.
    b.   Because it is frightening.*
    c.   With faith*, and come across from your ministry**, and see the truth*** fulfilled.

After the lamb has fulfilled the things that had been foretold concerning him, and has confirmed his Church in faith by the testimony of the prophets and of the angels, he reveals the sense to them so that they may understand the Scriptures, and announces on the outside through preachers that it is right to suffer for this faith, and what aids or what crowns he offers his people. Because, after reminding them of the renewal, if he passed over the tribulations in silence, they might now succumb if tribulation arose unexpectedly.

That the Lamb had opened. It was sealed because Christ opened everything either by himself or through his people. For he himself opened the meanings to his people so that they might understand these seals in the Scriptures. By the first seal opened out of which came the white horse is symbolized the whitening of the Church through baptism; by the second horse, the red one, is symbolized the open persecution of those who shed blood, whence tribulations arise for the baptized; by the third, the black one, the secret persecution of the heretics; and by the fourth, the pale one, the persecution of false brothers, both open and secret.[1]

With the seal being opened, the coming of the Son of God is declared, coming to the passion and giving example to his people so that they may follow his footsteps, which was previously hidden as if under a seal.[2]

6:1 (a) *Latin 588 has, "the beasts, John", as if the beasts and John (or the beasts that represented John?) were the ones who invited. Rusch has "John". I have chosen to follow Codex 24 as its version looked the most clear and probable to me, but I cannot be certain.] (b) *Not in Codex 24.] (c) *"With faith" not in Rusch. **Codex 24 and Rusch: "from mystery". The Latin words are very similar. ***Codex 24 and Rusch: "the truth, or justice".] 1 Not in Latin 588.] 2 Only in Latin 588.

6:2 And I saw: and behold ^(a)a white horse, and he that sat upon him had ^(b)a bow, and ^(c)there was ^(d)a crown given him, and ^(e)he went forth conquering that he might ^(f)conquer.

    a.   I.e. the Church whitened in baptism, or especially the preachers, who carry God everywhere.
    b.   I.e. the divine Scripture.
    c.   For preachers attribute what they do to God.
    d.   I.e. glory by his people.*
    e.   Sc. in the person of the Jews or in his own person.
    f.   Sc. the nations, or in the person of his limbs.*

He that sat upon him had a bow. Christ has a bow, i.e. the Scripture with[1] which he illuminates his people and kills his enemies[2].

A bow. The bow without the string is the Old Testament, which was, as it were, useless; but once the string, i.e. the New Testament, is put on it, it is useful for shooting arrows that transfix the hearts of the listeners.[3]

There was a crown given him. Or God is crowned in his people, because God is glorious in the saints. Or according to his humanity.[4]

6:2 (d) *Not in Codex 24. Rusch has "I.e. power".] (f) *Codex 24 and Rusch: "The nations with his limbs".] 1 "With" not in Codex 24 and Rusch.] 2 Codex 24: "the others, i.e. his enemies".] 3 Only in Latin 588.] 4 Codex 24: "God is crowned in the saints according to his humanity"; Rusch: "God is crowned in the saints or according to his humanity".

6:3 And when he had opened the ^(a)second seal, I heard the second beast, saying, Come, and see.

    a.   In the order and time in which these things were lived.*

6:3 (a) *Codex 24 and Rusch: "In the order in which he saw these things, not in time". The Latin corresponding to "in which these things were lived" and "in which he saw these things" differ only in one letter.

6:4 [a]*And there went forth* [b]*another horse, red: and* [c]*he that sat thereon, to him it was* [d]*given that he should* [e]*take* [f]*peace* [g]*from the earth, and that they should* [h]*kill one another, and* [i]*a great sword was given to him.*

   a.   Because what he has in his heart, he fulfills in deed.
   b.   Opposed to the previous one. That is, open and bloody persecutors.
   c.   I.e. the Devil.
   d.   I.e. conceded by God.
   e.   I.e. take away.
   f.   I.e. all peace of mind.
   g.   I.e. also* from those who are devoted to earthly things.
   h.   Sc. with a material sword or with that of persuasion.
   i.   I.e. a great power to kill, because it is not only over lesser people, but also over greater ones like Peter.

6:4 (g) *"Also" only in Latin 588.

The Devil, seeing that the Church is being set up to fill the place he fell from, first tries openly to destroy it.

6:5 And when he had opened the third seal, I heard the third beast, saying, Come, and see. And behold [a]*a* [b]*black horse, and* [c][d]*he that sat upon him,* [e]*had* [f]*a balance in* [g]*his hand.*

   a.   I.e. the Devil.*
   b.   Obscuring his vices with a few good works.
   c.   I.e. his people who trust in him.*
   d.   His people attribute to the Devil what they do through him.*
   e.   I.e. they say that they have.
   f.   I.e. true discernment with regards to the Scriptures.
   g.   Because what they preach, they confirm in deed.

6:5 (a) *Only in Latin 588.] (c) *Only in Latin 588.] (d) *In Latin 588, this is written in the margin with a sign repeated above interlinear (c) and it to indicate that it refers to (c). It is different in Codex 24 and Rusch, which have: "We attribute to the Devil himself what his people do through him".] 1 Codex 24 and Rusch: "open persecutions".] 2 Codex 24 and Rusch: "false reasonings". The Latin words are similar.] 3 The last part starting from "which we symbolize" is only in Latin 588.

Seeing that he has not succeeded through open persecutors[1], the Devil sends the heretics to contend with false speeches[2] so that they may deceive more easily; which we symbolize by the black horse because they obscure the Scriptures with perverse ideas so as to corrupt and lead astray simple people.[3]

6:6 [a]*And I heard as it were* [b]*a voice in the midst of the four beasts saying:* [c][d]*Two pounds of* [e]*wheat* [f]*for* [g]*a penny, and* [h]*thrice two pounds of* [i]*barley* [j]*for a penny,* [k]*and* [l]*wine, and* [m]*oil* [n]*you hurt not*[o].

   a.   Because they are coming into the greater danger constituted by the heretics, the help of Christ is presented.*
   b.   Sc. of an angel appearing.*
   c.   As if saying: Do not fear, faithful, because they shall not be able to harm you; and you devils, do not harm these people, because you shall not succeed, because two pounds of wheat, etc.*
   d.   I.e. the Church gathered out of two peoples.*
   e.   By wheat, the more perfect people are meant.*
   f.   Sc. is bought.
   g.   I.e. the blood of Christ.
   h.   For one ought to have at least faith in the Trinity.
   i.   By barley, the lesser ones.*
   j.   Sc. bought.*
   k.   Is likewise bought, as well as oil, for a penny, i.e. Christ.*
   l.   By wine, the preachers.*
   m.   By oil, those who have been anointed by the Holy Spirit.*
   n.   And therefore.
   o.   Sc. any of these.

A *bilibris*[1] is a container with a capacity of two pints, which is the Church consisting of two peoples and of faith and works[2].

The wheat is the more perfect people who, ground by tribulations and[3] cooked by fire, are a food sweet to God. The barley is the lesser ones of the same kind. The wine is the preachers who have indeed been ground in battle but are not so well cooked[4], but yet are strong in themselves and inebriate others with a desire to do good works. The oil is those who do not inebriate others, but anoint them with pure discourses[5]. Or the wine and oil are the confessors, on account of the fervor of their love and of the sweetness of their mercy which they have in themselves and towards others.[6]

By the wheat we understand the greater martyrs, who weigh two pounds, for, on account of their martyrdom, they have works and the love of God and of their neighbor, or faith and works. By the barley we understand the lesser martyrs, that is, those who have only faith in the Trinity without works and without any love, but for faith alone are saved in blood: these weigh thrice two pounds because of faith in the Trinity. Or otherwise: as wheat indeed is first ground a lot, and then becomes very good bread, so did Christ, ground a lot by various persecutions, become for us the bread of life by giving us his body and blood. And so are the faithful ground by many tribulations, and, once they have become a very good food for God, they become the imitators of wheat, i.e. of Christ. Or they are full of wheat, i.e. of wheaten preaching, because the preaching of faith refreshes the hearts of those who listen to it as wheat refreshes the taste more than any fruit of the land. And to those who are the imitators of wheat, preaching gave birth through one penny, i.e. those who unanimously obey the penny, i.e. the Decalogue, i.e. the ten commandments of the law[7].[8]

A pound consists of twelve ounces; by this are symbolized the twelve apostles, and by the two pounds the twofold love of God and neighbor. Or those who have the love of God and of their neighbor as well as faith in the Trinity and obey the four Gospels weigh two pounds, for three times four is twelve, which is the number the pound consists of; by three they have the faith in the holy Trinity, by four the four Gospels, and by the two pounds the love of God and neighbour.[9]

By the wheat we may understand the New Testament, and by the barley the Old. The wheat, i.e. the New Testament, is said to weigh two pounds because of its double meaning, namely the historical one and the spiritual one. As if saying: Do not fear, you faithful, for perfection will be given to you, through which you shall be able to resist the heretics.[10]

And wine and oil. I.e. those who have been refreshed by wine, i.e. by my blood, and anointed with oil, i.e. with the Holy Spirit.[11]

6:6 (a) *Codex 24 and Rusch: "Because the danger is greater here in the fight against the heretics, help is presented".] (b) *Not in Codex 24.] (c) *Codex 24: "I want you, faithful, not to fear... (the rest being the same as in Latin 588)"; Rusch: "I want you, faithful, not to fear those who used to be able to harm you... (rest the same)".] (d) *Only in Latin 588.] (e) *Only in Latin 588.] (i) *Only in Latin 588.] (j) *Only in Latin 588.] (k) *Codex 24 and Rusch have only "Wine is likewise bought for a penny".] (l) *Only in Latin 588.] (m) *Only in Latin 588 here, but see the marginal gloss on wine and oil.] 1 This is the Latin word translated as "two pounds" in the verse. The word is primarily an adjective meaning "weighing or containing two pounds", then it also came to mean the two pounds themselves. Here the glossator apparently understood it as the name of a container.] 2 Codex 24 and Rusch: ".... the Church consisting of two peoples, or having faith and works".] 3 Latin 588 has "i.e." instead of "and", but I have chosen to follow the other books here because it made more sense to me.] 4 Codex 24: "... The barley is the softer ones of the same kind, who have indeed been ground in oil, but are not so well cooked..."; In Rusch, this part is identical to Latin 588's version except that it has "those who have indeed been..." instead of "the preachers who have indeed been...".] 5 Latin 588 has "anoint God with pure reasonings".] 6 This last sentence, "Or the wine and oil are the confessors, etc.", is not in Latin 588.] 7 "Penny" translates Lat. *denarius*, which was an adjective meaning "containing ten", and then as a noun meant a silver coin worth ten asses.] 8 Only in Rusch.] 9 Not in Latin 588.] 10 Only in Rusch.] 11 Not in Latin 588.

6:7 And when he had opened [(a)]**the fourth seal, I heard a voice of** [(b)]**the fourth beast, saying, Come, and see.**

    a.   The secrets of the fourth seal.*
    b.   The fourth status.*

6:7 (a) *Not in Latin 588.] (b) *Not in Latin 588.

6:8 And behold [(a)]**a pale horse: and** [(b)]**he that sat upon him, his name was death, and** [(c)]**hell followed him. And power was given to him** [(d)]**over the four parts** [(e)]**of the earth,** [(f)]**to kill with** [(g)]**sword, with** [(h)]**famine, and with** [(i)]**death, and with** [(j)]**beasts of the earth.**

    a.   I.e. the dead and someone afflicting himself.*
    b.   I.e. the Devil.
    c.   I.e. the insatiable who imitate him with earthly things, or those who are to be put in hell.*
    d.   I.e. over all the wicked living everywhere, or over the Jews and the Gentiles, and the heretics and the false Christians.
    e.   Of the world.*
    f.   What power?

Seeing that he was able to succeed neither through open tribulations nor through open heresies, the Devil sends false brethren who, under the appearance of religion, possess the nature of both the red and the black horse in that they corrupt faith.

Death. Because it is through him that death came, or literally because he kills some in the flesh and some in the soul.

g.   A material one or that of persuasion.
h.   Of the divine word.
i.   Poisonous words.
j.   Beast-like ministers or literally.

6:8 (a) *Codex 24 and Rusch: "I.e. the dead or hypocrites afflicting themselves".] (c) *Codex 24 and Rusch have something phrased a little differently, which could mean either the same thing or "That is, those who are insatiable for earthly things imitate him. Or those who are to be put in hell".] (e) *Not in Latin 588. Rusch has "Or of the world".

6:9 *(a)***And when he had opened the fifth seal: I saw** *(b)(c)(d)***under the altar the souls of them that were** *(e)***slain** *(f)***for the word of God, and for** *(g)***the testimony which they** *(h)***had.**

a.   I.e. when he had revealed the secrets of the Church for what concerns the last status, i.e. in the time of the Antichrist.*
b.   Here is the place.*
c.   I.e. humbling themselves before their head.
d.   I.e. under the protection of Christ, who is the altar.*
e.   Sc. by some martyrdom or by some trouble.*
f.   I.e. for the commandment of God which they fulfilled.*
g.   Which he attests in front of others.*
h.   I.e. showed in deed by imitating Christ.*

After showing the tribulations that presently impend over the faithful, lest they should succumb somewhat, he comforts the suffering ones, assuring them of the crown present.

I saw under. Or *under,* i.e. in secret, because no one in this life can see how they are there.

The altar is Christ, upon whom they sacrifice[1], and whom they have as a bulwark. Or the souls themselves are the altar, from whom proceeds a smoke delightful to God, and who were smeared with blood[2], now appearing under, i.e. in a lesser dignity than they are to be in the future, because they have received but one stole yet.

6:9 (a) *Only in Rusch.] (b) *Only in Rusch.] (d) *Not in Latin 588. In the other ink in Codex 24.] (e) *Codex 24 and Rusch: "Either by open martyrdom or by some trouble".] (f) *Codex 24: "I.e. for the commandment of God which is being fulfilled". Not in Latin 588.] (g) *Not in Latin 588. The Vulgates of Codex 24 and Rusch read "for the testimony <u>of Jesus Christ</u> which they had. Is it Jesus Christ who attests, or is it a mistake for "they attest"?] (h) *Only in Rusch.] 1 Rusch: "sacrifice themselves".] 2 Codex 24 and Rusch: "and because they were smeared with blood", but the word "smeared" being missing in Codex 24.

6:10 And *(a)***they cried with a loud voice, saying,** *(b)***How long** *(c)***Lord,** *(d)***holy and** *(e)***true, do you** *(f)(g)***judge not and** *(h)***revenge not our blood of them that** *(i)***dwell** *(j)***on the earth*?**

a.   I.e. they cried great things with a great desire.*
b.   Why.*
c.   In proportion to your power.*
d.   I.e. loving holiness.
e.   Sc. in your promises.
f.   By making the separation between the good and the wicked.
g.   Absent from most versions.*
h.   By inflicting punishments on those who have deserved it.*
i.   By their love.
j.   I.e. in earthly things.

They long for a greater joy and for the society of angels[1], and agree with God's justice in the damnation of the wicked.

6:10 In the verse: *Codex 24 has: "How long, Lord, holy and true, how long do you revenge not our blood and do you judge not them that dwell on the earth?"; Rusch has: "How long, Lord, holy and true, how long do you judge not and do you revenge not our blood, taking vengeance on them that dwell on the earth?"] (a) *Codex 24 and Rusch have only "with a great desire". "A loud voice" in Latin is literally "a great voice".] (b) *Only in Latin 588.] (c) *Only in Rusch.] (g) *Only in Rusch.] (h) *Codex 24 has only "By inflicting punishments", placed above "judge" due to the inverted order of the verse in Codex 24; Rusch has "I.e. by inflicting punishment on the shedders of our blood", above "revenge" like in Latin 588, and has also "By inflicting punishments" above "taking vengeance".] 1 Codex 24 and Rusch: "saints".

6:11 And *(a)***white stoles were given, to every one of them one: and it was** *(b)***said to them, that they should** *(c)***rest yet a little time, until** *(d)***their** *(e)***fellow-servants be complete, and their brethren*, that are to be slain even as they.**

a.   Happiness of the soul.
b.   I.e. inspired by God.
c.   Wait patiently.

d. They must wait for the servants for the sake of the Lord himself, and wait for their brethren out of love.*

e. Because they have the same Lord.*

6:11 In the verse: *The Vulgates of all three books have "until the number of their fellow-servants be complete, and of their brethren".] (d) *Codex 24 and Rusch: "The servants must wait for the sake of the Lord himself, the brethren must wait out of love".] (e) *Only in Rusch.

6:12 And I saw, when he had opened the sixth seal, and behold (a)there was made (b)a great earthquake, and (c)the sun became (d)black as it were a (e)sackcloth (f)of hair: and the (g)whole (h)moon became as blood:

a. Sc. by the persecution of the Antichrist.
b. I.e. such a cruel torment that earthly people will be shaken violently, like an earthquake.*
c. I.e. a faithful man. Or those in whom God shines shall be considered guilty men and sinners, keeping their brightness inside of themselves. Or some will fall down to darkness. Or Christ, the old* sun, and now bright, in the time of the Antichrist will be dark, i.e. glittering with no miracles.
d. Sc. with tribulations.
e. Because the doctors will be considered worthless.*
f. Either after the place* or because of its roughness.**
g. Because it shall suffer everywhere.
h. I.e. the Church.

After having interposed some comfort for the suffering ones so that they not succumb in tribulation, he speaks again about the persecution in the time of the Antichrist.[1]

As it were a sackcloth of hair. A light put in a sack does not shine outside: the faithful will not shed the light of preaching.[2]

Previously bright by their virtues, they shall be considered as worthless by the impious as a sackcloth of hair, that is, a worthless garment. In the same way as, if a light were put in a sack, it would shine inside nonetheless, so will the faithful, in the time of the persecution, retain their brightness in their minds and consciences, even though they are afflicted on the outside. The word cilicinus[3] comes from "Cilicia" where it was invented, or from cilicium[4]. [5]

6:12 (b) *Only in Latin 588.] (c) *Codex 24 and Rusch: "true", which is perhaps the more likely reading. Only one letter differs in Latin.] (e) *Only in Rusch.] (f) *See notes 3 and 4 and the gloss they are about itself. **Only in Latin 588.] 1 Only in Latin 588.] 2 Not in Latin 588.] 3 Latin for "of (goat) hair(-cloth)".] 4 Latin for "a rug or blanket of goat's hair", indeed "apparently originating in Cilicia" (quoting the Oxford Latin Dictionary).] 5 This gloss is found only in Latin 588.

6:13 and (a)the stars (b)from heaven fell (c)upon the earth, as the fig tree casts (d)(e)her green figs when (f)it is shaken of a great wind:

a. I.e. they who were previously bright.
b. I.e. from their previous splendor.*
c. Resting upon.*
d. I.e. empty fruits, for God permits no one to fall if they serve him with true love.
e. I.e. fruits light and empty for lack of digestive heat.*
f. Sc. before they reach ripeness.*

6:13 (b) *Only in Latin 588.] (c) "Rusch has "resting upon earthly things".] (e) *Only in Rusch. "Lack of digestive heat" was associated with greed, pride and hypocrisy. The "digestive heat" is also compared figuratively to love.] (f) *Only in Rusch.

6:14 (a)(b)and heaven departed (c)as a book folded together: and every hill, and (d)islands (e)were moved out of their places.

a. I.e. the sacred Scripture, because it will be concealed.*
b. I.e. the Church will depart from the wicked in faith and deed, whence "Go out from her (i.e. from Babylon), my people" (Rev. 18:4) and "Touch not the unclean thing" (2 Corint. 6:17).
c. I.e. they will hide preaching from the impious.
d. Those who are buffeted by persecutions.
e. They will be separated from the wicked in faith and deed.

Or every hill, i.e. outstanding virtues. Or the hills, who are the proud, and the islands, who are those who busy themselves with businesses of the world, will be moved out of faith.

6:14 (a) *Only in Rusch.

6:15 And (a)the kings of the earth, and (b)princes, and (c)tribunes, and the (d)rich, and the (e)strong, and every (f)bondman, and (g)free-man hid themselves (h)in the dens and rocks of mountains.

    a.   I.e. the greater or lesser people who resist the flesh.
    b.   Of the earth.*
    c.   Those who render justice.*
    d.   Sc. in works.
    e.   Against the temptations of the Devil.
    f.   I.e. married man or bondman of God.
    g.   Free from sin or from marriage.
    h.   Literally.*

The kings of the earth, and princes, and tribunes, following the various honors of the world: as they will not want to lose them, they will abandon faith; the rich, fulfilling every bad desire they have; the strong in causing the ruin of others; bondman of sin; free from justice: these, despairing of receiving help from saints, will seek the help of demons, so that they in whom they trusted may deliver them.

6:15 (b) *Not in Latin 588.] (c) *Only in Rusch.] (h) *Only in Rusch. 588 has above "hid themselves" the sign that usually signifies the beginning of an interlinear gloss, but nothing follows. A copyist interrupted his work and then forgot to actually write the gloss when he came back to it, perhaps? Or did he just draw the sign by mistake?

6:16 (a)And they say (b)to the mountains and the rocks: (c)Fall upon us, and (d)hide us (e)from the face (f)of him that sits upon the throne, and from the wrath (g)of the Lamb:

    a.   I.e. they ask for the intercession of angels, who are the mountains by their superiority and the rocks by their firmness, so that the Judge's mercy may be obtained* through their prayers**.
    b.   They will implore the help of saints.*
    c.   With affection.*
    d.   With prayers.*
    e.   I.e. from the presence or judgment*.
    f.   Of the Father, of the Son and of the Holy Spirit.*
    g.   I.e. of Christ man.*

The good ask to be protected from the face of God angry by the intercessions of saints. He is said to be angry when he lets his people be thus afflicted, and that so great tribulation permitted by God is said to be like the face of God angry. Or the wicked ask the demons whom they have imitated to defend them from the wrath of the judge.[1]

6:16 (a) *Codex 24 and Rusch: "so that they may obtain". **"Through their prayers" not in Codex 24.] (b) *Only in Rusch.] (c) *Not in Latin 588.] (d) *Not in Codex 24.] (e) *"Or judgment" only in Latin 588.] (f) *Not in Latin 588.] (g) *Codex 24 has only "I.e. of Christ".] 1 Not in Latin 588.

6:17 (a)because the great day of (b)their wrath is come, and (c)who shall be able to stand?

    a.   You must fall.
    b.   Of the Father sitting and of the Lamb.*
    c.   Sc. unless he is helped by true prayers.

6:17 (b) *Codex 24 and Rusch have "of the reprobates" - by which they probably meant the great day of wrath against the reprobates.

CHAPTER 7

7:1 [(a)]**AFTER these things I saw** [(b)(c)]**four** [(d)]**angels** [(e)]**standing upon the four** [(f)]**corners of the earth, holding the** [(g)(h)]**four winds of the earth that they should not blow** [(i)]**upon the land, nor upon** [(j)(k)]**the sea, nor** [(l)]**on any tree.**

   a.   He does not mark the diversity of the visions but their order.*
   b.   I.e. a fourfold devil because of the four parts of the world.*
   c.   Because of the four kingdoms they rule.*
   d.   Because they are sent by God.*
   e.   I.e. dwelling.
   f.   I.e. in the most remote places.*
   g.   I.e. the fourfold order of preachers scattered in the four directions over the world.*
   h.   Because of the four things to be preached* or because of the Gospels.**
   i.   I.e. upon those who dwell on the earth or those who are devoted to earthly things.
   j.   Opposite to the former and different from it.*
   k.   I.e. those who dwell in islands or those who are flowing with various vices.
   l.   I.e. on anyone who has already risen even above earthly matters, or is ready to bear fruit.
   a.

7:1 (a) *Only in Rusch.] (b) *Only in Latin 588.] (c) *Only in Rusch.] (d) *Only in Rusch.] (f) *Rusch: "Even in the most remote places".] (g) *Only in Latin 588.] (h) *Only in Rusch.] (j) *Not in Latin 588.] 1 Codex 24 and Rusch: "of all".] 2 Not in Latin 588.] 3 Codex 24 and Rusch: "to detain the breath". The abbreviations look somewhat similar.

A Devil is called an angel, i.e. one sent, by God for the proof of the integrity of the good and the deception of the wicked, and by the chief Devil for the destruction of the just[1].

Having described the manifold war of the Church, he adds that in the time of this war the Devil is ready to harm, but restrained by God, so that his people should not somewhat be paralyzed or despair.

Four Angels. For the four parts of the world in which they do harm.[2]

Holding the four winds. Indeed, in time of tribulation, nothing has been more necessary than preaching, and therefore the Devil strives to detain it[3] in every place.

Winds. The wind makes the clouds move, irrigates the earth, makes it fruitful, and makes its face cheerful: so does preaching with the minds of men.

7:2 And I saw [(a)(b)]**another angel ascending from the rising of the sun, having** [(c)(d)]**the sign of the living God:** [(e)]**and he cried** [(f)]**with a loud voice to the four angels, to whom it was** [(g)]**given** [(h)]**to hurt** [(i)]**the earth and the sea,**

   a.   Against them.*
   b.   Because he announced new joys to the world.*
   c.   I.e. the cross to sign his people with. Or a power equal to that of the Father. Or immunity from sin, through which it appears clearly that he is God, because every man is a sinner.
   d.   The ensign of the cross, or the power to do miracles and forgive sins.*
   e.   Sc. when he restrained the demons in his passion. For God, crying is doing.
   f.   I.e. with a great authority.
   g.   I.e. permitted.*
   h.   Not as much as they want.*
   i.   I.e. the greedy, but who are nonetheless to be converted.*

7:2 (a) *Only in Latin 588.] (b) *Only in Rusch.] (d) *Only in Rusch.] (g) *Only in Rusch.] (h) *Only in Rusch.] (i) *Only in Rusch.] 1 Codex 24 and Rusch add "i.e. of the Father".] 2 Not in Latin 588.

Another angel. This angel is the stone cut out without hands that destroyed the statue made of four metals (Ref. Daniel 2:34); he releases the four winds.

Ascending. After Christ expired, he ascended when he bound the Devil and illuminated the world with faith little by little through preachers as the sun does with light. Or he ascended from the rising sun, i.e. from the Father he ascended, advancing in wisdom and age (ref. Luke 2:52). Or he is descended from himself, because he did not assume flesh through the sexual act of a man but he, who is the rising of the sun[1], created it himself.

The sign. Even if not in fact, the ancient fathers nonetheless wore this sign all the time by their faith.[2]

7:3 saying, [(a)]**hurt not the earth and the sea, nor the trees,** [(b)]**until we sign the servants of our God in their foreheads.**

   a.   As if saying "Do not work".
   b.   I.e. until we distinguish them within and without by the sign of the cross.*

7:3 (b) *Codex 24 and Rusch: "Until I distinguish them within and my people distinguishes them without with the sign of the cross".] 1 Not in Latin 588.

The sign of the cross is worn on the forehead so that it not be hidden in tribulation. For the signing of the breast is the confession of the heart.

When a child is catechized, he is anointed on his breast so that he may have the faith of the heart, on his forehead so that he should not blush, but confess, *for with the heart we believe unto justice; and with the mouth confession is made unto salvation* (Rom. 10:10), on his shoulders so that he may bear the burden of Christ, and on the top of his head so that he may keep reason, which is the top and head of the interior man.[1]

7:4 *(a)And I heard the number of them that were signed, (b)a hundred forty four thousand were (c)signed, (d)of every tribe of the children of Israel.*

    a.   I.e. I understood what kind of people had to be signed.
    b.   The finite for the infinite, or* because God includes all under a determined number.
    c.   Because of their perfection.
    d.   I.e. of every nation, of those that imitate the faith of Jacob.*

A hundred forty four thousand. With twelve we have those who have been signed by faith in the holy Trinity in the four parts of the world. And to show that these are perfect, we multiply twelve by four, and it makes forty-eight; now for this perfection to refer to the Trinity, we multiply forty-eight by three, and it makes a hundred forty four.

7:4 (b) *Codex 24 and Rusch: "He gives a finite number because God etc."] (d) *Codex 24 and Rusch: "I.e. of all those who imitate the faith of Jacob".

7:5 *Of the tribe of (a)Judah, twelve thousand signed. Of the tribe of (b)Reuben, twelve thousand signed. Of the tribe of (c)Gad, twelve thousand signed.*

    a.   "Judah" is interpreted as "confessing". This suffices for those who are not kept for works*.
    b.   "Reuben" = "seeing the son", i.e. "the works". This is for those who are kept for doing works*.
    c.   "Gad" = "Girded with a sword", in case tribulation should threaten.

Of the tribe of Judah. That is, of the children who, born and baptized, are saved just by the confession of their spiritual parents.[1]

Judah, who is put first, was fourth in order of generation: for this it is hinted that one should pay attention to spiritual lineage. The Antichrist will be born of the race of Dan, therefore it is omitted here in order to show that the Antichrist must be cast out of the whole number of the saints. Or Dan means the passing judgment of the Jews, because after the truth came, what was founded on the old law passed, and the Gentile people, forgetting idols, rose in truth after Christ's birth in the sixth age.

7:5 (a) *Codex 24 and Rusch: "... This suffices for those who are not kept here to live".] (b) *Latin 588: "... This is for those who will keep".] 1 Not in Latin 588.

7:6 *Of the tribe of (a)Asher, twelve thousand signed. Of the tribe of (b)Naphtali, twelve thousand signed. Of the tribe of (c)Manasseh, twelve thousand signed.*

    a.   "Asher" = "blessed", "not intent on worldly things".
    b.   "Naphtali" = "breadth", i.e. "liberality* giving bountifully to others, out of his love".
    c.   "Manasseh" = "having forgotten and not taking care to provide the things that concern the needs of life".

7:6 (b) *"Liberality" only in Latin 588.

7:7 *Of the tribe of (a)Simeon, twelve thousand signed. Of the tribe of (b)Levi, twelve thousand signed. Of the tribe of (c)Issachar, twelve thousand signed.*

    a.   "Simeon" = "A hearkening to sadness", i.e. always grieving at past sins for the preservation of virtue.
    b.   "Levi" = "added", doing even what he has not been enjoined to.
    c.   "Issachar" = "salary", striving for the reward, like "I desire to be dissolved and to be with Christ" (Philippians 1:23).

7:8 *Of the tribe of (a)Zebulun, twelve thousand signed. Of the tribe of (b)Joseph, twelve thousand signed. Of the tribe of (c)Benjamin, twelve thousand signed.*

    a.   "Zebulun" = "dewlling place of courage", i.e. those who do not refuse hard work, but sometimes come down from Mary to Martha (ref. Luke 10:38-42) for the needs of their brothers.

b. "Joseph" = "increase", i.e. those who enrich the Church in number of saints.

c. "Benjamin" = "son of the right hand", those who ascribe everything to God's mercy and nothing to themselves.

7:9 *(a)After these things I saw a great multitude (b)which no man could number, (c)of all nations, and (d)tribes, and (e)peoples, and (f)tongues: (g)standing before the throne, and (h)in the sight of (i)the Lamb, (j)clothed in white robes, and (k)palms in their hands:*

After seeing figuratively those that had to be elected under a determined number, and only of the children of Israel, he now clearly lets us know that by this number we must understand all the faithful, and by the twelve tribes all the nations.

a. As if he were saying: I saw it fulfilled just as it had been foretold.

b. The number, certain for God, is unknown to men.

c. Even of the most barbarous ones.

d. In each nation.

e. In each city.

f. In a same people there are various tongues.

g. I.e. ready to obey God the judge or their superiors. This in the present. And they must be placed like that *standing before the throne* so that they be seen*.

h. So that they see.*

i. I.e. Christ man.

j. Sc. first in baptism, and then thanks to tears. This in the present.

k. I.e. victory that results from works. This concerning the future.

7:9 (g) *The part starting from "And they must be placed like that" is only in 588, but the end of it and the next gloss look like the same having suffered mistranscription/reinterpretation one way around or the other.] (h) *Not in Latin 588, as you may have expected.

7:10 And (a)they cried (b)with a loud voice, saying, (c)Salvation to our God which sits upon (d)the throne, and to the Lamb.

a. In the present and particularly in the future.

b. I.e. with a great desire.

c. That is, it is not through ourselves, but through the Lamb that we have salvation, remission of sins*, good works and eternal glory.

d. I.e. ourselves in whom he judges.

7:10 (c) *Codex 24 and Rusch: "... salvation, i.e. the remission of sins...".

7:11 And all the angels (a)stood (b)in the circuit of the throne and of (c)the seniors and of the four beasts: and (d)they fell (e)in the sight of the throne (f)upon their faces, and adored God,

All the angels. By the angels mentioned earlier we may understand the greater superiors, and by these the lesser superiors or just the inferiors. Just as there are angels and archangels, and yet all are angels, i.e. messengers, so now too are there greater and lesser superiors, i.e. archbishops and bishops.[1]

He presents the angels rejoicing at the community of the saints and confirming their testimony, and thanks to whom the multitude he had seen had persisted in this faith. Or by what was said earlier we understand the judges in the Church, and here this is added concerning their inferiors.

a. As helpers.

b. I.e. in its protection.*

c. The preachers of the Old and of the New Testament.*

d. I.e. they humbled themselves before God.

e. Sc. in order to be seen.

f. Rationally.

7:11 (b) *Not in Latin 588.] (c) *Not in Latin 588.] 1 Not in Latin 588.

7:12 saying, (a)Amen. Benediction, and glory, and (b)wisdom, and (c)thanksgiving, (d)honor and (e)power, and (f)strength to our God forever and ever. (g)Amen.

a. I.e. truth be to God.*
b. Because he knows everything and makes us wise.*
c. As if he were enumerating* all the good things for which we must be grateful.
d. Which he has in himself and gives to us.
e. I.e. power to resist. Also in himself.*
f. I.e. the effect of power.*
g. Let it be done, let it be done.*

Amen. Concerning the good things attributed. Or "amen" will be read together with the things that follow, like this: *Amen*, i.e. truth in promises, *benediction*, i.e. exaltation, which he has above every creature, or our exaltation in virtues, and *glory*, i.e. impassibility, or ours in works.

7:12 (a) *Not in Latin 588.] (b) *Codex 24: "Because he knows everything or because he makes us wise"; Rusch: "Because he knows everything or because he makes us know".] (c) *Codex 24: "hinting at". Similar words.] (e) *"Also in himself" only in Latin 588.] (f) *The Latin word *virtus*, translated in the verse as "power", can also (and more often does) mean "courage, bravery" or "virtue".] (g) *Not in Latin 588.

7:13 And (a)one of the seniors (b)answered, and (c)said to me, These that are clothed in the white robes, (d)who are they? And from where did they come?

a. All the seniors are one, because they teach one and the same thing.
b. Satisfying the desire.
c. Explaining.*
d. How worthy are they?

After seeing so great a multitude in so great a dignity, he is advised to think about by what way it was able to come up there, so that he may teach others to examine the same question.

7:13 (c) *Not in Codex 24.

7:14 And I said to him, (a)My Lord, you know. And he said to me, These are they which (b)have come out of great tribulation, (c)and have washed (d)(e)their robes, and (f)made them white (g)in the blood of the Lamb.

a. As if he were saying, "I do not know, but you, teach me*".
b. Come and will come.
c. Because no one is without sin but Christ.
d. Because it does not only pertain to the martyrs.*
e. I.e. the innocence received in baptism, or their bodies.
f. Through good* works.
g. I.e. through faith in the Passion of Christ.

7:14 (a) *Codex 24 and Rusch: "I do not know, but teach me, because you know".] (d) *Not in Latin 588.] (f) *Rusch: "new".

7:15 Therefore they are (a)before the throne of God, and they serve him (b)day and night (c)in his temple: and (d)he that sits in the throne (e)shall dwell* over them.

a. Before God the judge, or in the community of the holy angels.*
b. I.e. continuously.
c. Either here in the Church or in heaven.
d. I.e. he that gave knowledge to the angels.
e. I.e. shall give them the same knowledge.

7:15 In the verse: *Codex 24 and Rusch have "dwells" instead of "shall dwell", Rusch mentioning the latter in a gloss.] (a) *Codex 24 and Rusch: "Before the Lord judge, or in the community of angels".

7:16 [a]*They shall no more hunger nor thirst, neither shall* [b]*the sun fall upon them, nor any heat.*

    a.   Because they shall enjoy true bread, and* living bread, and the fountain of life.

    b.   I.e. a greater or lesser tribulation.

7:16 (a) *The words "true bread, and" only in Latin 588.

7:17 *Because the Lamb which is in the midst of the throne,* [a]*shall rule them, and shall conduct them to the living fountains of waters,* [b]*and God will wipe away all tears from their eyes.*

    a.   In the present *from virtue to virtue* (Psalm 83:8)*, and through this he shall in the future *conduct them to the living fountains of waters*, i.e. to complete refreshment.

    b.   I.e. all suffering, whether for their own faults or for hardships or exile or all other things of the kind.

7:17 *The Latin verb for "to rule" can also mean "to lead".

CHAPTER 8

8:1 AND when he had opened the seventh seal, [(a)]there was made silence in heaven, as it were [(b)]half an hour.

    a.   Because after the death of the Antichrist there will be peace in the Church.

    b.   Because the judgment will come quickly.*

In this third vision, the subject is seven angels sounding with trumpets for the destruction of the enemies, similarly to those people who destroyed the walls of Jericho by sounding with trumpets (Joshua 6:20-21). The intention in this is clear enough: it is as if he were saying: As I had understood the salvation of the just, I understood on the other hand the damnation of the wicked through the duty[1] of preaching imposed upon the good.

As he is about to say that the damnation of the wicked will come from the preaching of these people[2], he gives an excuse[3] in advance so that the damnation of the wicked should not be blamed on them, because in itself their preaching is good and enjoined by a good teacher.[4]

8:1 (b) *Codex 24 and Rusch: "Because he will come quickly for the judgment".] 1 Codex 24: "through the effect".] 2 Codex 24 and Rusch: "of the just". The versions differ only in one letter.] 3 Codex 24 and Rusch: "kind of an excuse".] 4 In Codex 24 and Rusch, this gloss is to "having a gold censer" in verse 3.

8:2 And I saw [(a)]seven angels [(b)]standing in the sight of God: [(c)]and there were given to them [(d)]seven trumpets.

    a.   Because they are all the angels, or imbued with the sevenfold spirit.

    b.   I.e. working, not bent with fear.

    c.   Because the damnation of the wicked does not displease God.*

    d.   I.e. the duty of preaching.

8:2 (c) *Latin 588 has "Because the (word of uncertain meaning) of the impious displeases God", above "in the sight of God". It may be either a mistranscription or something else I cannot figure out.

8:3 [(a)]And [(b)]another angel [(c)]came, and stood before the altar, having [(d)]a [(e)]golden censer*: and [(f)]there were given to him many incenses, [(g)]that he should give of the prayers of all [(h)]saints [(i)]upon the altar of gold, which is [(j)]before the throne of God.**

    a.   By whom?*

    b.   I.e. a greater one, that is, Christ.

    c.   I.e. he united humanity to himself.

    d.   I.e. the apostles, who are vessels of fire, i.e. of the Holy Spirit, and out of whom come prayers that rise before God.

    e.   Because of their wisdom.*

    f.   I.e. there are offered by the saints prayers delightful to God.*

    g.   That he should present them to God the Father.

    h.   Who sometimes ask for what they should not.*

    i.   I.e. to the one who is above him according to his humanity according to which he is the altar, that is, to the Trinity.

    j.   I.e. in the good pleasure of him that sits in the throne.*

He *stood before the altar*, ready to sacrifice like a priest. Or Christ is the altar, who offered himself, and upon whom the Church offers its prayers to God. So he *stood before the altar*, i.e. before himself, because he has no mediator to please through. Or he *stood before the altar*, i.e. before he was the altar, i.e. before he offered himself, he stood, because he helped his people since the time of his nativity. Or he *stood before the altar*, i.e. the Church, which is inflamed with the fire of love, sends its offerings to God through Christ.

He said "of the prayers" and not "the prayers" because he does not present them all to the Father, but he listens to those that have to do with salvation.[1]

8:3 In the verse: *All three books add "in his hand" here, and Latin 588 has a gloss above it saying "I.e. in his power". **Codex 24 and Rusch have "which is in the sight of God before the throne of God", with in Rusch an gloss above the additional part, saying "Absent from most versions".] (a) *I.e. By whom were the trumpets of the previous verse given? Answer in this verse: By this other angel.] (e) *Only in Latin 588.] (f) *In Codex 24 and Rusch, this differs slightly and is in two glosses: a first one above "there were given to him", saying "there are offered to Christ by the saints", and a second one above "many incenses", saying "prayers delightful to God".] (h) *Codex 24 and Rusch: "Because they sometimes ask for what they should not, like Paul".] (j) *Codex 34 and Rusch have this gloss above "upon the altar of gold"; unless it refer to "in the sight of God", since the placement of glosses is not always absolutely precise.] 1 Not in Latin 588.

8:4 ^(a)*And* ^(b)*the smoke of the incenses* ^(c)*of the prayers of the saints ascended* ^{(d)(e)}*from the hand of the angel* ^(f)*before God.*

    a.   Because they were given to him.
    b.   I.e. the devotion produced by eagerness for prayer kindled by God's fire.*
    c.   Coming from.*
    d.   I.e. from his work, Christ's existence being the cause*, or Christ is God's hand through whom he has done everything.
    e.   Where did it ascend from?*
    f.   Where?*

8:4 (b) *Codex 24 and Rusch: "The devotion produced by eagerness for prayer and kindled within by the fire of the vision of God".] (c) *Not in 588. The Latin just says "coming", but the Latin word translated here by "of" in the verse, in its most basic meaning, indicates motion from a point — and so could have been translated here as "from".] (d) *Instead of "Christ appearing being the cause", Codex 24 has "where Christ ascended from", and Rusch only "Christ existing".] (e) *Not in Latin 588, nor in Codex 24 as such, but see previous note.] (f) *Codex 24 has "the word". Similar words, mistranscription would have easily happened.

8:5 ^(a)*And the angel took the censer, and filled it* ^(b)*of the fire of the altar, and cast it* ^(c)*on the earth, and there* ^(d)*were made* ^(e)*thunders and* ^(f)*voices and* ^(g)*lightnings, and* ^(h)*a great earthquake.*

    a.   I.e. those he had taken in order to illumine, he is here said to take for another task.*
    b.   I.e. of the same Spirit that he himself was full of.
    c.   I.e. on those who were apt to bear fruit.
    d.   Sc. by them.
    e.   I.e. threats.
    f.   I.e. suasions.
    g.   I.e. miracles.
    h.   Some are moved* with good consequences and some with bad ones.**

8:5 (a) *Codex 24 and Rusch: "Those Christ had taken in order to illumine, he is said to take for that task".] (h) *The Latin for "earthquake", *terrae motus*, means literally "earth motion". **Codex 24 and Rusch: "With good consequences for some and bad ones for others".

8:6 *And* ^(a)*the seven angels which had* ^(b)*the seven trumpets,* ^(c)*prepared themselves to sound with the trumpets.*

    a.   I.e. all the preachers who imitate the apostles.
    b.   The duty of preaching.*
    c.   I.e. they first fulfilled in deed the things they were going to say in word, and* considered beforehand what was suited to each person.

8:6 (b) *Not in Latin 588.] (c) *Codex 24 and Rusch, instead of "and": "or they prepared, i.e.".

8:7 *And the* ^{(a)(b)}*first angel* ^(c)*sounded with the trumpet, and there was made* ^{(d)(e)}*hail and* ^{(f)(g)}*fire,* ^{(h)(i)}*mingled in blood, and it* ^(j)*was cast on the earth, and* ^(k)*the third part* ^(l)*of the earth was* ^(m)*burnt, and* ⁽ⁿ⁾*the third part of* ^{(o)(p)(q)}*trees was burnt, and all green grass was burnt.*

    a.   Sc. in order of narration, or because this blinding of the Jews first occurred when the apostles were preaching.
    b.   Sc. the band of apostles in Judea.*
    c.   I.e. in a manner dreadful to the wicked and sweet to the good.*

And it was cast on the earth. All this, i.e. hail, fire, and blood, was cast on the earth, i.e. on the Jews, who had been cultivated by the law and the prophets.

The third part. There are two parts of the just, i.e. the perfect ones and the less perfect ones, while all the reprobates are to be understood in the third part.

51

d. I.e. their preaching, sweet to some, seemed beating and heavy to others.
e. I.e. the whip of persecution outside.*
f. Sc. eternal for the one who did not believe.*
g. Inside.*
h. And therefore they got angry with the preachers.
i. These two things, i.e. hail and fire, were the reason why they killed them, and this is why it is said "mingled in blood".*
j. Sc. by the wrath of God.*
k. Sc. all the reprobates.*
l. Those who were devoted to earthly things.*
m. Blinded by God and damned by his ministers.*
n. of the wicked has greater weight.*
o. The trees are the greater people* who used to live under the law without giving occasion for complaint.
p. I.e. of the greater people.*
q. That is, for what concerns the superiors who are neither contemplative nor active but devoted to earthly things.*

Grass. I.e. all those who rest in the flower of the world and who, like grass, quickly catch flame.[1]

8:7 (b) *Only in Rusch.] (c) *Only in Rusch.] (e) *Only in Rusch.] (f) *Only in Latin 588.] (g) *Only in Rusch.] (i) *Shorter in Codex 24 and Rusch: "Because these two things were the reason why they killed them".] (j) *Only in Rusch.] (k) *Only in Rusch.] (l) *Not in Codex 24.] (m) *In Rusch, this gloss is to the second "burnt" (that with the trees) — which was first omitted in Latin 588's Vulgate text and was then added below the line in the other ink.] (n) *Only in Rusch.] (o) *Codex 24 and Rusch: "the greater Jews".] (p) *Only in Rusch.] (q) *Only in Rusch.] 1 Codex 24 has "I.e. all those who rest in the flower of the world", and "and quickly catch flame" added in the other ink; Rusch has "I.e. all those who rest in the flower of the world and quickly catch flame", and a small gloss added saying "I.e. the voluptuous".

8:8 (a)*And the* (b)*second* (c)*angel* (d)*sounded with the trumpet: and* (e)*as it were a great* (f)*mountain* (g)*burning* (h)*with fire,* (i)*was cast* (j)*into the sea, and* (k)*the third part of the sea was made* (l)(m)*blood:*

a. In the time of the martyrs.*
b. In order of narration, according to what was fulfilled*. For, the Jews having been blinded and the apostles having turned** to the nations, the two parts, i.e. all the good, believed, and the third part, i.e. all the reprobates, were given to the reprobate opinion.
c. Order of preachers.*
d. For the nations.*
e. Sc. with regards to swelling.*
f. I.e. the Devil is a mountain because of his pride.
g. To do harm.
h. With envy.
i. Sc. with divine permission.*
j. I.e. into the Gentiles.*
k. Those who received the doctrine neither openly nor secretly.*
l. I.e. sinners.*
m. People shedding blood.*

Into the sea. The Gentiles are the sea, i.e. flowing into many vices. Although the Devil was already in them before, he is said to have been cast into them now because, as some of them are going away, he strives to detain the others.

8:8 (a) *Only in Rusch.] (b) *Codex 24: "uncompleted". **Codex 24: "having been sent".] (c) *Only in Rusch.] (d) *Only in Rusch.] (e) *Only in Rusch. It refers to the swelling of pride.] (i) *Only in Rusch.] (j) *Not in Codex 24. Rusch, on the other hand, has more: "I.e. into the Gentiles, who are swelling because of their pride and waving because of their idolatry".] (k) *Only in Rusch.] (l) *Instead of this, Codex 24 has "preachers" above "the third part", and Rusch has "I.e. of the sinners" above "of the sea". The Latin words for "preachers" and "sinners" are similar enough.] (m) *Only in Rusch.]

8:9 and (a)(b)*the third part of those creatures* (c)*died, which had* (d)*lives in the sea, and the third part of* (e)*the ships perished.*

a. I.e. that of those Gentiles who were considered worthier by them* because of a few good works.
b. I.e. the wise in matters of the world or the philosophers who were converted neither by the exercise of reason nor by preaching.*
c. I.e. was blinded.
d. I.e. capacity of discernment.*
e. I.e. those who governed others.

8:9 (a) *Codex 24 and Rusch: "by others".] (b) *Only in Rusch.] (d) *The word translated by "lives" in the verse also means "souls".

8:10 [a]*And the third angel sounded with the trumpet, and* [b][c]*a great star fell* [d]*from heaven,* [e]*burning as it were* [f]*a torch, and it fell on the third part of* [g]*the floods, and on the fountains of waters:*

    a.   Sc. in the time of the heretics.*
    b.   I.e. a heresiarch.*
    c.   I.e. the Devil, seeing* or wise**.
    d.   I.e. from the Church or literally.
    e.   I.e. heretic.*
    f.   Which sets on fire and is consumed.
    g.   I.e. the preachers, who irrigate others with their preaching.*

And the third. In order of narration, because* this happened after those two other events. For after the Devil was unable to blind all the Jews and Gentiles, he sent them the heretics and caused the downfall of some of them.

What is called fountains is where the sum and as it were the origin of all faith is contained, like the Gospel. The rivers that are drawn from there are as it were their interpretations, among which there are two understandings for the faithful: the historical one and the allegorical one; the third one is that of the heretics when they strengthen their heresies with perverse interpretations of the Scriptures.[1]

8:10 (a) *Only in Rusch.] (b) *Rusch: "and because".] (c) *Only in Rusch.] (d) *Codex 24 and Rusch: "envying" instead of "seeing" — the difference in Latin being only in two letters, *invidens* vs. *videns*. **Codex 24 and Rusch: "or a wise heretic", cf. (f). In the Latin word order, "burning" directly follows "great star".] (f) *Only in Latin 588 here, but see previous note.] (h) *Only in Latin 588.] 1 In Latin 588, this gloss is written in a different hand from all the rest.

8:11 *and the name of the star is called* [a]*Wormwood. And the third part of the waters was made into wormwood: and many men died of* [b]*the waters, because they were made bitter.*

    a.   I.e. bitterness.
    b.   I.e. the teachings wrongly interpreted by the heretics.*

8:11 (b) *Only in Latin 588.

8:12 [a]*And the fourth angel sounded with the trumpet, and the third part of* [b][c]*the sun was* [d][e]*smitten, and the third part of* [f][g]*the moon, and* [h]*the third part of* [i][j]*the stars, so that the third part of them* [k]*was darkened, and of* [l]*the day there shined not the third part, and of* [m]*the night in like manner.*

    a.   Sc. in the time of the hypocrites.*
    b.   The greater people.*
    c.   The superiors.*
    d.   Blinded.*
    e.   By the removal of grace.*
    f.   I.e. the lesser ones.*
    g.   I.e. clergymen.*
    h.   All the reprobates.*
    i.   I.e. simpler people.
    j.   I.e. the religious.*
    k.   I.e. lost knowledge and good works.
    l.   I.e. those who were illuminated by the greater ones.
    m.   I.e. those who were illuminated by the lesser ones.

The fourth angel. In order of narration, and in order of fact. For when the Devil had blinded some of the Jews and of the Gentiles and converted some to heresy, he eventually set himself to attack the children of the Church themselves, and seized a few of them, some greater ones as well as some lesser ones.

He has related these four damnations as past, inasmuch as they are seen everyday in the churches. But he has the three that are to follow announced beforehand, in order to inform us that there will be in the last times some still harder than the past ones; this can also be related to consolation for the present.

8:12 (a) *Only in Rusch.] (b) *In the other ink in Latin 588. Codex 24 and Rusch have "I.e. the greater teachers".] (c) *Only in Rusch. I could also have translated it as "prelates".] (d) *Not in Latin 588.] (e) *Not in Latin 588.] (f) *Codex 24 and Rusch: "The lesser preachers".] (g) *Only in Rusch.] (h) *Only in Codex 24.] (j) *Only in Rusch.

8:13 *And I looked, and heard the voice of one eagle flying through* [a]*the midst of heaven, saying* [b]*with a loud voice, Woe, woe, woe to* [c]*the inhabitants on the earth:* [d]*because of the rest of the* [e]*voices of the three Angels which were to sound with the trumpet.*

    a.   I.e. the Church, which hides divine secrets in itself.*
    b.   Because it does so in the whole world, or with a great steadfastness.
    c.   I.e. not the children of the Church.
    d.   Taking these three words.*
    e.   Trumpets.*

One eagle. By the eagle are symbolized all the preachers, who see faraway things with their minds, and fortify the Church by going round it foretelling the future; and they all are one because they aim at the same thing.

8:13 (a) *Rusch has at the end of this something that looks like an abbreviation for "or literally".] (d) *The first meaning of the Latin word translated by "because" here in the verse is "from"; so the idea is "taking "woe, woe, woe" from the rest of the voices of the three angels". This gloss is not in Codex 24 - and for a very good reason: its Vulgate lacks the part of the verse starting from "because".] (e) *Only in Latin 588.

CHAPTER 9

9:1 AND (a)the fifth angel sounded with the trumpet, and (b)I saw a star (c)to have fallen (d)from heaven (e)upon the earth, and there was given to him (f)the key of (g)the pit of bottomless depth.

    a.   Here the angel proclaims that the Devil has fallen.*
    b.   I saw the Devil falling and worrying that someone might enter the place that used to be his*.
    c.   Sc. into damnation.*
    d.   Either literally or from the Church.
    e.   Ruling the things of the earth.
    f.   I.e. power.*
    g.   I.e. the deep heretics.*

The fifth angel. In order of narration and of time. For this is the damnation of those whom the Devil sends to prepare the ways before the face of the Antichrist. But he also explains with what tinder the flame of the heretics, about which he had said little, has grown.

And there was given to him the key of the pit of bottomless depth. The bottomless depth is the dark heretics, and the pit is the deeper heretics, who drown others with perverse ideas; he is said to receive the key, i.e. power over these, because then he will not be restrained by God as he is now. Or *the key*, i.e. the princes through whom the heretics will work[1].

9:1 (a) *Latin 588: "The angel proclaims these things because the Devil has fallen". The difference in Latin is minimal (stands in a different abbreviation in one little word).] (b) *Codex 24 and Rusch add "I.e. paradise".] (c) *Codex 24 and Rusch: "By damnation".] (f) *Only in Latin 588.] (g) *Only in Latin 588.] 1 Codex 24 and Rusch: "worked" instead of "will work". They differ only in one letter in Latin.

9:2 And (a)he opened the pit of the bottomless depth: and the smoke of the pit (b)ascended, (c)as the smoke of a great furnace: and (d)the sun was darkened and the air (e)with the smoke of the pit.

    a.   Sc. he made them express the heresies that were hidden in their hearts.
    b.   I.e. caused the downfall of many, blinding their doctrine.*
    c.   I.e. similar to the doctrine of the Antichrist.
    d.   Sc. by this, some people who illuminated others and some people who were illuminated by them were smitten.
    e.   I.e. with their dark preaching.*

As the smoke. I.e. similar to the doctrine of the Antichrist, who is a smoke[1], cleansing the good and bringing the wicked back to ashes. Or *the smoke of the pit*, i.e. the vain and useless doctrine of the heretics, which prepares sorrow and distress for its followers.[2]

9:2 (b) *Codex 24 and Rusch: "Their blinding doctrine caused the downfall of many". The difference is made merely by an abbreviation sign above one letter.] (e) *Only in Latin 588.] 1 Codex 24 and Rusch: "who is a furnace".] 2 The part starting from "Or *the smoke of the pit*" is only in Latin 588.

9:3 And from the smoke of the pit there (a)issued forth (b)locusts into (c)the earth, and power was given to them, as the scorpions of the earth have power.

    a.   Throughout all the world.
    b.   I.e. disciples of the heretics and of the Antichrist.*
    c.   I.e. earthly people.*

There issued forth locusts. I.e. their disciples, who are compared to locusts because they neither fly on high[1] through knowledge nor walk firmly through good work, but jump through pride and fall back into the worse, and because they gnaw good things to pieces.

As the scorpions of the earth have power. The scorpion, charming in appearance, stings furtively with its tail. Or[2] he compares them to the scorpion because as the scorpion deceives[3] with its tail, so do the heretics deceive[4] with temporal things, which ought to be behind like the tail, which is the posterior part in an animal. Or they are compared to the scorpion because, when a scorpion stings, you do not feel it, but then the venom spreads: in the same way, those who are deceived by the heretics do not feel it, but they are eventually destroyed.

9:3 (b) *Not in Latin 588.] (c) *Only in Latin 588.] 1 Codex 24 and Rusch add "or into contemplation".] 2 The whole preceding part is not in Latin 588.] 3 and 4 Latin 588 has "strikes" and "strike" instead of "deceives" and "deceive".

9:4 And ^(a)***it was commanded them that they should not*** ^(b)***hurt*** ^(c)***the grass of the earth nor*** ^(d)***any green thing, nor any*** ^(e)***tree:*** ^(f)***but only men that*** ^(g)***have not*** ^(h)***the sign of God*** ⁽ⁱ⁾***in their foreheads.***

By the grass are symbolized those who need the watering of preaching, because as grass dries when it lacks rain, so do they dry up if they are not watered by the rain of heavenly teaching.[1]

a. Because God restrains their trickeries even if they do not know* it.
b. With death of the soul.*
c. I.e. those who are yet untrained in faith and easy to deceive.
d. Even if some of them* who are already advanced.**
e. Those who are already bearing fruit.
f. I.e. absolutely none but those who want to be mere and beast-like men.*
g. Sc. in truth.
h. In their minds.*
i. I.e. who do not dare to confess it openly.

By any green thing we understand those who make use of worldly things lawfully and bloom with the greenness of faith to a certain extent or a little.[2]

And by the tree are symbolized those who have taken root in the foundation of faith and already bear fruit.[3]

9:4 (a) *Codex 24 and Rusch: "realize".] (b) *Only in Latin 588.] (d) *The Latin corresponding to "nor any green thing" would translate literally to "nor every green thing", but with the same meaning as what we would say in English "nor any" ("they should not touch every green thing" = "every green thing should be untouched by them" = "they should not touch any green thing"); the glossator had the literal meaning in mind. **Codex 24 and Rusch have this in two glosses: "Even if some of them" above "any", and "Those who are already advanced" above "green thing".] (f) *Codex 24 and Rusch have only "Absolutely none".] (h) *Not in Latin 588.] 1 Only in Latin 588.] 2 Only in Latin 588.] 3 Only in Latin 588.

9:5 And it was given* unto them ^(a)***that they should not kill them: but that they should be tormented***** ^(b)***five months:*** ^(c)***and their torments as the torments of a scorpion*** ^(d)***when he strikes a man.***

That they should not kill them, but that they should be tormented. When the heretics cannot do it through deceits, they want to destroy by force; against this there is a commandment of God[1].

a. Sc. that they should kill their bodies but not their souls.*
b. I.e. in their bodies, which live with* five senses.
c. As if he were saying: Although the power to torture was given to them, they do not torment them openly, but accuse them in front of the princes of the world, and in the manner of scorpions*.
d. Furtively and deceitfully.*

Five months. Another version says six months because of the six ages through which this life is led and into which it is divided[2].

9:5 In the verse: *Codex 24 and Rusch have "said" instead of "given", Rusch mentioning the "given" variant in a gloss. **Codex 24 and Rusch have "that they should torment them".] (a) *Only in Latin 588.] (b) *Codex 24 and Rusch: "which need". The words have similar spellings.] (c) *"And in the manner of scorpions" only in Latin 588.] (d) *Only in Latin 588.] 1 Codex 24 and Rusch: "... against them there is a commandment of God that they should kill the bodies but not deceive the souls".] 2 Codex 24 and Rusch have only ".... into which this life is divided", without the "led" part.

9:6 ^(a)***And in those days*** ^(b)***men shall seek for death, and*** ^(c)***shall not find it: and they shall*** ^(d)***desire to die, and*** ^{(e)(f)}***death shall flee from them.***

a. And by this is the severity of the tribulation made known.*
b. Sc. fearing the fall.
c. Sc. in order that they be made worthier of credit.
d. And they shall not seek for it in just any manner, but they shall desire, i.e. wish for it.*
e. Because the care they have for their flock ties them to their labor.
f. This is said concerning superiors and inferiors.*

9:6 (a) *Only in Rusch.] (d) *Not in Codex 24.] (f) *Not in Latin 588. Codex 24 has "And this is not said concerning superiors and inferiors", which I surmise to be a mistake.

9:7 And ^(a)***the similitudes of*** ^(b)***the locusts,*** ^(c)***like to horses prepared unto battle: and*** ^(d)***upon their heads*** ^{(e)(f)}***as it were crowns*** ^(g)***like to gold: and their faces*** ^(h)***as the faces of men.***

And the similitudes of the locusts. After showing how they did harm both through deceits and through secret attack, and that they are restrained in both by God's control, he now shows what they are like

a. I.e. the symbolical locusts.
b. I.e. the heretics.*
c. Sc. were.
d. I.e. in their minds, where they are proud both in themselves and in front of others, or upon the teachers.
e. I.e. the victories they won over those they threw down, sc. by means of an untrue wisdom.
f. Because they are not true crowns.*
g. Not of true gold, i.e. wisdom.*
h. Because they make themselves look like they are men and pious while inside they are wild and wolves*.

and through whom they can operate[1].

Like to horses. Because they are fierce to attack and quick to run to and fro, and they do not look in advance whom they rush at, whether at enemies or at citizens.

9:7 (b) *Only in Rusch.] (f) *Not in Latin 588.] (g) *Not in Latin 588.] (h) *"And wolves" only in Latin 588.] 1 Codex 24 and Rusch: "what those through whom they can operate are like".

9:8 And they had (a)hair (b)as the hair of women: and their (c)teeth were (d)as of lions.

a. I.e. manners.
b. Sc. women's manners, which are without firmness and easily bent into every vice.
c. I.e. themselves tearing others to pieces.
d. Tearing to pieces and stinking.

Hair. Dissolute and effeminate manners that stick to them, and hang down from them to the deception of others. Or the hair is the lesser people whom they deceive when they stick to them.

9:9 And they had (a)habbergions as habbergions of iron, and (b)the voice of their wings as the voice of the chariots of many horses running into battle.

a. I.e. stubborn hearts.*
b. I.e. the uproar of opinions they make once they rage in their reasoning.*

Habbergions. I.e. stubborn hearts that the arrow of truth does not penetrate. Or opinions defended with deceptions, which the truth shatters.

As the voice of the chariots. Different chariots, by different ways[1], and by different horses, are snatched to the same war: in the same way, these, although with different heresies, attack the Church unanimously.

9:9 (a) *Only in Latin 588.] (b) *Codex 24 and Rusch: "I.e. the uproar of opinions they make once they fail".] 1 Latin 588 has "different in vices" instead of "by different ways". It looks like a mistake. The spelling is somewhat similar.

9:10 And they had (a)tails like to scorpions, and (b)stings were in their tails: and (c)their power was to hurt (d)men (e)five months.

a. Earthly princes or deceitful ideas.*
b. I.e. sin, because they make people sin.
c. As if he were saying: They are not to be feared because they can do nothing except in the body.*
d. Sc. wicked.
e. With regards to the five senses of the body.*

And they had tails like to scorpions. Once their reasoning or their uproar is of no avail, they seek the help of the princes, who are called tails because they frighten and flatter in order to bind people. Or the tails are deceitful ideas, with which they flatter people face to face and sting secretly.[1]

9:10 (a) *Only in Latin 588.] (c) *Codex 24 and Rusch: "But you good ones, do not fear, because" — after "because" understand the following part of the verse and its explanations.] (e) *Codex 24 and Rusch: "With regards to the five senses only".] 1 Not in Latin 588.

9:11 And they had over them a king, (a)the angel of the bottomless depth, whose name in Hebrew is Abaddon, and in Greek Apollyon: in Latin having the name (b)Exterminans.

    a.   I.e. the Devil ruling earthly matters.
    b.   I.e. separating from the country of life.*

And they had. After showing how they themselves are, he shows thanks to whom they are able to do this.

Whose name. As if he were saying: Because of this, beware, Jews, Greeks and Latins, because the law of Christ, i.e. the Gospel, has been written and found in one of these three languages.[1]

9:11 (b) *Exterminans* can translate to "expelling", "exiling", "banising", "killing", "abolishing" or "destroying". The Greek Ἀπολλύων (Apollyon) means "killing" or "destroying" and does not, as far as I can tell, share the "expelling" or "banishing", etc., meaning of the Latin. According to what I have found, the Hebrew Abaddon means "destruction".] 1 Codex 24 and Rusch: "As if he were saying: Because of this, beware, Hebrews, Greeks and Latins — so all the Church — because the Gospel of Christ has been written and received in one of these three languages". But in fact, St. John cannot have meant exactly that, since the original is in Greek, and the part "in Latin having the name Exterminans" was added afterwards by the Latin translator.

9:12 (a)One woe is gone, and behold two woes come yet (b)after these.

    a.   As if he were saying: We have talked about one severe persecution, and we are to talk about two.*
    b.   Or "After these, the sixth angel..."

9:12 (a) *Only in Latin 588.

9:13 And the (a)sixth angel sounded with the trumpet: and I heard one voice from the four horns of the golden altar, (b)which is before the eyes of God,

    a.   In order of narration and in order of time, for here is the damnation of the wicked that will take place in the time of the Antichrist.*
    b.   I.e. upon which whatever is offered is accepted by God.

From the four horns. By "four" are symbolized the things that are preached about Christ, which are the Nativity, the Passion, the Resurrection, and the Ascension; and everything revolves around these[1].

The altar means Christ; the horns of the altar the preachers supporting Christ and ready to die for him, as blood used to be put on the horns of the altar. Or the altar is the Church sacrificing itself, in which are the horns, i.e. the defenders of the others, who all aim at the same thing. Or the four horns are the four Gospels, which teach us to detect the deceits of the Antichrist.

9:13 (a) *In Codex 24 and Rusch, this gloss is found as a marginal gloss to "one woe is gone" in the previous verse.] 1 Codex 24 and Rusch: "and the other things revolve around these".

9:14 (a)saying to the sixth angel which had the trumpet, (b)Loose (c)the four angels which are bound in the great river Euphrates.

    a.   Because heralds of the past forewarn those who shall still be there in the time of the Antichrist of what they are to do.*
    b.   I.e. proclaim that they have been loosed* so that the elect should beware.
    c.   The four things said above, namely the Nativity, the Passion, the Resurrection and the Ascension.*

"Euphrates" means "fertility"; it is the river that surrounds Babylon, i.e. "confusion": these are the worldly princes through which the Devil worked secretly when he was in them. He orders them to be excommunicated so that the Devil, who was in them as if bound, may work through them more openly when they, i.e. the princes who mislead men by force, are handed over to him.[1]

9:14 (a) *The words "still" and "of what they are to do" only in Latin 588.] (b) *Codex 24: "I.e. preach against those that have been loosed". The same Latin word can translate to "proclaim" and "preach".] (c) *Not in Latin 588. Could this actually have been meant as a continuation to the previous gloss, specifying what they are to preach against them? In which case Rusch would have ended up with the same version of (b) as Latin 588, but yet also with (c) although it was meant to belong with Codex 24's version of (b) and no longer makes sense with that of Latin 588.] 1 Codex 24 and Rusch have it a little shorter: "Because the Euphrates is the river that surrounds Babylon, that is, it is the worldly princes through which the Devil worked secretly when he was in them. He orders them to be excommunicated so that he who was in them as if bound may work through them more openly when they are handed over to him.

9:15 **[a]And the four angels were loosed, who were prepared [b]for an hour, [c]and a day and a month and a year: that they might kill [d]the third part of men.**

    a.   Once those people were thus damned.
    b.   I.e. continuously.*
    c.   I.e. for a long time.
    d.   I.e. all the reprobates.*

The Devil being loosed, many rush headlong, who endeavor to blind others.[1]

The four angels. For the four parts of the world. Or because they attack the four things preached about Christ. Or the four angels are the unclean spirits reigning in the four parts of the world who had been restrained during Christ's passion.

For an hour, and a day, etc. By "an hour", understand half a year, by "a day", one year, by "a month", another year, and by "a year", a third one, for the persecution of the Antichrist will last for three years and a half.

9:15 (b) *We can assume that *in horam*, Latin for "for an hour", could also be interpreted as "each hour", similarly to *in diem* which can mean either "for a day" or "each day".] (d) *Codex 24: "The reprobates of the earth".] 1 This gloss is found twice in Latin 588, here and to the next verse. Codex 24 and Rusch have it only once; in Codex 24 it is placed close to the next verse, but in Rusch it is introduced by a tag to "were loosed that they might kill".

9:16 **[a]And the number of the army of horsemen was twenty thousand times ten thousand. And [b]I heard the number of them.**

    a.   The Devil being loosed, many rush headlong, who endeavor to blind others.*
    b.   I am right when I put them under a determined number, because I heard, i.e. I understood, that they were more numerous than the good.

Ten thousand are the saints fortified, i.e.[1] perfected, by the ten commandments of the law; against these is put a multiple number of wicked because the wicked are more numerous than the good.

9:16 (a) *See note 1 to the previous verse.] 1 "Fortified, i.e." only in Latin 588.

9:17 And so I saw the horses in the vision: and [a]they that sat upon them, had [b]habbergions [c]of fire and of [d]hyacinth and [e]brimstone, and [f]the heads of the horses were as it were [g]the heads of lions: and [h]from their mouths proceeded [i][j]fire, and [k]smoke, and [l]brimstone.

    a.   I.e. devils or men based upon the Devil.*
    b.   I.e. ideas.*
    c.   Because of the fire of anger and lust.
    d.   Hyacinth is a stone of a smoky and dark color; so is the Devil.*
    e.   I.e. stinking.*
    f.   I.e. the greater ones among the ministers of the Devil.
    g.   Because they tear to pieces and stink.
    h.   I.e. from their openly bad preaching proceeded...
    i.   Sc. eternal punishment.
    j.   I.e. cupidity.
    k.   I.e. pride.
    l.   I.e. the stench of bad works.*

So I saw. I.e. as I had understood that they were riding to the destruction of others, so did I understand that they were doing this through the Devil, whom they were carrying like horses. Or the horses are devils upon whom the wicked are based.

Had habbergions of fire. I.e. they defended them with ideas from which ensues an eternal punishment in which there is fire, smoke and stench. Or they *had habbergions of fire*, i.e. an eternal punishment which never lets go those it receives.

Of hyacinth because they are blind and in darkness.

Of brimstone because of the stench of vices and bad works.

And the heads of the horses were as it were the heads of lions. Above, in the plague of the locusts, he saw faces of men, because the heretics display a bit of humanity; here he saw faces of lions, because what the ministers of the Antichrist teach with words and signs[1], they even force people to confess it with tortures.

9:17 (a) *Codex 24 has two glosses here, one saying "devils" and another saying "many people based upon them". Rusch has "Devils or men based upon them".] (b) *Only in Latin 588.] (d) *Codex 24 and Rusch have only "A stone of a smoky color".] (e) *Only in Latin 588.] (i), (j), (k), (l) *Codex 24 and Rusch have all these interlinears in the form of one marginal gloss, which I would not even mention if the beginning of it did not differ slightly in substance: "*Proceeded fire.* The cause of eternal punishment, or *fire* i.e. cupidity, etc." (the tag *proceeded fire* being only in Rusch).] 1 Codex 24: "tongues" instead of "signs".

9:18 And by these three plagues was slain the third part of men, (a)of the fire and of the smoke and of the brimstone, which proceeded from their mouth.

    a.   Namely.*

9:18 (a) *Only in Latin 588.

9:19 (a)For the power of the horses is (b)in their mouth, and (c)in their tails. (d)For their tails be (e)like to serpents, having (f)heads: and in these they hurt.

    a.   Truly from their mouth, because...
    b.   I.e. in their bad preaching.
    c.   I.e. in secret deceptions if they cannot do as they want* openly.
    d.   They truly have power in their tails.
    e.   Because they* flatter with their faces and furtively inject venom.
    f.   I.e. other greater teachers* who bite.

9:19 (c) *Codex 24 and Rusch: "if they cannot do it".] (e) *Codex 24 and Rusch: "who" instead of "because they". The difference in Latin is very small (one more letter in a word to give "because they" or a different abbreviation).] (f) *Codex 24 and Rusch: "greater people".

9:20 (a)And (b)the rest of men which were not slain with these plagues, (c)neither have done penance from the works of their hands, not to adore devils and (d)idols of gold and silver and brass and stone and wood, which neither can see, nor hear, nor walk,

    a.   The third part is dead, i.e. all the reprobates from the Church; and similarly all the Jews or pagans who were never baptized or separated from the Church.*
    b.   Shall perish.*
    c.   Who perished because they did not do penance in such a way as not to adore devils etc.*
    d.   Which is more shameful.*

9:20 (b) *Not in Latin 588.] (c) *Codex 24 and Rusch: "Because they perish because they did not do penance" above "neither have done penance" and "They did not do penance in such a way as not to adore" above "not to adore".] (d) *In the other ink in Codex 24.

9:21 and have not done penance from their murders, nor from their sorceries, nor from their fornication, nor from their thefts.

CHAPTER 10

10:1 [(a)]*AND I saw* [(b)]*another angel,* [(c)]*strong,* [(d)][(e)]*descending* [(f)]*from heaven,* [(g)]*clothed with a cloud, and* [(h)]*a rainbow on his head, and his face was* [(i)]*as the sun, and* [(j)]*his feet as* [(k)]*a pillar of fire.*

a. Against those bad ones.*
b. Contrary to them.
c. I.e. Christ, strong in works, because, as a strong soldier, he has overcome the strong Devil.*
d. I.e. humbling himself.
e. Because he made himself capable of being known on earth.*
f. I.e. from the knowledge of angels, or from the bosom of the Father to the bosom of the Virgin.*
g. I.e. hidden in a cloud of flesh which is for us a refreshment like a cloud.*
h. God was in Christ, reconciling the world with himself. Or God's mercy which was in Christ.*
i. I.e. equal to the Father.*
j. I.e. the apostles, his carriers firm in faith and supporting others.*
k. And they thought this because they were kindled by the Holy Spirit and illuminating others with preaching.*

Since in the time of the Antichrist there will be so great a destruction, preaching will be forbidden to those who are there in his time, even if they wish to preach since they got the duty of preaching from their predecessors. But those predecessors preached because they were sent by God and appointed to preaching because then[1] it was the time to preach and he himself had come for this. But now, see the destruction of the time of the Antichrist, which is contrary to the construction that Christ did, and because of this, consider the consolation[2]. [3]

Or otherwise[4]: After describing the cruelty of the Antichrist, he mentions the consolation they will have then in the time of the Antichrist, namely that the faithful will consider in their hearts that such things, i.e. tribulations etc.[5], come from Christ, which will be for them a consolation.[6]

And a rainbow on his head. He who has true knowledge about God considers him as God.[7]

A rainbow. In a rainbow there are two colors: green and red. By the green we understand baptism; by the red the gifts of the Holy Spirit given by fire; or the past flood and the future judgment through fire.[8]

His face. I.e. those in whom the image of God truly shines, as in contemplative people, because when they have knowledge about him, they consider those who imitate him to be God, like the psalmist: "I have said: You are gods" (Ps. 81:6).[9]

10:1 (a) *Only in Latin 588.] (c) *Codex 24 and Rusch have only "Because, as a strong soldier, he has overcome the strong Devil."] (d) and (e) *In Codex 24 and Rusch, these two glosses are fused into one marginal gloss reading "That is, humbling himself by the assumption of the flesh, or because he made himself capable of being known".] (f) *The part starting from "or from the bossom" is only in Latin 588.] (g) *Codex 24: "Hidden in the flesh which is for us a refreshing against vices"; Rusch: same as Codex 24, but with "you" instead of "us".] (h) *"Or God's mercy which was in Christ" only in Latin 588.] (i) *Only in Latin 588.] (j) *Codex 24: "I.e. carriers firm in faith and carrying others". This gloss is not here in Rusch, but see the last gloss to the next verse.] (k) *Codex 24 and Rusch: "Because they were kindled by the Holy Spirit and illuminating others"] 1 Codex 24 and Rusch: "... But those predecessors preached because they were appointed to it by Christ, and Christ appointed them to it because then..."] 2 Codex 24 and Rusch: "... consider that it is for a good reason that preaching is removed".] 3 In Codex 24, this gloss is placed somewhere next to verse 6; in Rusch it begins with a tag to "the mystery of God shall be consummate" in verse 7.] 4 In Latin 588, "or otherwise" is written above the gloss in the other ink.] 5 "I.e. tribulations etc." only in Latin 588.] 6 In Codex 24 and Rusch, this gloss follows the previous one in the places I said in note 3.] 7 Not in Latin 588, but it is very similar to some of the words of the gloss on "his face", so it may be merely that the part in question accidentally got "detached", somewhat modified and repeated as a separate gloss. The Latin is a little ambiguous and could also possibly mean "He considers him who has true knowledge about God as God". It is not the interpretation that comes most naturally to mind, but considering the gloss on "his face" and the Psalm verse quoted there, it does not seem altogether impossible.] 8 Only in Latin 588.] 9 Codex 24 has only the part "I.e. those in whom the image of God truly shines, as in contemplative people". Rusch has "I.e. those in whom the image of God truly shines, as in contemplative people. Or preaching." preceded by a tag to "as a pillar of fire", but it definitely seems better to belong with "his face".

10:2 And he had in his hand [(a)]*a little book opened: and he put* [(b)]*his right foot upon* [(c)]*the sea, and* [(d)]*his left* [(e)]*upon the land.*

a. The works fulfilled by him or all the Scriptures.*
b. I.e. the firmer preachers, sc. the apostles*.
c. I.e. the more flowing* in sins, like the Jews and pagans**.
d. I.e. the less firm ones, like Gregory and Augustine, who are the lesser of the apostles.*
e. I.e. upon those who supported them in any way even if they did not believe, or who were ready to bear fruit*.

A little book. I.e. all the Scriptures fulfilled in part[1] by his work, in part by preaching, in part by fulfilling the things that had been said about him, and finally by revealing his[2] meaning to his people.

His right foot upon the sea, and his left upon the land. That is, he put the greater and firmer preachers upon the greater sinners, and the lesser preachers upon the lesser sinners.[3]

The feet are firm carriers, i.e. apostles, firm in faith and supporting others.[4]

10:2 (a) *Only in Latin 588.] (b) *"Sc. the apostles" only in Latin 588.] (c) *I.e. dissolute. **"Like the Jews and pagans" only in Latin 588.] (d) *Codex 24 and Rusch have "I.e. the less firm ones".] (e) *"Or who were ready to bear fruit" only in Latin 588.] 1 This first "in part" is only in Latin 588.] 2 No "his" in Codex 24 and Rusch, just "the meaning".] 3 Not in Latin 588.] 4 Rusch: "*His right foot.* That is, carriers firm in faith and supporting others". This gloss is not here in Codex 24, but see interlinear (j) of the previous verse.

10:3 ^(a)*And he cried with a* ^(b)*loud voice,* ^(c)*as when a lion roars.* ^(d)*And when he had cried,* ^{(e)(f)}*the seven thunders spoke* ^(g)*their voices.*

    a.   Through them, i.e. the apostles and their inferiors who preached.*
    b.   Treating great subjects, or he was about to speak about great things*.
    c.   As dreadfully.*
    d.   I.e. because these people, i.e. the apostles sent by him, preached, because they did everything by the commandment of his mouth.*
    e.   I.e. all the faithful successors, inflicting terror and threats.*
    f.   I.e. they will consider that they must fulfill all this just as it was foretold.*
    g.   Not so dreadful, but suitable for their time.*

The voice of the lion shows his strength in his resurrection, and when he roars he produces fervor, "If you do not do it you shall die".[1]

When the lion has made a furrow around the forest with his tail and roars, none of the wild beasts dares go out. In the same way, Christ, who is called a lion, shutting up, i.e. keeping, his people in faith, roars, i.e. threatens, so that no one should go out, i.e. go away from him.[2]

10:3 (a) *Only in Latin 588.] (b) *The second part, "or he was etc." only in Latin 588. Remember that a "loud voice" in Latin is literally a "great voice".] (c) *Not in Latin 588.] (d) *Codex 24 and Rusch have only "And because these people sent by him preached".] (e) *Only in Latin 588.] (f) *Only in Latin 588.] (g) *Codex 24 has only "Suitable for their time"; Rusch has "Suitable for their time, or which..." to "their voices" in the next verse.] 1 Codex 24 and Rusch: "The voice of the lion shows his strength and produces terror".] 2 All the "i.e.'s" and explanations that follow them as well as "who is called a lion" are only in Latin 588.

10:4 ^{(a)(b)}*And when* ^(c)*the seven thunders had spoken their voices,* ^(d)*I was about to write:* ^(e)*and* ^(f)*I heard a voice from heaven* ^(g)*saying to me:* ^(h)*Sign the things which the seven thunders have spoken: and* ⁽ⁱ⁾*write them not.*

    a.   I.e. and because.
    b.   Here he is playing the role of those who, in the time of the Antichrist, will wish to preach in imitation of those who preceded them, and this is why he says "I was about to write".
    c.   All the successors inflicting terror.*
    d.   I.e. I was about to preach, but it was not then the time.*
    e.   Sc. for "because".*
    f.   I.e. I understood that they will then understand.*
    g.   I.e. explaining, so that I should not cast pearls before swine (ref. Matt. 7:6), because preaching will then be useless.*
    h.   I.e. seal them so that they be visible to friends and hidden from enemies.
    i.   I.e. do not reveal them to the unfaithful among whom they have no place.

heard etc. Those who understand divine inspiration or the angelic admonition will understand the one given through me.[1]

Sign the things which the seven thunders have spoken. A divine inspiration or angelic admonition.[2]

10:4 (c) *Not in Latin 588, but see interlinear (e) of the previous verse.] (d) *Only in Latin 588.] (e) *Only in Latin 588. Codex 24 has, above "I was about to write", a little gloss saying "or "the things which"", which I cannot make sense of, but it visually resembles (e), with regards to spelling, so it may be it that got modified.] (f) *Not in Latin 588.] (g) *Only in Latin 588.] 1 Only in Latin 588, but the next gloss may be nothing else but the same one shortened and placed elsewhere.] 2 Not in Latin 588 (at any rate not as a separate gloss). The tag referring it to "sign the things etc." is from Rusch; in Codex 24, there is no tag, but its placement would not make it impossible for it to refer to "a voice", though I cannot say for sure.

10:5 And the angel which I saw ^(a)*standing upon the sea and upon the land,* ^(b)*lifted up* ^(c)*his hand to heaven,*

    a.   I.e. ready to help.*
    b.   I.e. exalted, or he rose again*.
    c.   I.e. his humanity, which he had worked as if by his hand, i.e. by his power*.

As there will be so great a desolation in the Church because even preaching will be taken away, so that the faithful may not despair, they receive the consolation that it is not to the detriment of their salvation that preaching is removed.[1]

10:5 (a) *Only in Latin 588.] (b) *"Or he rose again" only in Latin 588.] (c) *"As if by his hand, i.e. by his power" only in Latin 588.] 1 Not in Latin 588.

10:6 *(a)and he swore by him that lives (b)forever (c)and ever, (d)that created heaven and those things which are in it: and the earth, and those things which are in it: and the sea, and those things which are in it: that there shall be (e)(f)time no more.*

a. And by this he firmly declared that he was God, for if Christ rose again, we too shall.
b. In this age.*
c. And in the future one.*
d. He who created all things from nothing was able to recreate his people for the better.
e. I.e. corruption.*
f. Mutability, because then it will be the end of all temporal things.*

And those things which are in it. He refutes the heresy of some people[1] who say that some things were not created by God but by the Devil, like the toad etc.

There shall be time no more. Because the good shall be made immortal and impassible, but on the other hand the time, i.e. the corruption, of the wicked shall be forever; as the psalmist says, "Their time shall be forever" (Ps. 80:16).[2]

There shall be time no more. That is, no changeableness, but eternal stability, the immortality of souls.[3]

Those last people, considering this, will endure cheerfully.

10:6 (b) *Only in Latin 588.] (c) *Only in Latin 588. The Latin *in saecula saeculorum*, translated by "forever and ever", literally means "for the ages of the ages" or "for the centuries of the centuries". So interlinear (b) is above *saecula*, "ages/centuries", and is saying, "in this one", and (c) is above *saeculorum*, "of the ages/centuries". Besides, the word *saeculum*, "age", "century", can also mean "world".] (e) *Only in Latin 588.] (f) *Only in Latin 588.] 1 Codex 24: "some wicked".] 2 Codex 24 and Rusch have only "Because they shall be made immortal and impassible, while on the other hand the time of the wicked shall be forever".] 3 Not in Latin 588.

10:7 *but (a)in the days of the voice of the seventh angel, (b)when he shall begin to sound the trumpet, the mystery of God shall be consummate, (c)as he has evangelized by his servants the prophets.*

a. I.e. in the time of the Antichrist.*
b. I.e. when he proclaims that it shall not last long.
c. Because the first intention of the prophets was concerning the coming of the Lord and the consummation of the world.

The mystery. I.e. the reward of the saints, which is a secret because *eye has not seen, nor ear heard, etc.* (Corint. 2:9).

10:7 (a) *Only in Latin 588.

10:8 *And I heard (a)a voice from heaven (b)again speaking with me, and (c)saying: (d)Go, and take (e)the book that is opened, of the hand of (f)the angel (g)standing upon the sea and upon the land.*

a. I.e. a divine admonition.*
b. I.e. again speaking about the same things.
c. I.e. giving explanations.
d. Deserve the grace of God.
e. I.e. the Scripture fulfilled by God and made known to the faithful, and understand through it.*
f. I.e. Christ.*
g. Ready to help all those who come to him.

[1]After the destruction that will take place in the time of the Antichrist has been shown, preaching[2] then taken away, and consolation given to the faithful for this, he is told to preach[3] the things he has seen, as if he were told openly, "Behold I have revealed you everything; now go and preach, and do not shun these things because they are harsh, and do not be frightened by any tribulation, because you shall not suffer as great hardships as those who persist in the time of the Antichrist will suffer". For the consolation of the faithful and[4] of the present Church, this is added here, where a greater tribulation is announced.

John is admonished to understand that which he knew well, so that the others who are to preach be informed by this admonition.

10:8 (a) *In the other ink in Codex 24.] (e) *In Codex 24 and Rusch, this gloss was split; here they have only "I.e. understand through it", and the rest found itself, slightly modified, as a marginal gloss to "to the angel" in the next verse.] (f) *Only in Latin 588.] 1 In Codex 24 and Rusch, this gloss starts with "As if he were saying".] 2 Codex 24 and Rusch: "even preaching".] 3 Codex 24 and Rusch add "in the meantime".] "Of the faithful and" only in Latin 588.

10:9 *And (a)I went to the angel, (b)saying unto him, that he should give me (c)the book. (d)And he said to me, Take the book, and (e)devour it: and it shall make (f)your belly to be bitter, (g)but (h)in your mouth it shall be sweet as it were honey.*

To the angel. I.e. to the Scripture fulfilled by God and made known to the faithful.[1]

To be bitter. Because it is harsh for human nature, which is frail and

a. As an obedient man, and I extended, i.e. exalted*, my mind.
b. With work and reason*.
c. I.e. divine knowledge of the Scriptures.*
d. Because if God sees someone ready, he spontaneously offers him what is necessary.
e. I.e. handle it by inquiring into it and by working.
f. I.e. your humanity.*
g. But it shall please you when in reflecting and preaching, in eternal life, which is sweet*.
h. I.e. in your heart.*

unstable, to be filled with divinity.[2]

10:9 (a) *"I.e. exalted" only in Latin 588.] (b) *Codex 24 and Rusch have "prayer" instead of "reason". The two Latin words differ only in one letter.] (c) *Only in Latin 588.] (f) *Only in Latin 588.] (g) *"In eternal life, which is sweet" only in Latin 588.] (h) *Only in Latin 588.] 1 See interlinear (e) of the previous verse and the note to it.] 2 Codex 24 and Rusch: "Because it is harsh for human nature, which is weak and frail, to fulfill it". In Rusch, it starts with a tag to "standing upon the sea" in the previous verse.

10:10 And I took ^(a)the book of the hand of ^(b)the angel, and ^(c)devoured it: and it was in my mouth as it were honey, sweet. And ^(d)when I had devoured it, my belly was made bitter,

a. I.e. the work of Christ, by taking it over.
b. I.e. Christ.*
c. Sc. by work and preaching.*
d. I.e. when I received it.*

10:10 (b) *Only in Latin 588.] (c) *Only in Latin 588.] (d) *In Codex 24 and Rusch, this gloss is not here, but seems to have been merged with gloss (a) of the next verse. See the note there.

10:11 ^(a)and he said to me, ^(b)You must ^(c)again prophecy to nations, and peoples, and tongues, and many kings.

a. Although I understood that those things were bitter, he said to me, i.e. admonished me, not to let them go even in front of death.*
b. Because for now* you shall go out of prison.
c. After the apostles, judgment is at hand.*

10:11 (a) *In Codex 24 and Rusch, it begins with: "When I received it, although..." See the note on (d) of the previous verse, if you do not already come from there.] (b) *"For now" only in Latin 588.] (c) *Only in Latin 588.

CHAPTER 11

11:1 AND there was given me [(a)]**a reed like unto** [(b)]**a rod: and** [(c)]**it was said to me,** [(d)]**Arise, and** [(e)]**measure the temple of God, and the altar,** [(f)]**and them that adore in it.**

    a.   I.e. the Scripture written with a reed.
    b.   I.e. a scepter, because it has appointed kings.
    c.   I.e. admonishing.*
    d.   I.e. erect it in order to preach.
    e.   I.e. preach according to each person's capacity in such a way as to establish the Church, and the altar, i.e. Christ, in it.
    f.   And to establish in what manner they are to adore in it.

There was given me a reed. After charging him with the task of preaching, he gives him the Scriptures as an aid by which to carry it out.

If we take "temple" literally, we should indeed pray in it. But if it means also bishops and preachers, we should not pray in them, but let us pray to God through them.[1]

11:1 (c) *Instead of "and it was said to me", Latin 588's Vulgate has "saying".] 1 Only in Latin 588.

11:2 But [(a)(b)]**the court which is without the temple,** [(c)]**cast forth, and** [(d)]**measure not that: because** [(e)]**it is given** [(f)]**to the Gentiles, and** [(g)(h)]**they shall thread underfoot the holy city** [(i)]**two and forty months:**

    a.   I.e. the false Christians who pretend they are a church, but do not want to obey the commandments, and therefore are without.*
    b.   Christ's* narthex Christ.**
    c.   I.e. show that they are without by excommunicating them.
    d.   I.e. altogether take preaching away from them.
    e.   The court.*
    f.   I.e. they have become similar to the Gentiles.
    g.   I.e. they will persecute the Church, which is assembled to live truly* and fortified** with virtues; for as a city is fortified with a wall, so does the Church have a wall, i.e. Christ, who is its strength***.
    h.   And the Gentiles themselves.*
    i.   I.e. three years and a half during which the Antichrist reigns.

Two and forty months. As if he were saying: Know that all the persecutions there are in the present and that were in the past proceed, i.e. come[1], from the Antichrist just like those there will be in his own time.[2]

11:2 (a) *Codex 24 and Rusch: "The false Christians who pretend they are a church but deny it in their deeds".] (b) *Reading somewhat uncertain. **Only in Latin 588.] (e) *Only in Latin 588.] (g) *Codex 24 and Rusch: "rightly". **Rusch: "imbued". ***"For as a city etc." only in Latin 588.] (h) *Not in Latin 588.] 1 "I.e. come" only in Latin 588.] 2 In Latin 588, the sign that indicates what this gloss refers to, besides being found here above "two and forty months", is repeated above "two hundred sixty days" in the next verse.

11:3 and I will give to [(a)]**my two witnesses,** [(b)]**and they shall prophesy a thousand two hundred sixty days,** [(c)]**clothed with sackcloth.**

    a.   It concerns Elijah and Enoch, by whom the others* are understood.
    b.   I.e. they shall preach three years and a half as Christ himself did.
    c.   Preaching penance and showing it by the example of the sack*.

As if he were saying: When tribulation is lesser, you ought not to desist, because in his time, when it is more severe, I will make them preach, and these two shall then be killed by him. You indeed no one kills for preaching[1].

A thousand two hundred sixty days. Note that these days do not completely make three years and a half, just as Christ too did not complete the half year of his preaching.[2]

11:3 (a) *Codex 24 and Rusch: "the other preachers".] (c) *Codex 24 and Rusch: "... showing it by example".] 1 The part from "and these two" only in Latin 588.] 2 Not in Latin 588.

11:4 (a)*These are the two* (b)*olive-trees and the two* (c)*candlesticks that* (d)*stand* (e)*in the sight of the Lord of the earth.*

a.   These indeed...*
b.   Anointed by the Holy Spirit.
c.   Giving light to others and illuminating themselves.*
d.   I.e. help with their advice.*
e.   I.e. paying attention to* what pleases the Lord, in his good pleasure**.

Olive-trees. By the olive-tree the body is anointed and refreshed; so are these refreshed as they are anointed, i.e. illuminated, by the Holy Spirit.[1]

11:4 (a) *Codex 24 and Rusch: "And you ought to preach following their example; these indeed...".] (c) *Codex 24 and Rusch have only "Giving light to others", and in another place: above "that stand".] (d) *Only in Latin 588.] (e) *Rusch: "kindling". The words resemble each other. **"In his good pleasure" only in Latin 588.] 1 Only in Latin 588.

11:5 And if any man will (a)*hurt them,* (b)*fire shall come forth out of their mouths, and* (c)*shall devour their enemies, and if any man will* (d)*hurt them: so must he* (e)*be slain.*

a.   I.e. restrain them from pursuing their goal.
b.   I.e. a spiritual sentence by which they shall be excommunicated*.
c.   I.e. that fire shall damn them.
d.   Restrain them from pursuing their goal, or with physical death.*
e.   By the spiritual sentence, i.e. the fire*.

Let them be killed only in the body, but their enemies be killed in the soul. *It were better for him that a millstone should be hanged about his neck* (Matt. 18:6).[1]

11:5 (b) *"By which they shall be excommunicated" only in Latin 588.] (d) *Codex 24 and Rush have only "with physical death".] (e) *"I.e. the fire" only in Latin 588.] 1 Only in Latin 588.

11:6 These have power to shut (a)*heaven,* (b)*that it rain not in the days of their prophecy: and they have power over* (c)*the waters to turn them* (d)*into blood,* (e)*and to strike* (f)*the earth* (g)*with all plagues* (h)*as often as they will.*

a.   I.e. the Scriptures which hide secrets.
b.   Because there will be no preaching* except in the right time.
c.   I.e. their teachings, which for the faithful are irrigating waters.
d.   I.e. into sin.
e.   As far as those whom they will see convicted are concerned, because it was given to them to curse and to bless*.
f.   I.e. earthly people.
g.   With all damnation.*
h.   Not always.*

To shut heaven, that it rain not. It refers to the story of Elijah, who prayed that it should not rain upon the earth, and it did not rain for three years and six months (ref. 1 Kings 17).[1]

To turn them into blood. Whence Paul, "To the ones is given the odor of life unto life, to the others the odor of death unto death" (2 Corint. 2:16, not word for word).[2]

Into blood. Into sin: either when their teaching is heard but neglected or when people even disdain to hear it.[3]

All plagues. Remember the plagues; the Lord struck Egypt with plagues (see Exodus 7-11).[4]

11:6 (b) *Codex 24 and Rusch: "Because they will not preach".] (e) *The part starting from "because" only in Latin 588.] (g) *Only in Latin 588.] (h) *Only in Latin 588.] 1 Only in Latin 588.] 2 Only in Latin 588.] 3 Not in Latin 588.] 4 Codex 24 and Rusch have only "Remember the plagues of Egypt".

11:7 (a)*And when they shall have finished* (b)*their testimony:* (c)*the beast which* (d)*ascended* (e)*from the depth, shall make* (f)*war against them, and shall overcome* (g)*them, and* (h)*kill them.*

a.   Which will indeed* last for three years and a half.**
b.   I.e. their preaching testifying to Christ.*
c.   I.e. the Antichrist, who will overcome them* in a beast-like way.**
d.   Sc. to the kingdom, i.e. to strength*.
e.   I.e. from the dark places of hell.*
f.   Sc. with his arguments.
g.   Physically.*
h.   With death.*

11:7 (a) *"Indeed" only in Codex 24. **Not in Latin 588.] (b) *Only in Latin 588.] (c) *Or possibly "who will live", the reading is difficult. **Codex 24 and Rusch have only "the Antichrist".] (d) *"I.e. to strength" only in Latin 588.] (e) *Codex 24 and Rusch: "Through dark people".] (g) *In Codex 24 and Rusch, this gloss is above "kill".] (h) *Only in Latin 588.

11:8 [a]And their bodies shall lie in the streets of [b]the [c]great city, which is called spiritually [d]Sodom and [e]Egypt, where [f]their [g]Lord also [h]was crucified.

a. So that all who see them shall fear to become like them.
b. I.e. Jerusalem.
c. Great once in virtues, now in wickedness.
d. I.e. "mute", because no one will preach, or mute for the confession of God.*
e. I.e. "dark", without knowledge of God.
f. Elijah's and Enoch's.*
g. Christ.*
h. Contradicting the truth.*

11:8 (d) *Codex 24 and Rusch: "I.e. "mute", because no one will preach spiritually".] (f) *Not in Latin 588.] (g) *Not in Latin 588.] (h) *Not in Latin 588.

11:9 And there shall of tribes, and peoples, and tongues, and Gentiles, [a]see their bodies [b]for three days and a half: and [c]they shall not suffer their bodies to be laid in monuments.

a. Some with their eyes, others by report.
b. That is, for three days and a half, their bodies shall lie unburied, because this is the time his power shall last.*
c. So that their own renown should not diminish, and that the memory of those should not be held.*

11:9 (b) *Only in Latin 588.] (c) *Codex 24 and Rusch have only the part "that the memory etc.".

11:10 And the inhabitants of the earth shall [a]be glad upon them, and [b]make merry: and shall send gifts one to another, because these two prophets [c]tormented them that dwelt upon the earth.

a. The affliction of the just is the feast of the wicked.*
b. Whence the psalmist, "Well done, well done, our eyes have seen it" (Psalm 34:21).*
c. By opposing their iniquity and refusing to obey him.*

Gifts. Presents literally, or congratulations and conversations as they speak about them one to another.[1]

11:10 (a) *Not in Latin 588.] (b) *Only in Latin 588.] (c) *Codex 24 and Rusch have only "by opposing iniquity".] 1 Not in Latin 588.

11:11 And after [a]three days and a half, [b]the spirit of life from God [c]entered into them. And they [d]stood [e]upon their feet, and [f]great fear [g]fell upon them that saw [h][i]them.

a. Three years and a half, sc. after the Antichrist's death.*
b. I.e. the breath that gives life eternally.*
c. I saw that it would enter.*
d. Impassible and immortal.
e. I.e. upon themselves, who were previously the feet*; not needing anything to lean on, but they will be strong.
f. I.e. infernal punishment for the unjust*, or awe of God.
g. As an oppressing weight, or it touched them literally.
h. Or the others.*
i. Thus glorified.

Having shown the tribulation of those through whose example they invited to preach and, if necessary, to suffer, he also shows their crowns, so that they should similarly follow this example through the example of Elijah and Enoch so as to assure, in their own measure, their own crown as they did.[1]

11:11 (a) *Not in Latin 588.] (b) *Rusch has "Which eternally gives life to everything". *Anima*, "(vital) breath/soul" and *omnia*, "everything", look rather similar, especially when abbreviated, so a mistranscription would have easily happened.] (c) *Not in Latin 588.] (e) *"The feet" is lacking in Codex 24 and Rusch.] (f) *"For the unjust" only in Latin 588.] (h) *Only in Rusch.] 1 Rusch has "Having shown the tribulation of those through whose example he invited him to preach and, if necessary, to suffer with them, he also shows their crowns so as to make him — that is, John or anyone else — similarly certain of his own crown in his own measure", and Codex 24 has the same as Rusch minus "that is, John or anyone else".

11:12 And they heard a (a)loud voice (b)from heaven (c)saying to them, Come up here. And they (d)went up into heaven (e)in a cloud: and their enemies saw them.

    a.   I.e. of a great power.
    b.   From Christ or from an angel*.
    c.   I.e. working*.
    d.   Sc. to the community of the saints.*
    e.   I.e. borne by clouds* such as to refresh them and frighten their enemies**.

11:12 (b) *Codex 24 and Rusch: "archangel".] (c) *Codex 24: "I.e. working at this"; Rusch: "I.e. working at these things".] (d) *In Codex 24 and Rusch, this is above "come up".] (e) *The part "I.e. borne by clouds" only in Latin 588. **In Rusch, this second part is found as a marginal gloss proceeded by a tag to "a loud voice".

11:13 And (a)in that hour there was made a great (b)earthquake: and (c)the tenth part of the city (d)fell: and there were (e)slain in the earthquake (f)names of men (g)seven thousand: and (h)the rest were cast (i)into a fear, and (j)gave glory to the God of heaven.

    a.   I.e. at the very moment of their glorification, or when Elijah and Enoch were seen*.
    b.   I.e. earthly people were moved* to be punished in hell; or it was for the destruction of the Church after its masters were killed.
    c.   I.e. man.*
    d.   Sc. into punishments, or* from the Church.
    e.   Completely destroyed in hell, or they did not recover their senses afterwards.*
    f.   I.e. named men* whom God predestined to death, i.e. whom he deleted from the book of life**; let the faithful not be afraid in any way.
    g.   I.e. all those who are perfect in wickedness.
    h.   Those who did not fall into punishments or sin.*
    i.   I.e. into reverence for God, or they are afraid of falling.*
    j.   I.e. attributing nothing to themselves, but to God*.

The tenth part is man; the man Adam was created in order that the tenth order, which had fallen, might be restored. I.e. those who were subjected to the Antichrist, who hoped that they were good and hoped for the restoration of the tenth order that had been thrown down from heaven.[1]

11:13 (a) *Codex 24 and Rusch: "... or in that hour when Elijah and Enoch were killed".] (b) *See note to (h) in 8:5.] (c) Only in Latin 588.] (d) *"Or" not in Codex 24 and Rusch.] (e) *This is Codex 24's as well as Rusch's reading; 588's is different, but partially faded: "I.e. completely destroyed in hell [....] they do not rise again".] (f) *"I.e. named men" only in Latin 588. **"I.e. whom he deleted from the book of life" only in Latin 588.] (h) *Codex 24 and Rusch: "When they fell into punishments or sin".] (i) *Not in Latin 588.] (j) *"But to God" only in Latin 588.] 1 Codex 24 and Rusch: "That is, man, who seems to have been created in order that the tenth order might be restored".

11:14 The second woe is gone: and behold the third woe will come quickly.
11:15 And the (a)seventh angel sounded with a trumpet: and there were made loud (b)voices in heaven saying, (c)(d)The kingdom of this world is made (e)our Lord's and (f)his Christ's, and (g)he shall reign (h)forever and ever. Amen.

    a.   In order of narration and of time, because everything will end then*.
    b.   Sc. praises to God for the salvation of the just and the damnation of the wicked.*
    c.   As if he were saying: He who was previously despised and rejected now reigns, crowning the good and condemning* the wicked.
    d.   Because in this kingdom, the good and the wicked are not mingled as before.*
    e.   I.e. the Father's.
    f.   I.e. his Son's.
    g.   I.e. his kingdom shall remain.
    h.   Not as some heretics think that the saints will come back to the life of the world after a determined amount of time.*

The third woe, when judgment is done concerning the punishments of the wicked; but he first mentions the praises and thanks that the just give for their salvation. The woe is denoted where he says, *the Gentiles were angry* (in your sight); *your wrath is come* (Christ is come to judge).[1]

11:15 (a) *"Because everything will end then" only in Latin 588.] (b) *In Rusch, this is to "glory" in the previous verse.] (c) *Latin 588: "contemning". Same similarity between the two words in Latin as in English.] (d) *Only in Latin 588.] (g) and (h) *In Codex 24 and Rusch, these are fused into one marginal gloss saying: "I.e. his kingdom will remain in itself, sc. not as some heretics etc."] 1 Only in Latin 588.

11:16 And the four and twenty seniors ^(a)which sit ^(b)on their seats in the sight of God, ^(c)fell ^(d)on their faces, and ^(e)adored God,

a. I.e. considering in his good pleasure what pleases God; i.e. they judge what is in the present.*
b. Granted to them by God.*
c. I.e. they then humbled themselves.*
d. I.e. on their hearts.
e. So that he might keep them in their place.*

And the four and twenty seniors. As if he were saying: It is not only the lesser ones who will thus glorify God, but also the greater ones themselves, i.e. the judges of the others.[1]

On their faces. He falls on his face who recognizes his fault in this life and laments it by repenting. He falls backwards who leaves this life suddenly and does not know to what punishments he is being led.

11:16 (a) *Codex 24 and Rusch have "I.e. considering what pleases God" above "in the sight of God" and "I.e. they judge what is in the present" above "sit".] (b) *Codex 24 and Rusch: "Entrusted to them".] (c) *Rusch: "I.e. they will then humble themselves".] (e) *Rusch: "Sc. because he had kept them here"; Codex 24's reading is ambiguous between the two and does not really make sense as it stands.] 1 Codex 24 and Rusch have only "It is not only the lesser ones who thus glorify God, but also the greater ones".

11:17 saying: ^(a)We thank you Lord God Omnipotent, ^(b)which are, and ^(c)which were, and which shall come: ^(d)because you have received* your ^(e)great power, ^(f)and have reigned.**

a. Because you have saved us and damned our enemies.
b. Immutable.
c. Who were once despised.*
d. By rising again, giving the Spirit to your people, and assembling the Church.
e. For your kingdom.*
f. I.e. you have defended your people from the Devil, destroying the Devil's power*.

11:17 In the verse: *Latin 588's Vulgate has "which are, and which were, and which have received"; Codex 24 "which are, and which were, and which shall come, which have received". **Latin 588 does not have "your".] (c) *Codex 24 and Rusch: "Once when you were despised".] (e) *In Codex 24 and Rusch, this, with the addition of "and" at the beginning, is to the beginning of the next verse, "And the Gentiles were angry".] (f) *"Destroying the Devil's power" only in Latin 588.

11:18 And the Gentiles were angry, and your wrath ^(a)is come, and ^(b)the time of the dead, ^(c)to be judged, and ^(d)to render reward to your servants the ^(e)prophets and ^(f)saints, and to ^(g)them that fear your name, little and great, ^(h)and to destroy them that have corrupted ⁽ⁱ⁾the earth.

a. Sc. against them.
b. The right time for both good and wicked is come.
c. For the good to be separated from the wicked.*
d. Time is come to render.
e. Sc. those who exercise forethought for themselves and for others.
f. Those who are confirmed in faith.*
g. Not only the greater ones, but all the faithful.
h. And time is come to destroy, i.e. separate.*
i. I.e. themselves by wicked works and others by their bad example.

The Gentiles were angry. The reprobates shall be grieved at God's power by which they shall be damned.[1]

11:18 (c) *Codex 24 and Rusch add "or for them to judge as judges". Rusch has "to judge" in the verse instead of "to be judged".] (f) *The Latin word for "saint" or "holy", *sanctus*, is originally the past participle of a verb meaning "to render sacred or inviolable, to appoint as sacred or inviolable, to fix unalterably, establish, ordain, decree, enact, confirm, sanction..." (Lewis & Short).] (h) *Rusch has only "And time is come"; Codex 24 has nothing here. The Latin verb here translated as "to destroy", *exterminare* (which I have already talked about in the note to 9:11 (b)), can also mean "to drive out or away, to expel, exile, banish" or "to put away, put aside, remove" (definition Lewis & Short).] 1 Only in Latin 588.

11:19 [(a)][(b)]*And the temple of God was opened in [(c)]heaven: and [(d)]the ark of his testament was seen [(e)]in his temple, and [(f)]there were made [(g)]lightnings, and [(h)]voices, and [(i)]an earthquake and [(j)]great hail.*

a. In most versions, the twelfth chapter starts here.*
b. I.e. the Spirit was given, by which the mysteries of the Church, which were* symbolized by the second tabernacle, were revealed to the faithful.
c. I.e. the Church.
d. I.e. the ark, i.e. Christ, *in whom are hid all the treasures of wisdom* (Colossians 2:3), who fulfilled the Old Testament and instituted the New.
e. I.e. in the Church, which is in heaven thanks to good works*.
f. I.e. there was given understanding.
g. I.e. miracles.
h. I.e. exhortations.
i. Some were moved to faith and others to anger*.
j. Because to some people, preaching seemed intolerable*.

He here mentions the revelation of the mysteries which were in the second vision, and the enjoined duty of preaching which we had in the third one, so as to show that this forth vision, which concerns the fight of the Church[1], depends on these two.[2]

In this forth vision, his topic is a woman well adorned, i.e. the Church having good works, who is attacked by the Devil both openly and secretly. And he shows that she overcomes in all these things; by this he especially adorns, or arms, the faithful for them not to succumb in any tribulation.[3]

It depends on the fight of the Church, on the revelation of the woman, and it depends on the third vision, which concerns the enjoined duty of preaching.

11:19 (a) *Only in Rusch.] (b) *Codex 24 and Rusch: "was".] (e) *Codex 24 and Rusch: "good life". In Codex 24, "thanks to good life" is strangely separated and placed somewhere above "the arch of his testament was seen".] (i) *Codex 24: "life", certainly nothing more than a mistranscription.] (j) *Codex 24: "an intolerable sign".] 1 Codex 24 and Rusch add "and the Devil".] 2 In Rusch, this gloss is to 12:1.] 3 Codex 24: "In this forth vision, his topic is a woman well adorned and having good aids, who is attacked by the Devil both openly and secretly. And he shows that she overcomes in all these things; by this he especially arms the faithful for them not to succumb in any tribulation"; Rusch has the same as Codex 24 except this passage where it differs: "... a woman well adorned and having good aids, that is to say concerning the fight of the Church which is attacked by the Devil both openly and secretly".] 4 Not in Latin 588.

CHAPTER 12

12:1 ^(a)*AND* ^(b)*a great sign appeared* ^(c)*in heaven:* ^(d)*a woman clothed* ^(e)*with the sun, and* ^(f)*the moon* ^{(g)(h)}*under her feet, and* ⁽ⁱ⁾*on her head* ^(j)*a crown of twelve stars:*

 a. And from these things I saw this proceed, namely a figure signifying something great.*
 b. A signifying figure.*
 c. I.e. in the Church.
 d. I.e. the Church*, because it has clothed itself with Christ, who illuminates it.
 e. I.e. with Christ.*
 f. I.e. all earthly things, which wane like the moon.*
 g. I.e. under her mind.*
 h. Even though they are* sustained by worldly things, yet they do not* strive after them.
 i. I.e. on Christ, or in the beginning of the Church.
 j. I.e. the twelve apostles through whom the world has believed, or in whom the world lives.*

12:1 (a) *Codex 24 and Rusch: "And from these things I saw this proceed, namely the grace of faith, i.e. signifying something great."] (b) *Not in Latin 588.] (d) *"I.e. the Church" not in Codex 24.] (e) *Not in Rusch; in the other ink in Codex 24.] (f) *Codex 24 and Rusch: "All earthly things, which do not remain in the same state."] (g) *Only in Latin 588.] (h) *Codex 24 and Rusch: "... she is... she does not..."] (j) *Codex 24 and Rusch: "I.e. the twelve apostles whom the world has believed, or in whom she has overcome the world."

12:2 *and* ^(a)*being with* ^(b)*child, she* ^(c)*cried also* ^(d)*travailing, and* ^(e)*is in anguish to be delivered.*

 a. I.e. in the Virgin Mary.*
 b. Sc. the word of God.*
 c. I.e. preached.
 d. I.e. desiring to engender others.*
 e. I.e. she suffers hardships when she preaches, or she is tortured* by herself, i.e. she mortifies her flesh so that her preaching be suitable; she is delivered when she sends her people forth into the light.

12:2 (a) *The Latin here translated as "being with child" literally means "having in the womb", this gloss being above "in the womb". I have taken Codex 24 and Rusch's version; Latin 588 has something I cannot make sense of, probably a mistranscription.] (b) *This above the word that literally means "having".] (d) *The Latin word translated as "travailing", *parturiens*, is from one of a sort of Latin verbs called "desiderative", indicating a wish or need to do something, whose infinitives are formed by adding the ending - *rire* to the stem of the past participle of a verb. To illustrate: *esse* (past participle *esus*) = "to eat"; desiderative of *esse* = *esurire* = "to desire to eat, to need to eat, to be hungry"; *parere* (past participle *partus*) = "to give birth"; desiderative of *parere* = *parturire* = "to desire to give birth, to be in travail".] (e) *"Is tortured" = same Latin verb as the one translated in the verse as "is in anguish".

12:3 *And there was seen* ^(a)*another sign* ^(b)*in heaven, and behold a* ^(c)*great* ^(d)*red dragon having* ^(e)*seven heads, and* ^(f)*ten horns: and on his heads* ^(g)*seven diadems,*

He is not talking about how the dragon actually is, but about his power.

 a. I.e. against this woman.*
 b. I.e. in the Church to be attacked.
 c. Because of the strength of his great power.
 d. Because he is a murderer.
 e. I.e. all his faithful through whom he speaks.*
 f. I.e. kingdoms or riches with which the princes attack the Decalogue of the law as animals attack with their horns*.
 g. I.e. all the victories over those he has thrown down and who favor him*.

12:3 (a) *Only in Latin 588.] (e) *Codex 24 and Rusch: "I.e. all the princes through whom he works."] (f) *"As animals attack with their horns" only in Latin 588.] (g) *"And who favor him" only in Latin 588.

12:4 and his [(a)]**tail** [(b)]**drew** [(c)]**the third part of** [(d)]**the stars of heaven, and** [(e)]**cast them to the earth, and** [(f)]**the dragon** [(g)]**stood** [(h)]**before the woman** [(i)]**which was ready to be delivered: that** [(j)]**when she should be delivered, he might** [(k)]**devour her son.**

a. I.e. as shameful parts are hidden by the tail, so are their perverse manners hidden by deceits with which they hide their vices.*
b. From faith to faithlessness.
c. I.e. all the reprobates.
d. I.e. those who illuminate the Church.*
e. I.e. those whom he had drawn, he seduced by love of earthly things.
f. I.e. the Devil trusting in such a power.
g. Not just for a short while, but taking pains.
h. Against the Church.
i. I.e. who was suffering pain because she was sad on account of the dragon's power.*
j. I.e. when she should engender a son.*
k. I.e. draw him* to sin.

12:4 (a) *Codex 24 and Rusch: "I.e. the deceits with which they hide their vices, as shameful parts are hidden by the tail."] (d) *Codex 24 and Rusch add "by their teaching, not by their lives".] (i) *Codex 24 and Rusch have: "Who was suffering pain, and because of this he thought she would give up soon" as a marginal gloss, as well as a second one following it: "The Devil thought that the Church had been subjugated to him by the passion."] (j) *Codex 24 and Rusch: "I.e. when she should engender someone in faith".] (k) *Codex 24 and Rusch: "draw him back".] 1 Only in Latin 588. It would be John 16:21, were it not for the negation added.

A woman, when she is in labor, has sorrow because her hour does not come.[1]

12:5 And she brought forth [(a)]**a man child, who was to govern all nations** [(b)]**with an** [(c)]**iron rod: and** [(d)]**her son was taken up** [(e)]**to God and** [(f)]**to his throne,**

a. Either Christ or faith in Christ in the hearts of listeners.*
b. I.e. with power or justice.
c. Inflexible.
d. I.e. the flesh, by the force of the divinity.
e. I.e. to equality with God.
f. I.e. for him to judge with the Father.

12:5 (a) *Only in Latin 588.

Christ came forth from Abraham and David by carnal generation. Or the Church brought forth a child, i.e. faith in Christ in the hearts of listeners.

The dragon was ready to devour, but he was not able to because one was born who stopped him from it.

12:6 and [(a)]**the woman** [(b)]**fled** [(c)]**into the wilderness where she** [(d)]**had a place prepared of God, that there they* might** [(e)]**feed her** [(f)]**a thousand two hundred sixty days.**

a. I.e. the faithful.*
b. Sc. from the pleasures of the world, by this Son's help.
c. Into the desert* of the mind, rejecting the uproar** of the world.
d. Abandoning the world, she is heartened by God.
e. Sc. with the teaching of preaching.
f. I.e. all the time during which the Church subsisted on Christ's preaching, which lasted for three years and a half. There are as many days in that length of time.*

12:6 In the verse: *Codex 24's and Rusch's Vulgates have "that there he might feed her", instead of "they", and they have a gloss above it saying that it is God who will feed her.] (a) *Only in Latin 588.] (c) *Codex 24: "desire". **Codex 24 and Rusch add "or charm".] (f) *The second sentence, "There are as many days etc.", only in Latin 588.

12:7 [(a)]**And there was made a great battle** [(b)]**in heaven,** [(c)]**Michael and** [(d)]**his angels** [(e)]**fought with the dragon, and the dragon fought and his angels:**

a. Here is another aid.
b. I.e. in the Church.*
c. I.e. the strong one, i.e. the apostles.*
d. I.e. those under their authority.*
e. Sc. supporting the Church by praying and bringing help.

12:7 (b) *Not in Rusch. In the other ink in Codex 24.] (c) *Codex 24 and Rusch: "The greater ones."] (d) *Codex 24 and Rusch: "The lesser ones."

12:8 and they [(a)]**prevailed not,** [(b)]**neither was their place found any more** [(c)]**in heaven.**

a. Sc. to remove the helps of angels, because they were not able* to bring the Church into sin.*
b. I.e. they were expelled from the hearts of the faithful.*
c. But yet it was still found among the wicked, but not in the Church.*

12:8 (a) *The Latin translated as "to prevail" can also mean "to be able/have power to".] (b) *Only in Latin 588.] (c) *Codex 24 and Rusch: "In the Church, as far as the good are concerned."

12:9 And that [(a)]**great dragon** [(b)]**was cast forth, the** [(c)]**old** [(d)]**serpent, which is called the** [(e)]**Devil and** [(f)]**Satan, which** [(g)]**seduces** [(h)]**the whole world: and** [(i)]**he was cast into the earth, and his angels were thrown down with him.**

a. Because of his violence.
b. By their help. By the first baptism.*
c. As if he were saying, "Guard against him, you all".
d. Because of his cunning.
e. I.e. flowing* from the good to the wicked.**
f. I.e. adversary.
g. Sc. the reprobates.
h. Who would like if he could.*
i. I.e. falling away from the faithful, he attacks the more vehemently those who love earthly things.

12:9 (b) *"By the first baptism" only in Latin 588.] (e) *Codex 24 and Rusch: "flowing apart". **Interpretation of Latin *diabolus* < Greek διάβολος (diabolos) (from which the English "devil" is ultimately derived as well), literally "slanderer", from the verb διαβάλλειν (diaballein), "to throw across", "to set at variance", "to slander" or "to deceive", compounded of διά (dia), "through", "across" or "apart", and βάλλειν (ballein), "to throw", which can also mean "to throw oneself", "to fall", speaking for example of a river, whence the glossator's "flowing".] (h) *Only in Latin 588.

12:10 And I heard a great [(a)]**voice** [(b)]**in heaven saying:** [(c)]**Now is there made** [(d)]**salvation and** [(e)]**force, and the** [(f)]**kingdom of our God,** [(g)]**and the power of his Christ: because the** [(h)]**accuser of our brethren is cast forth, who** [(i)]**accused them** [(j)]**before the sight of our God** [(k)]**day and night.**

a. I.e. exultation.
b. I.e. from* the angels or the holy souls.
c. I.e. from the time of Christ which is not* in the nature of man, but in God**.
d. I.e. remission of sins.*
e. I.e. strength in baptism.*
f. He leads his people from virtue to virtue.
g. And he has carried all this out through Christ.
h. The Devil's office is to accuse, i.e. to make people blameworthy through sin.
i. He showed in his effect what he had according to his function, as in Job*.**
j. Because nothing is hidden from God, which is why he frightens most.
k. I.e. every day*, either by delighting them in success or by saddening them in hardships.

After showing that the Devil was overcome[1] by the Church in this secret struggle thanks to the help of the Son and of the angels, he mentions the exultations of the holy angels themselves or of the holy souls at the brethren's victory, so that they who hear that the angels or the holy souls exult at their victory should strive to overcome.

Remission of sins in baptism, strengthening of judgment in the confirmation.[2]

12:10 (b) *Codex 24 and Rusch have "in" or "among". Latin 588's Vulgate has "from heaven" instead of "in heaven" in the verse.] (c) *"Not" missing in Codex 24. **"But in God" only in Latin 588.] (d) *Codex 24 and Rusch: "Remission of sins in baptism".] (e) *Only in Latin 588.] (i) *"As in Job" only in Latin 588. **Not in Rusch.] (k) *Codex 24 and Rusch: "Continuously".] 1 Latin 588 has "bound". The two Latin words differ only in one letter.] 2 Only in Latin 588.

12:11 And they overcame ^(a)him ^(b)by the blood of the Lamb, and by the ^(c)word of ^(d)their testimony, and ^(e)they loved not their lives even unto death.

a. His incitement.
b. I.e. applying free-will, by God whom they imitate.*
c. Because when it is necessary, they do not stay silent.
d. I.e. their faith, which Christ has testified to.
e. I.e. they did not cherish their lives, i.e.* their flesh, in such a way as to cause their souls to die.**

They loved not their lives. I.e. they hated carnal life even unto the point of enduring death for Christ.[1]

12:11 (b) *Codex 24 and Rusch have "applying free-will" above "they overcame" and "whom they imitate" above "the Lamb".] (e) *"Their lives, i.e." only in Latin 588. **In Latin 588, the gloss goes on "as he that hates his life..." with two more letters abbreviating two words; when this happens, it is usually a quote from the scriptures: the first few words of the quote are written in full, and then follows only the first letter of each following word. Here, "he that hates his life" corresponds to words in John 12:25, but the two letters that follow in the gloss do not correspond to what follows in the verse, so I do not know what they abbreviate. I can only make very doubtful conjectures: they could abbreviate "keeps it", not with the same Latin word used in John 12:25 for "keeps", but with a synonym starting with another letter, or "for him"; or the scribe could have made a mistake and written "he that hates his life" while he should have written "he that loves his life", in which case the two following letters would correspond exactly to what follows "he that loves his life" in John 12:25, namely "shall lose it".] 1 Only in Latin 588.

12:12 Therefore rejoice O ^(a)heavens, and ^(b)you that dwell therein. Woe to ^(c)the earth and to ^(d)the sea, because the Devil is ^(e)descended ^(f)to you, ^(g)having great wrath, ^(h)knowing that he has a little ⁽ⁱ⁾time.

a. I.e. angels or holy apostles.*
b. The lesser saints dwell in the greater ones, or men* in the angels.
c. I.e. those who are fixed in the same vice.
d. I.e. those who are flowing in vices.
e. From heaven, or from the greater saints, in whom the Devil no longer has a place.*
f. Sc. to kill you.
g. Because he sees that many people are taken away from him*.
h. Whence he rages more violently.
i. Sc. to deceive people, because the day of the Lord is near.*

Therefore rejoice. At their victory, he exhorts the others with an apostrophe.[1]

Woe to the earth and to the sea. Those whom the Devil has gone away from must rejoice; those whom he is joining must be saddened.[2]

12:12 (a) *Codex 24 and Rusch: "Angels or saints."] (b) *Codex 24 and Rusch have "all" instead of "men". The two words, when abbreviated, resemble each other.] (e) *Codex 24 and Rusch: "From heaven, or from the lesser saints, in whom temptation no longer has a place."] (g) *Codex 24 and Rusch go on "and substituted in his place".] (i) *Only in Latin 588.] 1 Only in Latin 588.] 2 Only in Latin 588.

12:13 And after the dragon saw that he was ^(a)thrown ^(b)into the earth, he persecuted the woman ^(c)which brought forth the man child:

a. Sc. away from the minds of the elect.*
b. I.e. into the hearts of the reprobates.*
c. I.e. who also has help against open tribulation, from the same child from whom she had help against secret attack.

When the Devil sees that he cannot succeed through secret deceit, he sets about attacking with open tribulation.

12:13 (a) *Only in Latin 588.] (b) *Only in Latin 588.

12:14 and there ^(a)were given to the woman ^(b)two wings of a great eagle, ^(c)that she might fly ^(d)into the desert unto her place, where she is nourished for ^(e)a time and ^(f)times, and ^(g)half a time, ^(h)from the face of the serpent.

a. Sc. by God.*
b. I.e. the two Testaments, the two loves, or the two lives.
c. Because they make for heaven by their way of life and have their gaze on God.*
d. She is taken away in mind from evils.*
e. I.e. a year.
f. I.e. two years.
g. I.e. half a year.
h. I.e. from the present tribulation inflicted by the Devil.*

Of a great eagle. Christ is an eagle having wings, because he is the founder and strength of both Testaments, of the love of God and neighbor, or of the present and future life.[1]

For a time and times, and half a time. By "a time", we understand a year, by "times", two years, and by "half a time", half a year: that is, the whole time of the Church, which is sustained and protected by the preaching of Christ, which lasted for three years and a half.[2]

12:14 (a) *Only in Latin 588.] (c) *Codex 24 and Rusch have, as a marginal gloss, respectively: "*Eagle.* Because they make for heaven by their way of life and have their gaze fixed on God" and "*Eagle.* Those who make for heaven by their way of life and therefore have their gaze fixed on God".] (d) *Only in Latin 588.] (h) *Codex 24 and Rusch: "From the present attack".] 1 Only in Latin 588.] 2 Codex 24 and Rusch: "If we take this to refer to the situation of the Church of the time of the Antichrist, we shall say "for a time and times, and half a time" for the preaching of Elijah and Enoch. If we take it to refer to that of the Church in general, we shall say "for a time and times, and half a time", differently, for the preaching of Christ, which lasted for three years and a half, the preaching of Christ by which the Church is fed every day".

12:15 ^(a)*And the serpent cast* ^(b)*out of his mouth* ^(c)*after the woman* ^(d)*water as it were a flood: that he might make her to be carried away* ^(e)*with the flood.*

    a.   And although she was thus prepared...
    b.   I.e. out of his influence.
    c.   Because he does not reach her.
    d.   I.e. an overflowing tribulation.
    e.   I.e. in sins.*

12:15 (e) *Codex 24 and Rusch have "into sin" above "to be carried away".

12:16 ^(a)*And* ^{(b)(c)}*the earth helped the woman, and the earth opened her mouth, and* ^(d)*swallowed up the flood which the dragon cast out of his mouth.*

    a.   But Christ gave his Church the strength to endure, or the saints did by praying.
    b.   I.e. Christ.*
    c.   They who were hidden and dry in vices.*
    d.   I.e. he destroyed all pains in himself, having become impassible and immortal, and he will do* the same in his people.

Opened. I.e. he made himself ready and apt to receive whatever was inflicted on him, like someone who opens his mouth. Which is what he did in his passion, in which he offered himself to his people as an example of patience.

Or Christ opened his mouth, i.e. he provided the woman with good persuasions against the incitements of the Devil through inward inspiration.[1]

12:16 (b) *Codex 24 and Rusch: "The saints, who are stable like the earth."] (c) *Only in Latin 588.] (d) *Rusch: "does".] 1 Only in Latin 588.

12:17 ^(a)*And the dragon was angry against the woman: and* ^(b)*went to make battle* ^(c)*with the rest of her seed, which* ^(d)*keep the commandments of God, and* ^(e)*have the testimony of Jesus Christ.*

    a.   Because although he cannot subdue her, yet he does not stop envying* and seeking an occasion to attack.
    b.   Now leaving these.*
    c.   I.e. with the lesser members of the Church.
    d.   I.e. fulfill in deed.
    e.   I.e. are not afraid to declare what they believe.

12:17 (a) *Latin 588 has "attacking". The two Latin words differ only in one letter.] (b) *Only in Latin 588.

12:18 And he stood* upon the sand of the sea.

Yet he did not overcome all those lesser people, but he nonetheless[1] made halt upon the sand, i.e. the unfruitful ones, and the traces of his feet are visible on them.

12:18 In the verse: *Codex 24 and Rusch have "sat" instead of "stood", Rusch having a gloss above it, saying "elsewhere, "stood"".] 1 Rusch: "only". Similar abbreviations.

CHAPTER 13

13:1 AND I saw ^(a)a beast coming up from the sea, having ^(b)seven ^(c)heads, and ^(d)ten horns, and upon his horns ^(e)ten diadems, and upon ^(f)his heads ^(g)names of blasphemy.

    a.   I.e. the whole collection of wicked princes exalting itself through the other wicked.*
    b.   I.e. all.*
    c.   I.e. princes.
    d.   I.e. all those through whom the princes attack the Decalogue.
    e.   Because there is not any commandment that is not broken by the princes and with which they are not crowned.
    f.   I.e. the princes.
    g.   Because they say that Christ was not God but a magician.

A beast. The beast is either the Antichrist in particular, or the whole collection of the wicked in general, or the entire Antichrist, head and body.[1]

Having seven heads. And in order to be well able to overcome them, he set up such a body of servants for himself.

Ten. Sarecens, Persians, Vandals, Goths, Lombards, Burgundians, Franks, Huns, Alemanni, Suebi: these are the ten kings through whom he will reign and be glorified throughout all the earth.[2]

13:1 (a) *Codex 24 has "I.e. from the collection of the wicked" above "from the sea" and "The beginning, or exalting itself through the others" as a marginal gloss presumably meant to refer to "coming up". Rusch has the same as Codex 24 above "from the sea", and "Because it is the beginning, or exalting itself through the other wicked" above "coming up". The Latin for "the beginning" and "of the princes" differ only in one letter, which would have made misreading and mistranscription easy.] (b) *Rusch: "All the wicked".] 1 Not in Latin 588. It is Rusch's version; it is different in Codex 24: "One beast is the Antichrist in particular, the other the whole collection of the wicked in general. Or the entire Antichrist, head and body."] 2 Only in Latin 588.

13:2 And ^(a)the beast which I saw, was like to a leopard, and his ^(b)feet as of a bear, and his ^(c)mouth, as ^(d)the mouth of a lion. ^(e)And the dragon gave him his own ^(f)force and great ^(g)power.

    a.   Full of various heresies, or hiding his vices with various simulations.
    b.   I.e. the people sent by the princes, fast and crushing*.
    c.   I.e. those who are greater in speech.
    d.   Because they devour and stink.
    e.   Another thing by which he does* harm.
    f.   To do miracles.
    g.   To seduce many.

13:2 (b) *"Fast and crushing" only in Latin 588.] (e) *Codex 24 and Rusch: "they do".

13:3 And I saw ^(a)one of his heads ^(b)as it were slain to death: and the ^(c)wound of his death ^(d)was cured. And all the earth was in admiration ^(e)after ^(f)the beast.

    a.   I.e. the Antichrist.
    b.   Pretending to be dead.
    c.   I.e. pretense.*
    d.   Sc. by an ascension.
    e.   Imitating beast-like people.
    f.   I.e. the Antichrist.*

As it were slain. The Antichrist will pretend to be dead, and after hiding for three days, he will then appear, saying that he has been resurrected.[1]

And the wound of his death was cured. He will ascend into the air by means of magic, with demons bearing him, and so will his death's wound be cured, because he who was previously thought to be dead will be considered alive afterwards.[2]

13:3 (c) *Instead of this, Codex 24 and Rusch have "pretended" above "death".] (f) *Not in Latin 588.] 1 Not in Latin 588.] 2 Not in Latin 588.

13:4 And they adored ^(a)the dragon which gave ^(b)power to the beast: and they adored ^(c)the beast, saying, ^(d)Who is like to the beast? And who shall be able ^(e)to fight with it?

    a.   I.e. the Devil.
    b.   Sc. to rise again.*
    c.   I.e. the Antichrist.
    d.   Since it has risen again.
    e.   I.e. to resist its will.

13:4 (b) *Codex 24 and Rusch add "as it seemed".

13:5 And there ^(a)**was given to it a mouth** ^(b)**speaking great things and** ^(c)**blasphemies: and** ^(d)**power was given to it** ^(e)**to work** ^(f)**two and forty months.**

a. With God's permission.
b. I.e. exalting itself with grandiloquence.
c. Because he will say that he is the son of God.
d. I.e. power was conceded to it to exercise its wickedness for three years and a half.*
e. I.e. to work for two and forty months.*
f. Three years and a half.*

13:5 (d) *Only in Latin 588.] (e) *The Latin has in the verse a word literally meaning "do" or "make" rather than "work", which is why the glossator felt the need to explain the unusual and potentially ambiguous phrasing — which happens to be less ambiguous in Latin 588, where this gloss is not found, due to a slightly different grammatical construction of the Latin for "two and forty months" (which makes no difference in English translation).] (f) *Only in Latin 588.

13:6 ^(a)**And he opened his mouth unto blasphemies** ^{(b)(c)}**toward God, to blaspheme** ^(d)**his name, and** ^(e)**his tabernacle, and** ^(f)**those that dwell in heaven.**

a. That is, he has broken out into such confidence that he now dares to blaspheme openly what he previously blasphemed secretly.
b. Denying that he is God.
c. I.e. against God or as far as God.*
d. All his institution through which it appears clearly that he is laudable.*
e. I.e. those who serve him as soldiers.*
f. I.e. all those who are protected by those greater ones.

13:6 (c) *Not in Latin 588.] (d) *Rusch has this as a marginal gloss with a tag to "and his tabernacle". In Codex 24, it is unclear what it is meant to refer to.] (e) *Only in Latin 588.

13:7 And ^(a)**it was given unto him to make battle with the saints, and** ^(b)**to overcome them. And power was given him upon every tribe and people, and tongue, and nation,**

a. It was permitted.*
b. Physically.

13:7 (a) *Not in Latin 588.

13:8 and all ^(a)**that inhabit the earth, adored it,** ^(b)**whose names be not written in** ^(c)**the book of life of the Lamb, which was slain from the beginning of the world.**

a. I.e. those who are devoted to earthly things.
b. I.e. only the reprobates.
c. This book is the Lamb. Indeed the same is the Lamb and the book.*

Slain. In his people, as in Abel. Or because it was determined previously[1] that he should be slain at the end of time. Or he was prefigured[2] in the lamb that Abel offered, or in Abel himself when he was killed by his brother (Gen. 4).

13:8 (c) *Not in Latin 588.] 1 Codex 24 and Rusch: "previously to everything".] 2 Codex 24 and Rusch: "mystically prefigured".

13:9 ^(a)**If any man have** ^(b)**an ear,** ^(c)**let him hear.**

a. As if he were saying, "Beware, everyone".
b. Understanding.*
c. Let him understand.*

13:9 (b) *Not in Latin 588.] (c) *Not in Latin 588.

13:10 (a)*He that shall lead into captivity, goes into* (b)*captivity:* (c)*he that shall kill with the sword,* (d)*he must be killed with the sword,* (e)(f)*here is the patience and the faith of saints.*

When considering the punishment of the wicked and the reward of the good, they become patient and keep faith.[1]

- a. He who takes men captive away now from faith, and eventually from salvation: namely the Antichrist, or the Devil himself.
- b. I.e. infernal punishments.
- c. Sc. the Antichrist or* his people kill with a material sword and with that of persuasion.
- d. I.e. they shall perish by the sword of the judgment*.
- e. The reason why they will endure and keep faith is because they know that once he is destroyed, they must be rewarded.
- f. I.e. in the fact of considering punishments and reward.*

13:10 (c) *Codex 24 and Rusch: "and".] (d) *Codex 24 and Rusch: "eternal judgment".] (f) *Not in Latin 588.] 1 Not in Latin 588.

13:11 *And I saw* (a)(b)*another beast* (c)*coming up* (d)*from the earth: and he had* (e)*two horns,* (f)*like to a lamb, and* (g)*he spoke as a dragon.*

After describing the tribulation there will be in the time of the Antichrist and by the agency of his princes[1], he mentions another one, which will be done by his apostles, whom he will send[2] throughout all the world to seduce men[3].

- a. I.e. pseudo-apostles.
- b. Lesser than the first one.
- c. Advancing to pride or preaching*.
- d. Through those who loved earthly things.
- e. I.e. he usurped for himself the two Testaments, or love of God and neighbor.*
- f. Because if there seems to be anything good in them, it will be simulation.*
- g. I.e. they* will speak in the same way as the Devil had spoken in the Antichrist.

Horns. Because they pretended that they had[4] the innocence, the pure life, the true doctrine, and the miracles that Christ had and gave his people.[5]

13:11 (c) *Codex 24: "betrayal"; Rusch: "perdition".] (e) *Codex 24 and Rusch have "Or they will usurp the two testaments for themselves" at the end of the gloss on "horns". They do not have the part "or love of God and neighbor" at all.] (f) *Not in Latin 588.] (g) *Codex 24: "the apostles"; Rusch: "the pseudo-apostles".] 1 Codex 24 and Rusch: "by the agency of the Antichrist and his princes".] Codex 24 and Rusch: "scatter".] 3 "To seduce men" only in Latin 588.] Codex 24 and Rusch: "Because they will pretend that they have".] 5 In Latin 588, this gloss is written next to verse 12, without anything indicating which word(s) it refers to, whether in verse 11 or in this one. Maybe it was written there because space was somewhat lacking on the previous page, where verse 11 ends and verse 12 starts.

13:12 *And* (a)*all the power of the former beast he did* (b)(c)*in his sight: and he made the earth and* (d)*the inhabitants therein, to adore* (e)*the* (f)*first beast,* (g)*whose wound of death was cured.*

The earth. I.e. people of the earth, and persisting in the love of the earth.[1]

- a. I.e. all the methods for deceiving with which the Antichrist deceived.
- b. I.e. in his good pleasure.*
- c. Because they will place* their head, namely the Antichrist, before themselves in everything.
- d. I.e. those who are fixed in earthliness.*
- e. I.e. the Antichrist.
- f. I.e. supreme.*
- g. Because here, with the simulated resurrection, they throw the foundation of their preaching as Christ's apostles did.

13:12 (b) *Only in Latin 588.] (c) *Codex 24 and Rusch: "placed".] (d) *Only in Latin 588.] (f) *Only in Latin 588.] 1 Codex 24 and Rusch add: "Or "the earth" for the body and "the inhabitants therein" for the soul".

13:13 And ^(a)**he did many* signs,** ^(b)**so that he made also fire to come down** ^(c)**from heaven unto the earth** ^(d)**in the sight of men.**

a. For the corroboration of his preaching.
b. As the Holy Spirit was given to the apostles in the appearance of fire, so will they too give a malign spirit in the appearance of fire.
c. I.e. from the air upon the earth.*
d. So that all men can see it, as the apostles did in a room, i.e. in their houses*.

Fire. I.e. he will make a malign spirit come down upon his people so that they may speak with divers tongues.[1]

13:13 In the verse: *Latin 588: "evil"; Codex 24 and Rusch: "great".] (c) *Only in Latin 588.] (d) *Codex 24: "... as the apostles received it in a room"; Rusch: "... while the apostles received it in a room".] 1 Not in Latin 588.

13:14 And he seduced the inhabitants on the earth through the signs which ^(a)**were given him to do** ^(b)**in the sight of the beast,** ^(c)**saying to them that dwell on the earth,** ^(d)**that they should make the image of the beast which** ^(e)**has the stroke of the sword, and** ^(f)**lived.**

a. With God's permission.*
b. I.e. in the invocation of the name of the Antichrist.
c. I.e. enjoining.
d. That they should make themselves similar to the beast, or literally.*
e. I.e. had death.*
f. I.e. rose again.

13:14 (a) *Not in Latin 588.] (d) *Codex 24 and Rusch add: "i.e. a statue".] (e) *Instead of this, Codex 24 and Rusch have "of death" above "of the sword".

13:15 And it ^(a)**was given him to give** ^(b)**spirit** ^(c)**to the image of the beast, and that** ^(d)**the image of the beast** ^(e)**should speak: and** ^(f)**should make, that whosoever shall not adore** ^(g)**the image of the beast,** ^(h)**be slain.**

a. By the Devil with God's permission*.
b. Similar to him, or a malign spirit.*
c. To those who are like the Antichrist.*
d. I.e. those who are like the beast*.**
e. With divers tongues.
f. Through the princes of the world.
g. Those who make themselves similar to him, or literally.*
h. By the death of the body.

That the image of the beast should speak. He will, by means of magic, make the statue speak and foretell the future.[1]

13:15 (a) *"With God's permission" not in Codex 24.] (b) *Only in Latin 588.] (c) *Not in Latin 588.] (d) *Rusch: "like him". **Not in Latin 588.] (g) *Not in Latin 588.] 1 Not in Latin 588.

13:16 ^(a)**And he shall make all, little and great, and rich, and poor, and freemen, and bondmen, to have** ^(b)**a character** ^{(c)(d)}**in their right hand, or** ^(e)**in their foreheads.**

a. Because they will say that their God rejects no one.
b. I.e. conformity to his wickedness.*
c. Signs are put both on the hand and on the forehead so that everyone should confess their God in word and in deed.
d. I.e. in deed.*
e. I.e. in word.*

13:16 (b) *Only in Latin 588.] (d) *Only in Latin 588.] (e) *Only in Latin 588.

13:17 And that no man may (a)buy or sell, (b)but he that has the character, (c)or the name of the beast, or the (d)number of his name.

a. Literally.*
b. I.e. but he who makes himself similar to him, or they who are signed with his name and confess him.*
c. I.e. those who expect a minor, middling, or very great reward from him.
d. Or name.*

13:17 (a) *Codex 24 and Rusch: "Literally, or acquire servants of God, or in a spiritual sense".] (b) *Codex 24: "Because they are signed with his name and confess him"; Rusch has the same but with "were" instead of "are".] (d) *Not in Latin 588.

13:18 (a)Here is wisdom. He that has understanding, (b)let him count the (c)number of the beast. (d)For it is the number of a man: and the number of him is six hundred sixty six.

a. Because the thing is obscure, he makes people attentive.
b. I.e. let him beware lest he be deceived.*
c. Or name.*
d. Although through these things he seems to be a god, to a wise man it will clearly appear that he is a mere man.

And the number of him is six hundred sixty six. Since this book was published in Greek, the number should be sought in the manner of the Greeks, among whom letters symbolize a number. His name is ANTEMOS, which is suitable to him who is said to be the contrary of Christ: A = 1; N = 50; T = 300; E = 5; M = 40; O = 70; S = 200; or ARNOYME, that is "I deny", he who denies that Christ is God; in which there is the same number: A = 1; R = 200; N = 50; O = 70; Y = 300: M = 40; E = 5; or TEITAN, that is "giant sun", which fits Christ truly, and fits the Antichrist by usurpation: T = 300; E = 5; I = 10; T again = 300; A = 1; N = 50. With Latin letters, DIC LUX[1], because he will say that he is the light: D = five hundred; I = one; C = one hundred; L = fifty; V[2] = five; X = ten, and thus we get the same sum. Six is the first perfect number, and it symbolizes those less perfect people who are married, and fulfill the Ten Commandments in their own measure. [3] A hundred symbolizes the most perfect who do not violate the integrity of their minds and bodies, and keep the ten commandments most perfectly. These bring forth fruit, some a sixfold[4], some sixtyfold, some hundredfold (ref. Matt. 13:8). And the disciples of the Antichrist will then say that no one can be saved unless he offer the Antichrist one of these fruits. By six we symbolize those who keep the six works of mercy we read in the Gospel (*I was hungry*, etc. (Matt. 25:35-36)) in the six ages of the world; by a hundred, the perfect people, or the hundredth sheep brought back (ref. Matt. 18:12 etc.; Luke 15:4 etc.); by sixty, which consists of the number six multiplied by ten, the keepers of the ten commandments and of the six works; by six we symbolize those who follow faith in unity, in the Trinity, and in the love of God and neighbor, because that number consists of unity, the number two, and the number three[5].

13:18 (b) *Only in Latin 588.] (c) *Not in Latin 588.] 1 In English, "Say Light".] 2 V and U used to be the same letter in the Roman alphabet; V was used in capitals and u in small letters.] 3 A sentence is here missing in Latin 588, which Codex 24 and Rusch have: "Sixty symbolizes the middlingly perfect ones who, renouncing lawful unions, remain in chastity, and, again, fulfill the ten commandments in their own measure".] 4 Codex 24 and Rusch: "thirtyfold".] 5 The whole part starting from "By six we symbolize those who keep, etc." is only in Latin 588.

14:1 AND ^(a)**I looked, and behold** ^(b)**a Lamb** ^(c)**stood upon** ^(d)**mount Sion, and with him** ^(e)**a hundred forty four thousand** ^(f)**having** ^(g)**his name, and** ^(h)**the name of his Father** ⁽ⁱ⁾**written** ^(j)**in their foreheads.**

a. I.e. this is with me seeing.*
b. I.e. Christ who was sacrificed for us.
c. As one helping.
d. I.e. the Church high in virtues and contemplating God.
e. Most perfect in virginity, gathered in faith in the Trinity from the four parts of the world.
f. He sees them* such as they were.
g. Because they will be called Christians.
h. Because they will be called gods.
i. Indelibly.*
j. Because they confess it openly.

14:1 (a) *Only in Latin 588.] (f) *"He sees them" only in Latin 588.] (i) *Not in Codex 24.

After showing the most grievous persecution the Church shall suffer inflicted by the Antichrist and his apostles, as a consolation, he shows what helper it has, and what body of servants he has.

14:2 And I heard ^(a)**a voice** ^(b)**from heaven, as the voice** ^(c)**of many waters, and** ^(d)**as the voice of a great thunder:** ^(e)**and the voice which I heard,** ^(f)**as of** ^(g)**harpers harping on** ^(h)**their harps.**

a. A desire or an admonition.
b. From those who were with him.
c. I.e. of many peoples, because they were assembled from many peoples, for by water, a people is symbolized*.
d. Because it frightens those who shun coming to its community.
e. Because they are those who have determined to stretch their devoted hearts* over the wood of the cross.
f. Or "was".*
g. Fulfilling in deed what they had according to their office.
h. Not those of someone else.

14:2 (c) *"For by water, a people is symbolized" only in Latin 588.] (e) *The Latin words for "heart" and "string" resemble each other, so there is perhaps sort of a wordplay here.] (f) *Only in Rusch.

14:3 And ^(a)**they sang as it were a new song** ^(b)**before the seat and before** ^(c)**the four beasts, and** ^(d)**the seniors, and no man could** ^(e)**say the song, but** ^(f)**those hundred forty four thousand,** ^(g)**that were bought** ^(h)**from the earth.**

a. I.e. they exulted in the integrity of their souls and bodies, and this joy will never grow old for them, but it is always new.
b. I.e. in the presence of those in whom God sits.
c. I.e. the preachers.
d. I.e. the judges.
e. I.e. rejoice in that integrity.
f. I.e. those virgins.
g. Whom the blood of Christ lifted up to be virgins.
h. Do not despair because you are from the earth.

14:4 These are they which ⁽ᵃ⁾were not defiled with women. For they are virgins. These ⁽ᵇ⁾follow ⁽ᶜ⁾the Lamb ⁽ᵈ⁾wheresoever he shall go. These were bought ⁽ᵉ⁾from among men*, the first-fruits ⁽ᶠ⁾to God and ⁽ᵍ⁾the Lamb:

- a. Either literally or with any filth of the world.
- b. I.e. imitate.
- c. I.e. Christ.
- d. I.e. in integrity of soul and body.
- e. As the good* horse from among the herd or the first-fruits from among the fruits.
- f. To the Father.*
- g. Christ.*

14:4 In the verse: *Codex 24 and Rusch have "from among all". The Latin words for "men" and "all" look somewhat similar.] (e) *Codex 24 and Rusch: "best".] (f) *Not in Latin 588.] (g) *Not in Latin 588.

14:5 and in their mouth ⁽ᵃ⁾there was ⁽ᵇ⁾found no ⁽ᶜ⁾lie, for they are without ⁽ᵈ⁾spot ⁽ᵉ⁾before the throne of God.

- a. Even if there was once.
- b. It is in those in whom it remains that it is found.*
- c. In word.
- d. I.e. perverse work.*
- e. I.e. before God the judge.

14:5 (b) *Not in Latin 588.] (d) *Codex 24 and Rusch: "In work".

14:6 And I saw ⁽ᵃ⁾⁽ᵇ⁾another angel ⁽ᶜ⁾flying ⁽ᵈ⁾through the midst of heaven, ⁽ᵉ⁾having ⁽ᶠ⁾the eternal Gospel, ⁽ᵍ⁾to evangelize unto ⁽ʰ⁾them that sit upon the earth, and ⁽ⁱ⁾upon every nation, and tribe, and ⁽ʲ⁾tongue, and people:

After the attack by the two beasts has been described, and then the help of the lamb mentioned and the dignity of his body of servants shown, an admonition is added for them to join this body of servants, and a threat for them to turn away from the other one.

- a. I.e. the preachers, who are the others* after Christ, pursuing his mission.
- b. Lesser.*
- c. Betaking himself away from earthly things, or preaching speedily*.
- d. I.e. through the common Church.*
- e. According to the duty enjoined to him.
- f. I.e. a preaching that promises eternal things, and leads those who fulfill it to eternity.
- g. And he had it for this purpose.
- h. I.e. those who live in contempt of the world.
- i. Sc. in order to overcome them by making them similar to himself.*
- j. That is, the complete diversity of those tongues that dwell in earthly things.*

14:6 (a) *The Latin word translated in the verse by "another" had most properly, in classical Latin, the meaning "the other" or "a/the second", "another" being expressed by a different word. The distinction sometimes got lost in later Latin.] (b) *Not in Latin 588.] (c) *"Or preaching speedily" only in Latin 588.] (d) *Codex 24 and Rusch add: "which they draw along with them by their words and examples".] (i) *Only in Latin 588. The Latin seems to be playing on words: *super* = "upon", "above", "over"; *superare* = "to climb over", "to surpass", "to overcome".] (j) *Codex 24 and Rusch have, starting above "upon every nation", "I.e. the complete diversity of those who dwell in earthly things".

14:7 saying with a loud ⁽ᵃ⁾voice, ⁽ᵇ⁾Fear ⁽ᶜ⁾our Lord*, and ⁽ᵈ⁾give him honor, because ⁽ᵉ⁾the hour of his judgment is come: and ⁽ᶠ⁾adore him ⁽ᵍ⁾that made heaven and earth, the sea and all things that are in them, and ⁽ʰ⁾the fountains of waters.

- a. I.e. persuasion.
- b. With a pure mind and love.*
- c. Not those beasts.
- d. By doing good works and announcing good things concerning him, so that he may clearly appear glorious through you.
- e. As if he were saying, "Do not succumb, because you shall not suffer for a long time".
- f. By making yourselves similar to him.*
- g. Even if you fear failure, ask him for help.*
- h. Whence flow teachings and preachings.*

14:7 In the verse: *Codex 24 and Rusch add here "you all his saints", and Rusch has a gloss above it saying "absent from most versions".] (b) *Codex 24 and Rusch have only "With a pure love".] (f) *Not in Latin 588.] (g) *Not in Latin 588.] (h) *Only in Latin 588.

14:8 And ^(a)another angel ^(b)followed, saying, ^(c)Fallen, fallen is ^(d)that ^(e)great Babylon, ^(f)which of the ^(g)wine of the wrath of her fornication ^(h)made ⁽ⁱ⁾all nations to drink.

a. According to the different announcement.
b. Because preachers succeed one another.
c. Repeated twice, it means infinity; by which one understands complete destruction.
d. All those who were confounded in vices.*
e. Because of their great number or because of their pride.
f. Defended with a perverse doctrine.
g. I.e. delight.*
h. Gave to drink or made drunk.*
i. Those who live heathenly.

The previous angel was exhorting people to fear and praise God who made all things, because he will deliver his people in a short time; this other angel exhorts them not to make themselves similar to the beast and to the dragon, because that great Babylon is fallen, i.e. all the wicked and all those who were confounded with vices were destroyed in soul and body; I mean Babylon which makes to drink, i.e. pollutes, all nations, i.e. those who live heathenly, of the wine, i.e. with the delight, of her fornication; by fornication I mean God's wrath, because God is made angry by it. Or *the wine of her fornication*, i.e. vices, and especially idolatry, which is a sweet drink to those who sin; vices with which they pollute others and make them drunk so that they cannot walk in the straight path, whence God's wrath is owed to them.[1]

14:8 (d) *Not in Latin 588.] (g) *Only in Latin 588.] (h) *Only in Latin 588. The purpose of this gloss is to clarify the meaning of the Latin verb used in the verse, which is frequently used in the Vulgate with the meaning "to make/give to drink", like here, but normally means "to drink".] 1 Only in Latin 588 except the last sentence starting from "the wine of her fornication, i.e. vices..." which is in the other books as well. 588's and Codex 24's Vulgates have in the verse "of the wine of her fornication" instead of "of the wine of the wrath of her fornication".

14:9 And ^(a)the third angel followed them, saying ^(b)with a loud voice, If any man ^(c)adore ^(d)the beast and ^(e)his image, and receive ^(f)the character ^(g)in his forehead, or ^{(h)in} his hand:

a. He says three because of faith in the holy Trinity, when these three things can be considered in the same person.
b. Not being fearful.
c. Even forced.*
d. I.e. the Antichrist.
e. And makes people similar to him.*
f. I.e. the sign of his name.
g. He who confesses him.
h. He who imitates him in deed.

14:9 (c) *Only in Latin 588.] (e) *Rusch: "I.e. makes himself similar to him".

14:10 ^(a)he also shall drink ^(b)of the wine of the wrath of God, ^{(c)(d)}which is mingled with pure wine in the cup of his wrath, and shall be tormented with fire and ^(e)brimstone ^(f)in the sight of the holy angels* and ^(g)before the sight of the Lamb.

a. Like Babylon.
b. I.e. of eternal damnation.
c. Which God angry offers*, i.e. has mingled**.
d. As if he were saying, "He who is not corrected by the penalty he gives for reproof* shall be punished with eternal punishment".
e. I.e. stench.
f. So that he should be consumed with envy when seeing their splendor.
g. Because all consciences will there be open to sight.*

The wine of the wrath of God. Pure wine is drunk when he scourges someone to correct them, the lees[1] when eternal damnation is inflicted on them.

In the cup. The cup is God's vengeance, where above there is pure wine, with which he punishes here for correction, and below the lees, i.e. damnation, which the wicked shall drink in the end. Therefore, concerning the wine, i.e. the lees, as he wants to show that this wine is turbid in comparison with pure wine, he adds *"which is mingled"*.

The predictions he puts in the present are announced as things that are to happen in the future.[2]

And shall be tormented with fire, etc. If he enumerates some things about the damnation of the wicked, he does not say it in order to describe damnation, but just to inspire terror in those whom he frightens off from their company.

14:10 In the verse: *Latin 588: "in the sight of the angels and of the saints".] (c) *Codex 24: "Which God offers reluctantly". **"I.e. has mingled" only in Latin 588.] (d) *Codex 24 and Rusch: "correction". As already mentioned in a previous note (4:1 (i)), the two Latin words differ only in one letter.] (g) *Only in Latin 588.] 1 Codex 24 and Rusch: "turbid wine".] 2 Only in Latin 588.

14:11 And the ^(a)smoke of their torments ^(b)shall ascend forever and ever: ^(c)neither have they rest day and night, which have adored ^(d)the beast, and ^(e)his image, and ^(f)if any man take ^(g)the character of his name.

When he says *"shall ascend forever"*, he means that the punishment will be eternal; when he adds *"neither have they rest"*, that it will be continuous.

    a.   I.e. darkness.
    b.   I.e. shall last.
    c.   As if he were saying, "It is not surprising if those who have adored the Antichrist in his own time are punished, because even his preceding ministers shall have the same punishment".
    d.   I.e. the Antichrist.*
    e.   I.e. his statue or those who are similar to him.*
    f.   Similarly, he has no rest.*
    g.   Any sign whatsoever of the things previously mentioned.*

14:11 (d) *Only in Latin 588.] (e) *Only in Latin 588.] (f) *Not in Latin 588.] (g) *Not in Latin 588.

14:12 ^{(a)(b)}Here is the patience of saints, ^(c)which ^(d)keep ^(e)the commandments of God and ^(f)the faith of Jesus.

Here is the patience of saints. That is, here must saints endure patiently in order not to come to eternal punishment.[1]

    a.   Or "this".*
    b.   In front of the sight of eternal punishment.
    c.   And of those.*
    d.   I.e. fulfill in deed.
    e.   I.e. concerning the two loves.
    f.   Because they confess that he is God.

14:12 (a) *Only in Latin 588.] (c) *Not in Latin 588.] 1 Not in Latin 588.

14:13 ^(a)And I heard a ^(b)voice from heaven, saying to me, ^(c)Write, Blessed are the ^(d)dead which ^(e)die ^(f)in our Lord, ^(g)from henceforth now, says ^(h)the Spirit, ⁽ⁱ⁾that they rest from ^(j)their labors, for ^(k)their works follow them.

Works. I.e. the reward of their works which follows them. As if he were saying: While they were in the world, quite great tribulations would fall on them for a quite great crown; whence it followed that they were regarded as abandoned by God, but now they shall not suffer anything anymore.

    a.   As if he were saying, "Those are wretched, these are blessed".
    b.   I.e. admonition.*
    c.   Sc. in your heart and in those of listeners.
    d.   To the world.
    e.   When body and soul are unfastened.
    f.   In the confession of the Lord.*
    g.   I.e. from the time of resurrection and death*.
    h.   The whole Trinity.
    i.   I.e. let them not suffer any more.
    j.   Which they have suffered so far.
    k.   Not those of others.*

14:13 (b) *Only in Latin 588.] (f) *In Latin 588, (e) and (f) are one gloss reading "In confession, the soul is unfastened when the body is".] (g) *"And death" only in Latin 588.] (k) *Only in Latin 588.

14:14 And I saw, and behold ^(a)a white cloud: and ^(b)upon ^(c)the cloud one sitting ^(d)like to the Son of man, ^(e)having ^(f)on his head ^(g)a crown of gold, and ^(h)in his hand ⁽ⁱ⁾a sharp sickle.

Having shown the reward of the good, by which he invited us to their community, he then adds the damnation of the wicked so as to lead us to the same purpose through terror.

Like to the Son of man. Because he was no longer really the son of man, because he was immortal.[1]

    a.   I.e. the saints or the Lord's flesh.
    b.   Christ sits upon the saints*, or his divinity sits upon his humanity.
    c.   I say.*
    d.   Because now impassible and immortal.
    e.   Sc. like one celebrating a triumph.
    f.   In himself or in his divinity.
    g.   Because he has overcome the Devil by wisdom.
    h.   I.e. in his power.
    i.   I.e. a judicial sentence dividing the wicked from the good.

14:14 (b) *Codex 24: "the heavens".] (c) *Not in Latin 588.] 1 Not in Latin 588.

14:15 And (a)(b)another angel came forth from (c)the temple, crying with a loud voice to (d)him that sat upon the cloud, (e)Thrust in your sickle, and (f)reap, (g)because the hour is come* to reap, (h)for (i)the harvest of the earth is dry**.

    a.   In that he is a servant.
    b.   Other than Christ.*
    c.   I.e. the Church.*
    d.   I.e. Christ.
    e.   Pass your judgment.
    f.   I.e. gather your people.*
    g.   Because it is now opportune that the number of your people be completed*.
    h.   Because the villainy of the wicked is consummate* and no longer has a place, and the justice of the saints also is**.
    i.   I.e. the wicked.*

Another angel came forth. I.e. the saints who had thus far been hidden appear in splendor to judge, begging with desire that God should make the separation between good and wicked.

Saints are said to come forth from the temple when they appear no longer as they used to be, but as they will remain forever.[1]

14:15 In the verse: *Codex 24 and Rusch have "it is the hour" instead of "the hour is come", and Rusch has a gloss above it mentioning the "is come" variant. **Codex 24 and Rusch have "ripe" instead of "dry", and Rusch again mentions the variant.] (b) *Not in Latin 588.] (c) *Only in Latin 588.] (f) *Latin 588 has "reap your people" in the verse, and so only "I.e. gather" above "reap".] (g) *Codex 24 and Rusch: "Because it is now opportune since the number of your people is completed".] (h) *Codex 24 and Rusch: "kept". **"And the justice of the saints also is" only in Latin 588.] (i) *Only in Latin 588.] 1 Not in Latin 588.

14:16 And he that sat upon the cloud, thrust his sickle into the earth, and (a)the earth was reaped*.

    a.   I.e. he separated the good from the wicked.

14:16 In the verse: *Latin 588 and Codex 24 have "and reaped the earth"; Rusch "and reaped it".

14:17 And (a)another angel (b)came forth (c)from the temple which is in heaven, (d)himself also having a sharp sickle.

    a.   The aforementioned saints, with another duty.
    b.   I.e. it appeared how he was.
    c.   I.e. from a secret place.
    d.   Like Christ.

After showing that God, having the power to judge, was implored by the saints, and that the judgment was thus being done, he shows that the saints have the same power, and that Christ orders them to judge and that they obey his order.

14:18 And (a)another angel came forth (b)from the altar, (c)which had power over (d)(e)the fire: and he cried with a loud (f)voice (g)to him that had (h)the sharp sickle, saying, (i)Thrust in your sharp sickle, and (j)gather the clusters of the vineyard of the earth: (k)because the grapes thereof be ripe.

    a.   I.e. Christ.*
    b.   I.e. from a more secret place.*
    c.   Who could well receive it because he could give it.
    d.   I.e. eternal punishment.
    e.   Or over demons and wicked men.*
    f.   I.e. authority.
    g.   I.e. to the saints.
    h.   Judicial power.*
    i.   I.e. pass your judgment.*
    j.   I.e. separate those who are ripe in villainy.*
    k.   I.e. because their wickedness is completed.

Another angel. Christ, who used to be hidden and considered worthless, appeared among the faithful, bright, coming from the altar, i.e. from a more secret place than the other saints, that is, he was recognized by men[1] as being consubstantial with God.

By the harvest of the earth and by the grapes of the vineyard of the earth we understand damnation[2]; but, however, the ones we see indicated by the vineyard are those[3] who do evil with greater zeal, just as greater care is applied to a vineyard to make it bear fruit than to the earth.

14:18 (a) *Not in Rusch. In the other ink in Codex 24.] (b) *Codex 24: "From a more secret place than the others", in the other ink again; Rusch: "From a more secret place in which the saints were" (perhaps a mistake for "From a more secret place than the saints"?).] (e) *Only in Rusch. Rusch's Vulgate text, as well as Codex 24's, have "fire <u>and water</u>".] (h) *Only in Rusch.] (i) *Not in Latin 588. Codex 24 has "I.e. exercise your judicial power" in the other ink. Note that what I translate as "exercise" here and as "pass" in Rusch's version is the same Latin word, but I wanted to avoid saying "exercise your judgment", which usually means something else than what is meant here.] (j) *This is from Codex 24 and Rusch. Latin 588 seems to have a mistranscription.] 1 Codex 24 and Rusch: "by all".] 2 Codex 24 and Rusch: "the damnation of the same wicked".] 3 Codex 24 and Rusch: "... the ones we understand by the vineyard are more especially those...".

14:19 (a)And the angel thrust (b)his sharp sickle (c)into the earth, and gathered the vineyard of the earth, and cast it (d)into the great press of the wrath of God:

And cast it into the great press. Whence the prophet, *"the pit wherein is no water"*, i.e. no solace[1] (Zach. 9:11).[2]

a. At such an order.
b. Sc. companies of the good.*
c. Into the people of the earth who must be judged.*
d. I.e. into hell, where many shall suffer the wrath of God.

14:19 (b) *Only in Rusch.] (c) *Only in Rusch. Latin 588's Vulgate text lacks the words "into the earth".] 1 In Latin *refrigerium*, literally "refreshing", "cooling", figuratively "solace", "comfort".] 2 Not in Latin 588. The same Latin word, *lacus*, is used here for both "press" and "pit".

14:20 (a)and the press was trodden (b)without the (c)city, and (d)(e)blood came forth out of the press, (f)(g)up to the horse bridles, (h)for (i)(j)a thousand (k)six (l)hundred furlongs.

Horse bridles. The horses that carry the others are wicked masters; the bridles by which they are directed are devils, who shall be heavily punished with those they have seduced.[1]

a. I.e. they were punished and put in hell.
b. Because that punishment will not be purgatory.
c. Sc. heavenly.*
d. That is the punishment for sin.*
e. Not wine which would be put* in God's cellar.
f. I.e. up to the point of punishing the leaders of the wicked themselves, i.e. the devils.
g. I.e. up to the leaders of the inferiors.*
h. I.e. throughout* all the voluptuous people playing with vanities.**
i. All those who are detained by the games* of the world, i.e. by riches**: those who are simply perfect in this, which we have in "six" — i.e. they are wicked in all their works*** — the more perfect in "hundred", the most perfect in "a thousand".
j. Those who are perfect in evil.*
k. The lesser ones.*
l. The middling ones.*

14:20 (c) *Instead of this, Codex 24 has: "The Church and the congregation of the good, which is the sanctified city". Codex 24 has nothing.] (d) *Codex 24 and Rusch: "Eternal punishment for sin".] (e) *Codex 24 and Rusch: "is put".] (g) *Only in Rusch.] (h) *Same Latin word as "for" in the verse, but translating differently depending on context. **Only in Rusch.] (i) *The Latin equivalent of "furlong" is *stadium*, whose principal meanings are those the word has kept in English. **Rusch: "vices". The Latin words look similar enough. ***The words between the dashes are only in Latin 588.] (j) *Only in Rusch.] (k) *Only in Rusch.] (l) *Only in Rusch.] 1 Only in Latin 588.

CHAPTER 15

15:1 *(a)AND I saw (b)another sign (c)in heaven great and (d)marvelous: (e)seven (f)angels having (g)(h)the seven last plagues. Because (i)in them (j)the wrath of God is consummate.*

    a.   In addition.*
    b.   I.e. a figure signifying something else.
    c.   Because those who are signified live* in heaven.
    d.   Because it is amazing that a man should have such great power that he is able to damn others.
    e.   All the just.*
    f.   I.e. preachers.
    g.   Enjoined to them by God.
    h.   I.e. all blinding and destruction of those who shall be there in the time of the Antichrist.
    i.   I.e. through those just people.*
    j.   They will really have the plagues because they will carry out the wrath of God*, and they will really have the last ones because after these God will not inflict any others in the world.

In the three visions described above, that is, in the revelation of mysteries, in the giving of the trumpets, and in the woman's fight against the Devil, he has followed the order from the beginning of redemption to the Day of Judgment. In the three following ones, on the other hand, he dwells on the last times, because, about the preceding ones, things have been said more clearly in other divine Scriptures, whereas about the following ones but little has been said and more obscurely. So, in this fifth vision, the subject is seven angels holding vials in which are contained plagues, i.e. the destructions of the wicked who shall be there in the time of the Antichrist; and this destruction very much encourages the people of the present to endure.

In the three visions. He says "three" whereas four were mentioned earlier, but, omitting the first one that concerned the correction of the churches, he mentions the three others; this should be considered. [1]

On the virtue and power of the just against the wicked.[2]

15:1 (a) *Only in Latin 588.] (c) *Latin 588: "the one who is signified lives".] (e) *Only in Latin 588.] (i) *Only in Latin 588.] (j) *Codex 24 and Rusch add "on the wicked".] 1 Not in Latin 588] 2 Only in Latin 588.

15:2 *And (a)I saw (b)as it were a sea of glass (c)mingled with fire, and them (d)that overcame (e)the beast and (f)his image and (g)the number of his name, (h)standing upon the sea of glass, (i)having the harps of God:*

    a.   With them.*
    b.   I.e. baptism, where purity of faith is achieved and people are cleansed of vices.
    c.   Because to those who are baptized in it, the Holy Spirit is given.
    d.   I.e. that were not seduced.*
    e.   I.e. the Antichrist.
    f.   Either literally or similarity to him.*
    g.   Those who were not deceived by it.
    h.   They stand who keep the grace of baptism unimpaired.
    i.   I.e. mortifying the flesh, as God has enjoined to them, or as he first did himself.

15:2 (a) *Codex 24 and Rusch: "With those angels".] (d) *Only in Latin 588.] (f) *Codex 24 and Rusch: "Those who imitated his similarity or his life."

15:3 *and (a)singing the song of Moses the servant of God, and (b)the song of the Lamb, (c)saying, (d)Great and (e)marvelous (f)are your works Lord God Omnipotent: (g)just and true are your (h)ways King of the worlds*.*

    a.   I.e. fulfilling with exultation the song, i.e. the old law, which is an exultation to those who understand it well*.
    b.   I.e. the New Testament.
    c.   I.e. reminding others.
    d.   In the first creation.
    e.   In the resurrection.*
    f.   Because you fashioned man marvelously and remolded him still more marvelously.*
    g.   Faith and mercy.*
    h.   God's dispositions by which we come to him or he himself comes to us. They are just because they give back* to each person according to their merit and true because they lead where they promise to.

15:3 In the verse: *Codex 24 and Rusch have "King of saints" instead of "King of the worlds", and both books mention the "worlds" variant in a gloss.] (a) *Codex 24 and Rusch add: "i.e. spiritually".] (e) *Codex 24 and Rusch: "In the recreation".] (f) *Only in Latin 588.] (g) *Only in Latin 588.] (h) *Latin 588: "are given back".

15:4 (a)*Who shall not* (b)*fear you O Lord, and* (c)*magnify* (d)*your name?* (e)*Because you only are holy,* (f)*because all nations shall* (g)*come, and* (h)*adore* (i)*in your sight,* (j)*because your judgments be manifest.*

    a.   Therefore.
    b.   I.e. serve you out of love*.
    c.   By work and preaching.
    d.   Not that of another.*
    e.   And they will really fear, because you freely save.
    f.   And they will really magnify it, because all nations, i.e. some people out of all...
    g.   Sc. with faith.
    h.   In spirit and truth (John 4:24).
    i.   I.e. in your good pleasure.*
    j.   And they will really magnify, because the faithful will realize that if you choose some and reject some others, it is according to justice.*

15:4 (b) *Codex 24 and Rusch: "out of fear".] (d) *Only in Latin 588. The reading is actually *non aliis*, which would mean "not for others" (unless it be *non alus*, which does not mean anything; two i's and one u can look very much alike in those manuscripts), but since it does not make a lot of sense to me, and given the similar glosses already met (14:2 (h); 14:13 (k)), I think it is likely to be a mistranscription for *non alius*, "not that of another".] (i) *Not in Codex 24.] (j) *Codex 24 and Rusch have "And they will really magnify it" as an interlinear above "because your judgments be manifest", and "Because you choose some and reject some others for the faithful to realize that it is according to justice" as a marginal gloss, preceded in Rusch by a tag to "your judgments be manifest".

15:5 And after (a)*these things* (b)*I looked,* (c)*and behold* (d)*the temple of* (e)*the tabernacle* (f)*of testimony was opened* (g)*in heaven:*

    a.   Sc. the things that were said before.*
    b.   I.e. I learned from the Spirit revealing it to me.*
    c.   The mysteries of the Church, in which God dwells and which fights for God's honor, were revealed. Or the Scriptures were opened, which truly testify to God, i.e. which contain in themselves Old and New Testament.*
    d.   I.e. the secrets or sacraments of Christ.*
    e.   The Church.*
    f.   I.e. which is contained in the Old and in the New Testament.*
    g.   I.e. in the Church.*

After showing that those angels have the power to strike with plagues, as he is about to say what plagues they will inflict, he gives a reason that shows that those who shall suffer those plagues are worthy of it, that is, because all mysteries of the Church were revealed to all those who wished to enter, and those people cannot understand them due to their bad merit.

15:5 (a) *Only in Rusch.] (b) *Only in Rusch. The Latin word translated in the verse as "I looked" basically means "I saw".] (c) *The part starting from "Or the Scriptures, etc." is only in Latin 588, but see (f).] (d) *Only in Rusch.] (e) *Not in Latin 588. Rusch: "The Church Militant".] (f) *Not in Latin 588 as such, though it is clearly a variant of the end of (c). Rusch has still a different variant: "I.e. which contains in itself Old and New Testament." The "which" of Rusch's version should refer to the Church, while that of Codex 24 should refer to the testimony (it is possible to tell thanks to the difference of grammatical gender between those words in Latin).] (g) *Only in Latin 588.

15:6 (a)*and there issued forth the seven angels, having* (b)(c)*the seven plagues,* (d)*from* (e)*the temple:* (f)*dressed with* (g)*clean and* (h)*white* (i)*linen,* (j)(k)*and girded about the breasts* (l)*with girdles of gold.*

    a.   And because the mysteries are revealed, preachers will issue forth and convict those who do evil. By the seven angels we understand all the preachers sent by God.*
    b.   I.e. plenitude of understanding of the Scriptures, which are the plagues.*
    c.   Judicial sentences. Seven for the whole number of the damned.*
    d.   Sent by Jesus Christ.*
    e.   For those who are the Church.
    f.   I.e. strengthened.*
    g.   From vices.
    h.   With virtues.*
    i.   I.e. strength, Christ, or innocence.*
    j.   Sc. as a sign of the mystery* of the superiors.
    k.   Restraining even evil thoughts.
    l.   With the bond of love.

15:6 (a) *Codex 24 does not have the second sentence, and instead of it Rusch has "I.e. all the preachers" as a separate gloss above "the seven Angels".] (b) *Only in Rusch.] (c) *Only in Latin 588.] (d) *Only in Rusch.] (e) and (f) *In Codex 24 and Rusch, these two glosses are modified and conflated into one gloss saying "after they strengthened those who are the Church".] (g) *Rusch has here "because without sin" and has "from vices" above "white". Latin 588 has "great" instead of "clean" in the verse.] (h) *Rusch has here, beside "from vices" which I mentioned above, "because of their way of life", and it has "with virtues" above "and girded about".] (i) *Codex 24 only has "strength". Rusch has "Christ in baptism" and "strength". The Vulgate texts of all three books are actually saying "stone" instead of "linen".] (j) *Lat. *misterii*. Maybe a mistranscription for *ministerii*, "of the office". This gloss is only in Rusch.

15:7 And (a)*one of the four* (b)*beasts* (c)*gave to the seven* (d)*angels seven* (e)*vials of gold full of the wrath of the God that* (f)*lives* (g)*forever and ever.*

a. Because they will have what they preach from the teaching of the first fathers, who are all said to be one because they teach one and the same thing.

b. I.e. the earliest preachers, or Christ himself, who was the four beasts.*

c. I.e. it made them into vessels containing the wrath of God, illumined with divine wisdom.

d. I.e. preachers.*

e. I.e. hearts.*

f. Sc. and can punish.*

g. I.e. for eternity.*

Of the wrath (Lat. iracundiae). I.e. of the wrath (Lat. *irae*)[1], because they correct, reprove, and threaten sinners with the wrath of God, and sometimes even excommunicate.[2]

15:7 (b) *Only in Rusch. Latin 588 has at this place the sign which serves to indicate the beginning of an interlinear gloss, but with nothing following, as if the scribe had either forgotten to write the gloss or put the sign where he should not have.] (d) *Only in Rusch.] (e) *Only in Latin 588.] (f) *Only in Rusch.] (g) *Only in Rusch. This gloss (Lat. *in aeternum*) could as well be translated as "forever", which would make it look as if it were simply repeating the same word as the verse; but see note to 10:6 (c) concerning the literal meaning of Lat. *in saecula saeculorum*, translated by "forever and ever".] 1 Lat. *iracundia* basically means "irascibility", the meaning "wrath" being a secondary one developed later, whereas *ira* is the basic word for "wrath".] 2 Not in Latin 588.

15:8 (a)*And* (b)*the temple was filled* (c)*with smoke* (d)*at the majesty of God, and at his power: and* (e)(f)*no man could* (g)*enter into the temple,* (h)(i)*till the seven plagues of the seven angels were consummate.*

a. And although all things will then be open to all the faithful's view, they will however be closed and obscure to the unfaithful.

b. I.e. the Scripture, sc. as far as the wicked are concerned.*

c. I.e. with obscurity.

d. I.e. from the presence of God.

e. Of the reprobates.

f. Because to him to whom he shuts, no man opens (Rev. 3:7).

g. Sc. through true understanding, because *their malice has blinded them* (Wisdom 3:21).*

h. He opens in punishment the eyes which fault shuts.*

i. Nor afterwards.*

It makes reference to the story of the old law.[1]

Enter. I.e. understand that secret judgment of God, why he chooses some and rejects some others, till the saints get to know it clearly in the end of the world. Or enter the Church, till the thorough damnation of the wicked is complete in the judgment, because it is certain that they will not enter after that.

15:8 (b) *Only in Rusch.] (g) *Only in Rusch.] (h) *Only in Rusch.] (i) *Only in Latin 588.] 1 Only in Latin 588. The reference in question might be to Exodus 19:18.

CHAPTER 16

16:1 AND I heard a great ^(a)voice ^(b)out of the temple, saying to the seven angels: ^(c)Go, and ^(d)pour out the seven vials of the wrath of God ^(e)upon the earth.

    a.   A divine inspiration or some injunction.
    b.   I.e. from heaven or the Church.
    c.   For they must not preach unless they are sent.*
    d.   I.e. announce to the sinners the punishments owed to them.*
    e.   I.e. upon those who are attached to earthly things, or upon people of the earth.*

Go, and pour out. You who are good, as far as you are concerned, progress, and carry out damnation on the wicked.

"Progress" refers to "go" and "carry out" to "pour out".[1]

16:1 (c) *Only in Rusch.] (d) *Only in Rusch.] (e) *Not in Codex 24. Rusch has only "upon people of the earth".] 1 Not in Latin 588.

16:2 And ^(a)the first went, and poured out his ^{(b)(c)}vial ^(d)upon the earth, and ^(e)there was made ^{(f)(g)(h)}a cruel and ^{(i)(j)}very sore wound upon ^{(k)(l)}men that had the ^(m)character ⁽ⁿ⁾of the beast, and upon them that ^(o)adored ^(p)the image thereof.

    a.   I.e. the first order of preachers.*
    b.   Judicial power, even while, at present, they announce that they are to be damned.*
    c.   I.e. preaching.*
    d.   Literally, the apostles first preached to the Jews, i.e. upon the Jews loving earthly things.*
    e.   Upon those who had been seduced.*
    f.   Disobedience is the reason why that wound is made.*
    g.   A noxious and also incurable damnation.*
    h.   Sc. they were blinded with regards to understanding.*
    i.   Because they do not want to receive Christ.*
    j.   Sc. with regards to effect.*
    k.   Who are the seat of the Antichrist.*
    l.   Sc. those who will receive the Antichrist instead of Christ.*
    m.   I.e. faith.*
    n.   Of the Antichrist; or those who are designated are the greedy who live similarly to the beast.*
    o.   PSAL. *The idols of the gentiles are silver and gold* (Ps. 113:12).*
    p.   I.e. those who are similar to him.*

As these angels are already preaching and the things they preach are manifest, and yet some people refuse to enter, they have the occasion to strike with plagues, and a divine injunction to do so.

16:2 (a) *Only in Rusch.] (b) *Only in Latin 588.] (c) *Not in Codex 24.] (d) *Only in Rusch.] (e) *Only in Latin 588.] (f) *Not in Latin 588.] (g) *Codex 24 and Rusch have only "I.e. a noxious damnation".] (h) *Only in Rusch.] (i) *Only in Rusch.] (j) *Only in Rusch.] (k) *Only in Latin 588.] (l) *Only in Rusch.] (m) *Only in Rusch.] (n) *Only in Rusch.] (o) *Only in Rusch.] (p) *Rusch has "I.e. upon those who are similar to his preachers". Codex 24 has nothing here.

16:3 And ^(a)the second angel poured out ^(b)his vial ^{(c)(d)}upon the sea, ^(e)and there was made ^(f)blood ^(g)as it were of one dead: and ^(h)every ⁽ⁱ⁾living soul ^(j)died ^(k)in the sea.

    a.   In office.*
    b.   His preaching of the divine vengeance.*
    c.   Upon those who beat the saints.
    d.   Upon the lustful.*
    e.   I.e. damnation was inflicted on them for the blood they shed.
    f.   I.e. vengeance for the blood they shed.*
    g.   Because they shall not rise again from that damnation.
    h.   I.e. all those who consent; because they seem to live, because they do not persecute openly, but they shall be damned for their consent.
    i.   I.e. which seemed to live.*
    j.   Like the philosophers.*
    k.   I.e. in the bitterness of heathenism.*

Blood. I.e. that damnation will be as it were of one dead, i.e. irrevocable. For as a dead man does not come back to life, so will that sentence of damnation not be revoked.[1]

16:3 (a) *Not in Codex 24.] (b) *Only in Rusch.] (d) *Only in Rusch.] (f) *Only in Rusch.] (i) *Only in Rusch.] (j) *Only in Latin 588.] (k) *Only in Rusch.] 1 Not in Latin 588.

16:4 And the third poured out his vial (a)upon the rivers and the fountains of waters: (b)and there was made (c)blood.

    a.   Against the Antichrist's pseudo-apostles who will pervert either more important or less important Scriptures.

    b.   Because these people shall similarly be damned for the blood they have shed corporally and spiritually.

    c.   I.e. vengeance and retribution for their sins.*

16:4 (c) *Only in Rusch.

16:5 And I heard (a)the (b)angel (c)of the waters, (d)saying: You are (e)just O (f)Lord, (g)(h)which are, and (i)which were, (j)the Holy One, (k)because you have* judged these things:

    a.   I.e. the leading preachers, sc. the apostles.*

    b.   Guardian.*

    c.   Of the Scriptures or of the peoples.*

    d.   I.e. praising in his inward emotion.*

    e.   Sc. by keeping equity.*

    f.   Sc. by presiding over all.*

    g.   He does not say "which shall come" because he understands that it will happen soon.

    h.   Sc. immutably.*

    i.   Sc. essentially.*

    j.   Sc. formally and effectively.*

    k.   Who have damned those wicked by our agency.

I heard, i.e. I understood, the very preachers[1] who will do this retribution attributing it not to themselves, but to the Lord, and affirming that it is done justly.

In the sixth seal and in the sixth angel he often spoke of the same wicked, but in this respect, that he showed what and how great tribulations they inflicted on saints, and even if there was some word there concerning the damnation of the wicked, it was put incidentally in order to encourage the suffering ones; here, on the other hand, he speaks only about the plagues which they themselves inflict on the wicked[2]. [3]

16:5 In the verse: Latin 588 and Rusch have "who have" instead of "because you have". Only one letter of a word differs between the two in Latin.] (a) *Only in Latin 588.] (b) *Not in Latin 588.] (c) *Only in Rusch.] (d) *Only in Rusch.] (e) *Only in Rusch.] (f) *Only in Rusch.] (h) *Only in Rusch.] (i) *Only in Rusch.] (j) *Only in Rusch.] 1 Codex 24: "all the preachers".] 2 Codex 24 and Rusch: "which the saints themselves will inflict on the wicked".] 3 In Codex 24 and Rusch, this gloss is placed earlier, somewhere near verse 1 or 2.

16:6 because (a)they have shed the blood of the (b)saints* and (c)prophets, and you have given them (d)(e)blood to drink. (f)For they are worthy.

    a.   And they have perverted the Scriptures.*

    b.   The lesser ones.

    c.   The greater ones.

    d.   I.e. an eternal punishment for the shedding of blood, which they took pleasure in deserving.

    e.   I.e. an eternal punishment, and dreadful like blood.*

    f.   Because he who makes a sword, shall perish by the sword.*

16:6 In the verse: *Codex 24 and Rusch: "of the holy apostles".] (a) *Only in Latin 588.] (e) *Only in Rusch.] (f) *Only in Latin 588. Perhaps a mistranscription for something more like Matt. 26:52?

16:7 (a)And I heard (b)another (c)saying: (d)(e)Yes Lord God Omnipotent, (f)true and (g)just are your judgment.

    a.   I.e. the disciples confirm what the masters say.

    b.   I.e. their disciples*.

    c.   I.e. approving.*

    d.   Out of a great emotion, they turn their speech to the Lord.

    e.   What you say is true.

    f.   I.e. doing what they promise.

    g.   For it is just that he who has shed blood should drink the vengeance of blood.

16:7 (b) *Codex 24 and Rusch have "disciple" in the singular.] (c) *Only in Rusch.

16:8 And the fourth angel poured out his vial (a)(b)upon the sun, and it was (c)given unto (d)him to afflict men with (e)(f)heat and (g)fire:

   a. I.e. upon the Antichrist, who says that he is the sun of the world.
   b. Upon vainglory.*
   c. I.e. permitted by God.
   d. The Antichrist.
   e. Sc. of vanity.*
   f. I.e. a lesser tribulation.
   g. I.e. a greater one.*

16:8 (b) *Only in Rusch.] (e) *Only in Rusch.] (f) and (g) *In Rusch, there are inverted.

16:9 (a)and (b)men boiled (c)(d)with great heat, and (e)(f)blasphemed the name of God (g)having power over the plagues, (h)neither did they penance (i)to give him glory.

   a. I.e. some succumbed in that tribulation.
   b. Sc. faithful.*
   c. Sc. afflicted.*
   d. I.e. overcome by fear of the Antichrist.*
   e. Sc. with their hearts and with their mouths.*
   f. That is, saying, "God is unjust because he lets us be afflicted".*
   g. Because he gives to whom he wants and takes back from whom he wants.
   h. I.e. they did not return to their senses.*
   i. Even if they were sorry in their hearts, they did not dare to profess it.

And men boiled. Or the afflicted will cause their torturers to be affected with the heat of wrath when they are found to be unconquerable[1], and so they "boiled" with envy and wrath.[2]

Neither did they, etc. Inwardly, they repented and were sorry, but they did not dare to confess it outwardly.[3]

16:9 (b) *Only in Rusch.] (c) *Only in Rusch.] (d) *Only in Latin 588.] (e) *Only in Rusch.] (f) *Only in Latin 588.] (h) *Rusch adds: "and did not confess their sin".] 1 Rusch has "inseparable". Most probably a mistranscription: the difference is only in two letters: unconquerable = *insuperabiles*; inseparable = *inseparabiles*, and *per* and *par* are abbreviated the same way.] 2 Not in Latin 588.] 3 Not in Latin 588.

16:10 And the fifth angel poured out his vial (a)upon the seat (b)of the beast: and (c)his kingdom was made (d)dark, (e)(f)and they together did eat their tongues (g)for pain:

   a. I.e. upon all those in whom he sits.*
   b. Of the Antichrist.*
   c. I.e. the seat itself.
   d. I.e. more blinded.
   e. I.e. they fed themselves with one another's evil speech.*
   f. By detracting from the truth.*
   g. I.e. for the envy they have towards saints.

Upon the seat. Because it is only bodies, and not spirits, upon which he will sit, because he will give physical things and not spiritual ones.[1]

They together did eat their tongues, etc. All feeding themselves with mutual evil-speaking against one another.[2]

16:10 (a) *Codex 24 has "I.e. upon each body", going on in the other ink, "of the wicked in which he sits"; Rusch has two glosses; "I.e. upon each body" and "I.e. ministers".] (b) *Only in Rusch.] (e) *Another interpretation is in theory possible: "They fed themselves with evil speech against one another", which would agree with the second marginal gloss; but, as you see, this second marginal gloss is not in Latin 588, which is the most ancient of the three books I have used, so there is always a possibility for it to be a later reinterpretation.] (f) *Only in Rusch.] 1 Not in Latin 588.] 2 Not in Latin 588.

16:11 and they (a)blasphemed the God of heaven because of their (b)pains and (c)wounds, and (d)did not penance from their works.

   a. Saying that he was a magician.*
   b. The plagues inflicted on them by which they are blinded.
   c. Which they did to themselves by the eating of the tongues.
   d. I.e. they were unrepentant to the very end.*

16:11 (a) *Rusch adds: "and a mere creature".] (d) *Only in Rusch.

16:12 And the sixth angel ^(a)poured out his vial ^(b)upon that great river ^(c)Euphrates: and ^(d)dried up the water thereof that a way might be prepared to the kings from the rising of the sun.

    a.   I.e. preached the wrath of God.*
    b.   Upon those who overflow with all riches and afflict others with them.*
    c.   Fertile.*
    d.   I.e. they will proclaim that the affluence of the world must be dried up soon.

He saw the pouring out of the vial upon them, and that they were not corrected but precipitated into a greater blinding.[1]

That a way might be prepared, etc. Because when the world has ended, there will be the resurrection of the faithful, who will come from the rising of the sun, i.e. from Christ, when he has started shining, i.e. manifesting himself. Another translation has "to the king", i.e. to Christ[2].

The rising of the sun. Christ is the risen sun; God the Father is what he rises from; the kings are the just who come from God the Father, and go through Christ to God the Father.[3]

16:12 (a) *Only in Rusch.] (b) *Codex 24 and Rusch: "Upon all those who overflow with riches".] (c) *Codex 24: ""Euphrates" translates as "fertile""; Rusch: ""Euphrates" translates as "fertility"".] 1 In Codex 24 and Rusch, this gloss is to the beginning of the next verse with "I saw" (clearly as a tag in Rusch) in the beginning instead of "he saw".] 2 The part concerning the other translation is not in Latin 588.] 3 Only in Latin 588.

16:13 ^(a)And I saw ^(b)from the mouth of the dragon, and ^(c)from the mouth of the beast, and ^{(d)(e)}from the mouth of the false prophet ^(f)three ^(g)unclean spirits in manner of ^(h)frogs.

    a.   Sc. to attack the Church.*
    b.   I.e. from the inspiration of the Devil.
    c.   I.e. from the words of the Antichrist.*
    d.   I.e. from the words of the apostles of the Antichrist.
    e.   I.e. from the counsel.*
    f.   Sc. because of the subtlety of their wickedness in denying faith in the Trinity.*
    g.   Because of their works of uncleanness.*
    h.   Such are the hypocrites.*

Three unclean spirits. That is, all the wicked, who, for their excessive evilness, are worthy to be called unclean spirits; or the very demons they generate in the hearts of others.[1]

Frogs. Frogs live in mud, are garrulous, and take quietness away from others: so do those people. And they jump on high with pride, but soon fall back.[2]

16:13 (a) *Only in Rusch.] (c) *Missing in Codex 24 and Rusch. Rusch also has (d) instead of (b) and (b) instead of (c), and Codex 24 has (d) instead of (c), but Latin 588's order obviously makes more sense.] (e) *Only in Rusch.] (f) *Only in Rusch.] (g) *Only in Rusch.] (h) *Only in Rusch.] 1 Codex 24 and Rusch add: "As the faithful by their teaching generate Christ's faith in the hearts of others, so do these people by their evilness generate a devil".] 2 The part "And they jump, etc." only in Latin 588.

16:14 ^(a)For they are the spirits of devils working ^(b)signs, and ^(c)they go forth to the kings ^(d)of the whole earth ^(e)to gather them ^(f)into battle ^(g)at the ^(h)great day of Omnipotent God.

    a.   Really unclean.
    b.   I.e. miracles.
    c.   Sc. sent by the Antichrist.*
    d.   I.e. of this world.*
    e.   Sc. not with regards to unity of place but to unity of agreement and evil will.*
    f.   Sc. against the faithful.
    g.   But to their own detriment, because they shall quickly be led to the Day of Judgment.
    h.   Future.*

16:14 (c) *Only in Rusch.] (d) *Codex 24 and Rusch: "Of the world".] (e) *Only in Rusch.] (h) *Only in Latin 588.

16:15 ^(a)Behold I come ^(b)as a thief: ^(c)Blessed is he ^(d)that watches, and keeps ^(e)his garments, that he ^(f)walk not ^(g)naked, and ^(h)they see ⁽ⁱ⁾his shame.

    a.   He will really come, because he himself affirms it.
    b.   Surprising* people in their sleep.
    c.   And therefore.
    d.   I.e. that worries about his salvation.
    e.   I.e. the innocence received in baptism.
    f.   I.e. rise.
    g.   In virtues.
    h.   I.e. the saints.*
    i.   I.e. his sins.

16:15 (b) *Codex 24 and Rusch: "killing".] (h) *Rusch: "The saints and angels".

16:16 ^(a)*And* ^(b)*he shall gather them into a place which in Hebrew is called* ^(c)*Armageddon.*

    a.   They go forth to gather, and they shall gather.
    b.   The Devil himself, who is in all of them.*
    c.   I.e. "mont of thieves" or "spherical* mont", i.e. the Antichrist**.

They go forth[1]/he shall gather. The demons go forth and the Devil shall gather, because they are all one.[2]

And he shall gather them into a place. That is, they will make them have trust in the Antichrist, who is a consolation[3] for all those who want to steal their faith from saints, and[4] to whom all the wicked of various sects will conglomerate[5].

16:16 (b) *Not in Latin 588.] (c) *The noun *globus*, "sphere", of which the adjective *globosus*, "spherical", is derived, can also mean a band, crowd, or clique. Might something of this meaning be intended here? **"I.e. the Antichrist" only in Latin 588.] 1 From verse 14.] 2 Not in Latin 588.] 3 Codex 24 and Rusch: "refuge".] 4 Codex 24 and Rusch: "or".] 5 Rusch: "will pride themselves". Most probably just a mistranscription. The Latin words look somewhat similar.

16:17 And the seventh angel poured out his vial ^(a)*upon the air, and there* ^(b)*came forth a* ^(c)*loud voice* ^(d)*out of the temple from* ^(e)*the throne, saying:* ^(f)*It is done.*

    a.   I.e. against the Devil*, whose place is the air.
    b.   I.e. came manifestly.
    c.   I.e. announcing great things.
    d.   I.e. out of the Church.
    e.   Which the Church received from God.
    f.   I.e. all things are consummate; the end of the world is there.

Having shown upon whom the angels pour out the vials, he adds what happens to the wicked themselves because of this pouring out: that is, that here they will resist as much as they can, as if they had received an increase in strength[1] from that pouring out, but they shall eventually be thrust down into hell.

16:17 (a) *Codex 24 and Rusch have "devils" in the plural.] 1 Codex 24: "as if they had received a sacrament". The Latin words look similar enough.

16:18 ^(a)*And there were made* ^(b)*lightnings, and* ^(c)*voices, and* ^(d)*thunders, and* ^(e)*a great earthquake was made, such a one as never has been* ^(f)*since men were upon the earth,* ^(g)*such an earthquake* ^(h)*so great.*

    a.   And there were made by those wicked, or by those seven good angels...*
    b.   I.e. miracles.
    c.   I.e. flatteries.
    d.   I.e. threats.
    e.   I.e. the wicked will be roused against the saints.*
    f.   Since the time of Abel, who was the first one to tread the earth.*
    g.   I.e. so ugly in quality*.
    h.   So severe in quantity*.

It is about the effect of the pouring out of the vials.[1]

16:18 (a) *Codex 24 and Rusch: "By those wicked or by those good ones".] (e) *Not in Latin 588.] (f) *Codex 24 and Rusch: "Since the time of Abel, who was the first one to tread, i.e. to despise, the earth, or who was the first just man".] (g) "In quality" only in Latin 588.] (h) *"In quantity" only in Latin 588.] 1 Only in Latin 588.

16:19 ^(a)*And* ^(b)*the* ^(c)*great city was made* into ^(d)*three parts: and the cities* ^(e)*of the Gentiles fell. And* ^(f)*Babylon the great* ^(g)*came* ^(h)*into memory before God, to give her the cup of wine* ⁽ⁱ⁾*of the indignation of his wrath.*

    a.   Because there is before the law, under the law, and after the law.*
    b.   I.e. the collection of the reprobates.*
    c.   For the heap of its vices.*
    d.   Sc. Jews, pagans, and bad Christians.*
    e.   I.e. of those who lived heathenly.*
    f.   I.e. the collection of sinners.*
    g.   I.e. God remembered the sins which he previously seemed to have forgotten.
    h.   Sc. to punish.*
    i.   Which comes from him when he is indignant and angry.*

And the great city was made into three parts. Because of this damnation and because of their sins which they add, the city itself was damned, and punishment was distributed to each one according to their merit, that is, to the Jews, to the Gentiles, and to the false Christians.

The cities. I.e. all the collections of the wicked remaining in the first generation fell[1].

In the carnal generation, not in the second spiritual regeneration.[2]

As if he were saying, "When I saw them condemned for every bit of money, I understood that they were to be punished".[3]

To give her the cup. So that God himself might give them a punishment proportional to the pleasures they had in the world[4].

God requites the wicked according to their merits, i.e. he requites them what they deserve, but not as much as they deserve[5], so that in the very retribution, where justice is obvious, there is also mercy. For *all the ways of the Lord are mercy and truth* (Ps. 24:10). To the good also he gives according to their merits, and more than they deserve, so that mercy there prevails over justice.[6]

16:19 In the verse: *Rusch: "broken". Only one letter differs.] (a) *Only in Latin 588.] (b) *Only in Rusch.] (c) *Only in Latin 588.] (d) *Not in Latin 588. Codex 24 has "Jews, Gentiles, and false Christians" in the other ink.] (e) *Only in Rusch.] (f) *Only in Rusch.] (h) *Only in Rusch.] (i) *Codex 24 goes on "in the world". Possibly words that went astray from the marginal gloss on "to give her the cup".] 1 Codex 24 and Rusch: "shall be damned" instead of "fell".] 2 Only in Rusch.] 3 Only in Latin 588.] 4 "In the world" only in Latin 588. But see note to (i).] 5 "But not as much as they deserve" is missing in Codex 24.] 6 Not in Latin 588.

16:20 And every [(a)(b)]island [(c)]fled, and [(d)]mountains were not [(e)]found.

a. I.e. congregation of saints.*
b. People beaten by the waves, sc. the waves of the world.*
c. Sc. the society of the reprobates and their punishment.*
d. I.e. people high in virtues.*
e. Sc. by the torments of the Antichrist.*

That is, I saw that all those who were afflicted for God in the world and outstanding in virtues, by consideration of these punishments, avoided the frequentation of the wicked during their lives, and therefore were not found in their punishments.

16:20 (a) *Only in Rusch.] (b) *Only in Latin 588.] (c) *Only in Rusch.] (d) *Only in Latin 588.] (e) *Rusch: "Sc. in the punishment". Codex 24 has nothing here.

16:21 And [(a)]great hail [(b)]like a talent came down from [(c)]heaven upon men: and [(d)(e)]men [(f)]blasphemed God for the plague of the hail: because it was made [(g)]exceedingly great.

a. I.e. eternal punishment that will beat them.
b. Heavy and proportional.
c. Sc. sent by God.*
d. I.e. suffering*, put in hell, even though they know that they are punished deservedly, they will nonetheless be grieved at the fact that God has such great power that he inflicts plagues on them.*
e. I.e. impatient ones.*
f. Sc. saying that he is unjust.*
g. I.e. torturing them intolerably.*

The big talent weighs a hundred twenty pounds, the medium one seventy-two, and the small one fifty. Here he is talking about the medium one, because sinners in the seventy-two tongues shall not escape this vengeance.

16:21 (c) *Only in Rusch.] (d) *"Suffering" only in Latin 588. **Codex 24 and Rusch add "and this is blasphemy". Codex 24 has "etc." after it, as if it were supposed to be the beginning of a quote, but the words "this is blasphemy" are too little to enable me to find where it is from, if indeed it is a quote.] (e) *Not in Latin 588. Rusch has "I.e. impatient and lustful ones".] (f) *Only in Rusch.] (g) *Only in Rusch.

CHAPTER 17

17:1 ^(a)*And there came one of the seven angels which had the seven vials, and spoke with me, saying, ^(b)Come, I will show you ^(c)the damnation of the great harlot, which sits upon many waters,*

    a.   The angel here has the role of the one who teaches, and John that of the one who learns.

    b.   Through understanding.*

    c.   I.e. the cause of the damnation of the wicked, who, forsaking the Creator, fornicate with the Devil by worshiping idols, loving earthly things, and serving uncleanness.

After describing the plagues preachers will inflict in the time of the Antichrist and the eternal damnation the wicked shall suffer from that, he is reminded[1] to consider the causes of damnation itself. As if he were saying: I have shown you what will happen in that future; now beware, you in the present, because the same Devil who will then deceive thus openly, secretly deceives every day and will lead people to the same destruction as he will then lead them.

This great harlot is the Antichrist and the wicked who are there in his time. She already sits upon the waters, i.e. he already reigns over the wicked of the present, all of whom he is the head of.

Which sits, i.e. reigns over many peoples, which she attracts to her by lust. Whence the Lord to Job, *"His (the Devil's) strength is in his loins"* (Job 40:11) when he deceives men, whose seed-store is in their loins, and *"in the navel"* when he deceives women, whose seed is in their navels. Whence the prophet said to Jerusalem, as if to a harlot, *"In the day of your nativity",* i.e. in this time, *"your navel was not cut",* i.e. you did not restrain your lust (Ezekiel 16:4).

17:1 (b) *In Codex 24 and Rusch, this gloss is duplicated; Codex 24 has it above "came" and above "come", Rusch above "one" and above "I will show".] 1 Rusch: "he reminds"; Codex 24: "... and the eternal damnation they shall suffer from that, the wicked are reminded...".

17:2 *with whom ^(a)the kings of the earth have fornicated, and ^(b)they which inhabit the earth have been drunk of the ^(c)wine of her ^(d)whoredom.*

    a.   I.e. the princes of the world.

    b.   Just as a drunk man is afraid of nothing, so are those who are eager for earthly things blinded to such a point* that they neither love God nor fear punishments.

    c.   I.e. delight.*

    d.   I.e. flagrant fornication.

17:2 (b) *Codex 24 and Rusch: "... so will those who are attached to earthly things be blinded to such a point by love of the earth..."] (c) *Only in Latin 588.

17:3 *And he took me away ^{(a)(b)}in spirit ^(c)into the desert. And I saw a woman sitting upon a ^(d)scarlet-colored beast, full of ^(e)names of blasphemy, having ^(f)seven heads, and ten horns.*

    a.   In a spiritual vision.*

    b.   Because such things cannot be seen with the physical eyes.*

    c.   I.e. into the reprobates' hearts.*

    d.   I.e. red with the shedding of the blood of saints.*

    e.   Because they say that the evil things they do please God.

    f.   I.e. the five senses of the body, then error, and finally the Antichrist: the seven things through which the Devil leads men to sin.

A woman. I.e. those voluptuous people who make themselves similar to Eve, from whom sin started, and who have the Devil as a foundation, who is bloody both in himself and in his people, either because they have shed blood, or because they understand God's words wrongly.

Ten horns. That is, the ten kingdoms there will be in the time of the Antichrist, by which others are understood.[1]

17:3 (a) *Only in Rusch.] (b) *Not in Latin 588.] (c) *Codex 24 and Rusch: "Into the reprobates' hearts deserted by God's grace".] (d) *Only in Latin 588.] 1 Not in Latin 588.

17:4 [a]*And the woman was clothed roundabout with* [b]*purple and scarlet, and* [c]*gilt with gold, and* [d]*precious stone, and* [e]*pearls,* [f]*having a golden cup in her hand, full of the* [g]*abomination and filthiness of her fornication.*

    a.   And because of that beast, such is this woman.
    b.   Because they kill those who refuse to assent to them.*
    c.   Because they will seem to be illuminated by divine wisdom.
    d.   I.e. carbuncle, that is, love, which they will say they possess.
    e.   I.e. other virtues.
    f.   I.e. having the divine Scripture, by which the faithful are given to drink for their salvation, in her hand, that is, in perverse interpretations.
    g.   I.e. because they ought to be rejected by men similarly to those interpretations, because they teach uncleanness of the flesh and to be unfaithful to God.

17:4 (b) *Above "scarlet" in Codex 24 and Rusch.] 1 "Fools" only in Latin 588.

Clothed roundabout with royal cloth, because they say that they are kings in order to deceive fools[1].

17:5 [a]*And in her forehead a name written,* [b]*"Mystery":* [c]*Babylon the great,* [d]*mother of the fornications and the abominations of the earth.*

    a.   Though she is so skillful in deceiving, yet do not despair, you faithful, because she has on her forehead, i.e. conspicuously, a sign, which is a mystery to the ignorant.
    b.   Sc. namely, this one.*
    c.   I.e. the great* confusion.
    d.   I.e. giving the example of doing sins for which earthly people shall be rejected from the faithful's salvation.

17:5 (b) *Not in Latin 588.] (c) *Codex 24: "insane".

17:6 [a]*And* [b]*I saw the woman* [c]*drunken of the blood* [d]*of the saints, and of the blood* [e]*of the martyrs of Jesus. And I marveled when I* [f]*had seen* [g]*her, with great admiration.*

    a.   I.e. I saw sin, and I also saw her damned for the sin.*
    b.   Namely, this.*
    c.   I.e. brought so low by the vengeance for the shedding of blood that she does not know where she is due to her excessive pains.
    d.   Of the lesser ones.
    e.   Of those who are not afraid to testify that Christ is God.
    f.   Elsewhere "was seeing".*
    g.   The woman.*

17:6 (a) *Codex 24: "I saw the sin of the world, and I also saw her damned for the sin"; Rusch: "I saw the sin of the world, and I also saw it damned for the sin."] (b) *Not in Latin 588.] (f) *Only in Rusch.] (g) *Only in Latin 588.

And I marveled. Here he has the role of those who, as they have seen wicked people exalted in the world, marvel when they hear the punishments promised to those same wicked. And since they are to be thus punished, they ask why God permits them to be exalted like that; but they are taught to understand that that exaltation has been given for a greater blinding, and that finally eternal damnation is justly inflicted on them.

17:7 And the angel said to me, [a]*Why do you marvel?* [b]*I will tell you* [c]*the mystery of the woman,* [d]*and of the beast that carries* [e]*her, which has the seven heads and the ten horns.*

    a.   As if he were saying, "Do not marvel, but understand what it is".
    b.   I.e. I will disclose it to you in such a way that you can understand.
    c.   I.e. what this woman signifies.*
    d.   I.e. why these wicked and the Devil who made them sin are punished, which is unknown except to the learned.
    e.   Sc. the woman.*

17:7 (c) *Only in Latin 588.] (e) *Only in Latin 588.] 1 Not in Latin 588.

The beast that carries her. The beast, i.e. the Devil, carries, i.e. governs, the woman, i.e. all the effeminate wicked; for he who governs others is said, as it were, to carry the burden of command.[1]

17:8 ^(a)*The beast which you saw,* ^{(b)(c)(d)}*was, and is not, and* ^{(e)(f)}*shall come up out of the bottomless depth, and* ^(g)*go into destruction: and* ^(h)*the inhabitants on the earth (whose names are not written in the book of life from the making of the world) shall marvel, seeing the beast that was, and is not.*

- a. I.e. the Devil, who makes people beast-like before the Antichrist's coming*.
- b. Before Christ's coming.*
- c. He reigned but a little.*
- d. Because he lost the right* when Christ was born.
- e. Because in the time of the Antichrist he will recover power.*
- f. He will have a place because he will find wicked people.
- g. Because once the Antichrist is dead, he shall no longer have a place*.
- h. When the wicked see their power thus annihilated, they will grieve, not as repentant ones, but only as marveling ones.

Was. Before Christ's coming, the Devil had very great power; but after it, though he did not completely lose his power, it was nonetheless not slightly weakened.[1]

Shall come up out of the bottomless depth. I.e. through those who are deep in sins, he shall come up into exaltation.[2]

17:8 (a) *"Before the Antichrist's coming" only in Latin 588.] (b) *Not in Latin 588. This gloss and the part of (a) that is found only in Latin 588 were very probably one, which was modified one way around or the other through mistranscription.] (c) *Only in Rusch.] (d) *Codex 24 and Rusch: "strength".] (e) *Not in Codex 24.] (g) *Codex 24 and Rusch: "the opportunity to tempt". The same word can translate as "place" and "opportunity", so there is only one more word in Codex 24 and Rusch, for "to tempt".] 1 Not in Latin 588.] 2 Not in Latin 588.

17:9 ^(a)*And here is understanding that has wisdom*.* ^(b)*The seven heads: are seven hills,* ^(c)*upon which the woman sits, and they are seven kings.*

- a. As if he were saying, "By a regard to this punishment, you can look out for yourselves".
- b. Because the Devil raises men to pride through these seven things.
- c. I.e. on which the unfaithful rely. Because he also leads to hell through these same things*.

17:9 In the verse: *The three books have "And here is understanding for him that has wisdom".] (c) *Codex 24 and Rusch: "Because he rules hell through these same things". The same verb, *regere*, means both "to lead" and "to rule", and the noun *rex*, "king", is from the same root as this verb.

17:10 ^(a)*Five are fallen,* ^(b)*one is, and* ^(c)*another is not yet come: and when he shall come,* ^(d)*he must tarry a short time.*

- a. Infancy being over.
- b. Error in mature age.
- c. I.e. the Antichrist, who will make the greatest violence, and will make people sin in other things.*
- d. But he is not to be feared, because...

Five are fallen. If Adam had continued in obedience, he would not be turned to any pleasure by the senses of the body[1]; but they have been so corrupted by sin that it is now natural to seek things that are soft to the touch, good-tasting, melodious[2], sweet-smelling, and beautiful to see. These are the five kings through whom the Devil governs men in childhood, because he was himself the cause for their being corrupted. These are the five husbands of the Samaritan woman (ref. John 4:18). In youth succeeds error; for once one has got discernment, if one sins, it is no longer imputed to the senses, but to error, concerning which the Lord said, *"he whom you now have is not your husband"*, because it is the spirit of error, which is an adulterer in the house of our flesh; because the legitimate husband is the spirit of reason, which rules over the five senses of the body as a master in his house rules over his servants. This spirit of reason the elect assume in the age of discernment[3].

Five. The five senses of the body, which error succeeds; the seventh is the Antichrist and his people; the Devil himself contains the seven; he who sins and shall be punished in himself and in others contains eight.[4]

17:10 (c) *Codex 24 and Rusch: "I.e. the Antichrist, who makes people sin most."] 1 Codex 24 and Rusch: "... the senses of the body would not be turned to any pleasure (sc. evil pleasure)...".] 2 "Melodious" only in Latin 588.] 3 The part starting from "because it is the spirit of error" is only in Latin 588.] 4 Only in Latin 588.

17:11 And (a)the beast which was, and is not: the same also is the eighth, and is of the seven, and goes into destruction.

    a.   The Antichrist.*

17:11 (a) *Not in Latin 588.

He *is of the seven* because he sins similarly, and shall be punished similarly, and *the eighth* because he surpasses them all in both wickedness and punishment.

17:12 (a)And the ten horns which you saw: are ten kings, which have not yet received kingdom, (b)but shall receive power as kings (c)one hour (d)after the beast.

    a.   In the time of the Antichrist, as Daniel says, there will be ten kingdoms (ref. Daniel 7:24), whose kings are signified by the horns.
    b.   Not really kings, but tyrants.
    c.   Therefore do not fear.
    d.   I.e. coming second after their head.

17:13 These have one (a)counsel and (b)force: and (c)their power (d)they shall deliver to the beast.

    a.   Sc. to deny Christ.
    b.   To believe in the Antichrist.*
    c.   Sc. which they have over themselves and others.*
    d.   Because they attribute him everything.

17:13 (a) and (b) *In Codex 24 and Rusch, these form one gloss above "one counsel".] (c) *Codex 24 and Rusch have "which they have in themselves" above "force" and "which they have over others" above "their power".]

17:14 (a)These shall fight with the Lamb, and (b)the Lamb shall overcome them, because he is (c)Lord of lords, and (d)King of kings, and they that are with him, (e)called, and elect, and (f)faithful.

    a.   Sc. in word and in work in order to take the faithful away from him.
    b.   Sc. by making his people resolute, and damning them in their head, i.e. with the Antichrist*.
    c.   Using even the wicked for the benefit of the faithful.
    d.   Therefore he will overcome the kings.
    e.   Either from eternity or through the preachers.*
    f.   Going on with the works.*

17:14 (b) *"I.e. with the Antichrist" only in Latin 588.] (e) *Codex 24 and Rusch have "through the preachers" above "called" and "from eternity" above "elect".] (f) *This gloss differs in Codex 24 in that it has one more word meaning "their", but not their own, "their" of other people (Latin can make this difference) — so maybe those of the preachers or Christ.

17:15 And he said to me, The waters which you saw where the harlot (a)sits: (b)are peoples, and nations, and tongues.

    a.   I.e. reigns through ministers.*
    b.   I.e. the present wicked gathered from the diversity of men. And therefore you should not make yourself similar to him, because those who are now attached to him shall grieve one day.*

17:15 (a) *Codex 24 and Rusch have "I.e. the Antichrist already reigns through the mystery". The Latin words for "ministers" and "mystery" resemble each other a lot. I am of the opinion that "ministers" is more likely to be the original reading.] (b) *In Codex 24 and Rusch, the second sentence, "And therefore etc.", is to the next verse.

17:16 And the ten horns which you saw in the beast: these shall hate the harlot, and shall make her (a)desolate and naked, and (b)shall eat her flesh, and (c)her they shall burn with fire.

    a.   Because the consolation of the Devil is the perdition of the wicked, which* he shall lose once the number of the pious** is completed.

    b.   I.e. they shall be tortured for her delights which they have become accustomed to, or they shall delight in the Devil's damnation.*

    c.   Sc. the flesh, because the Devil shall be punished with them and for their money.

The Devil has the power to make signs so as to deceive; he shall lose it once the number of the good is completed, because afterwards fornication[1] shall have no place.[2]

They are said to eat the flesh of the harlot because they will delight in inflicting torments.[3]

17:16 (a) *Codex 24 and Rusch: "whom". The Latin word used here for "lose" can also mean "to cause the destruction of"; but I think Latin 588's reading, with "which" referring to the consolation he shall lose, is the original one. **Codex 24 and Rusch: "impious".] (b) *Codex 24 and Rusch have, "That is, they shall be tortured for her delights which they have followed" (with, in Rusch, a tag to "shall burn with fire"), and do not have the second part.] (c) *Codex 24 and Rusch: "Because the Devil shall be punished with them and for their sins". "Money" in Latin 588's version most probably means something like "debts of sins", and a later copyist felt the need to clarify the meaning, giving the "sins" of Codex 24 and Rusch.] 1 Codex 24 and Rusch: "temptation".] 2 In Latin 588, the sign indicating what the gloss refers to is simply put at the beginning of the verse, but in Codex 24 and Rusch the gloss is preceded by a tag to "and naked".] 3 Not in Latin 588.

17:17 (a)For God has given (b)into their hearts, (c)to do that which pleases (d)him: (e)that they give their kingdom to the beast, (f)(g)till the words of God be consummate.

    a.   Deservedly, because he has blinded them according to their merits.

    b.   He has left it up to free will.*

    c.   Namely.

    d.   I.e. the beast.*

    e.   I.e. that they let themselves be ruled by the Devil.

    f.   Till they be fulfilled in deed. Concerning the promise of rewards or punishments.

    g.   I.e. the good and the wicked shall receive the things promised.

17:17 (b) *Only in Latin 588.] (d) *Only in Latin 588.

17:18 And the woman which you saw: is (a)the great city, which has kingdom (b)over the kings of the earth.

    a.   I.e. the multitude of the great*.

    b.   Because they* are extremely proud.

17:18 (a) *Codex 24 and Rusch: "of the wicked."] (b) *Codex 24 and Rusch: "the kings themselves."

CHAPTER 18

18:1 AND after these things I saw another (a)angel (b)coming down (c)from heaven, (d)having great power: and (e)the earth (f)was illuminated (g)of his glory.

- a. I.e. Christ.
- b. Sc. in* the flesh.
- c. I.e. from equality with the Father.
- d. With the Father according to his divinity, and according to his humanity; whence, now *all power is given to me in heaven and in earth* (Matt. 28:18).*
- e. I.e. the Church.
- f. Sc. the darkness of ignorance having been driven away.
- g. I.e. of his glorious preaching.

In this sixth vision, he treats the subject of the last punishments the wicked shall suffer in hell for every one of their sins; and he first shows what happens concerning Babylon, then concerning the beast and the false prophets, and finally concerning the Devil himself, in which the end is manifest[1]. As he is about to describe this damnation, he says by whom it was foretold[2], so as to be given more credence.

18:1 (b) *Codex 24 and Rusch: "into".] (d) *Only in Latin 588.] 1 Codex 24 and Rusch add: "in whose damnation the end will be".] 2 Codex 24 and Rusch: "he says that it was foretold by Christ."

18:2 And he (a)cried out (b)in force, saying, (c)Fallen fallen is Babylon the great: (d)and it is become (e)the habitation of devils, and (f)the custody of every unclean spirit, (g)and the custody of every unclean and hateful* bird:

- a. I.e. preached.
- b. What he said will not remain unaccomplished.
- c. Twice for the double damnation of soul and body, or because it* shall be punished eternally.
- d. And it shall fall because...
- e. I.e. a collection of devils.
- f. Because it keeps* itself for the Devil, or the Devil keeps it for himself.
- g. Devils in perverse hearts are unclean because of the enticements of the flesh, and they are birds because of the pride of the mind, or because they run about through this air.

18:2 In the verse: *"And hateful" not in Latin 588.] (c) *Codex 24 and Rusch: "they".] (f) *In Latin *custodire* = "to keep" > *custodia* = "custody", "the fact of keeping".

18:3 (a)because (b)all nations have drunk (c)of the wine of the wrath of her fornication*: and (d)the kings of the earth have fornicated with her: and (e)the merchants of the earth were made rich (f)by the virtue of her delicacies.

- a. And this for this reason.*
- b. I.e. some people of all nations.*
- c. I.e. of fornication, because of which God gets angry.
- d. I.e. the princes.*
- e. I.e. those who sell their souls by ambition for secular things.
- f. I.e. by the sins through which riches are acquired, because every rich man is either an unjust man or the heir of an unjust man.

18:3 In the verse: *Latin 588: "have drunk of the wrath of her fornication".] (a) *Only in Latin 588.] (b) *Only in Latin 588.] (d) *Codex 24 and Rusch: "I.e. the princes of the world".

18:4 And I heard another (a)voice from heaven, saying, (b)Go out from her my people: that you (c)be not partakers of her sins*, (d)and receive not of her plagues.

- a. I.e. a divine inspiration, either from Christ or from his preachers.*
- b. I.e. do not do her works.
- c. I.e. do not give your assent to those who sin.
- d. Because if you are different in life, you shall not be similar in punishment.

He follows with that future damnation as a warning to people of the present.[1]

18:4 In the verse: *The three books have "and be not partakers of her sins" instead of "that you be not...".] (a) *Codex 24 and Rusch: "I.e. a divine inspiration, either Christ's or his people's preaching." The difference in Latin is made but by the ending of the last word.] 1 Codex 24 and Rusch: "Mentioning that future damnation, he follows with a warning to people of the present".

100

18:5 ^(a)*Because her sins are come* ^(b)*even to heaven, and* ^(c)*God has remembered her iniquities.*

    a.   Because there is but a short time left, within which they shall receive according to their merit.*

    b.   I.e. even to the contempt of God through impenitence.

    c.   Even though he seemed to have forgotten them when he permitted her to prosper.

18:5 (a) *Not in Codex 24. Might the intended meaning have been "... before they receive according to their merit", but the grammar flawed?

18:6 ^{(a)(b)}*Render to her* ^(c)*as she also has rendered to you: and* ^(d)*double you* ^(e)*double* ^(f)*according to her works:* ^(g)*in the cup wherein she has mingled, mingle you double unto her.*

    a.   Go out from her, I say, and, separated from her, render...*

    b.   And therefore, because vengeance is now desired to such a point...*

    c.   I.e. just as my vengeance for you, who shall be cleansed, has increased, so avenge on them the wrong done to me.

    d.   In soul and body.*

    e.   Inflict greater pains on their souls and bodies than they did to you.

    f.   According to how they themselves have sinned.

    g.   I.e. just as they have* inflicted torments on you, so do to them too with your judgment.

18:6 (a) *Only in Latin 588.] (b) *Not in Latin 588.] (d) *Only in Latin 588.] (g) *Codex 24 and Rusch: "she has".

18:7 ^(a)*As much as she has glorified herself, and has been in delicacies, so much give her* ^{(b)(c)}*torment and* ^(d)*mourning: because* ^(e)*she* ^(f)*says in her heart,* ^(g)*I sit* ^(h)*a queen, and* ⁽ⁱ⁾*widow I am not, and* ^(j)*mourning I shall not see.*

    a.   Because some do so more and others less, he repeats the reason for this distinction, although he had already said it above*.

    b.   Here is denoted quantity in the cup of quality.*

    c.   In her body.

    d.   In her soul.

    e.   Unwilling to repent.*

    f.   Or "has said".*

    g.   As if saying, "I shall not be moved".*

    h.   In honor and dignity.

    i.   Because I have comfort in temporal things.

    j.   Because she does not* take precautions against future evils.

18:7 (a) *Codex 24 and Rusch: "... for the sake of this distinction, he repeats what he had said above."] (b) *Only in Latin 588.] (e) *Only in Latin 588.] (f) *Only in Latin 588.] (g) *Codex 24: "As if not to be moved"; Rusch: "As if without moving".] (j) *Codex 24: "they do not".

18:8 Therefore ^(a)*in one day shall her plagues come,* ^(b)*death, and* ^(c)*mourning, and* ^(d)*famine, and with fire she shall be burnt: because God is* ^(e)*strong that shall judge her.*

    a.   I.e. in Judgment Day.

    b.   That is, the absence of life, i.e. of God.*

    c.   As opposed to their having laughed here.

    d.   Because they shall lack God, who is the nourishment.

    e.   He can be bent by no prayers.

18:8 (b) *Codex 24 and Rusch add: "because his presence is life".

18:9 *And* *(a)the kings of the earth, which have fornicated with her, and have lived in delicacies, (b)shall weep, and (c)bewail themselves (d)upon her, (e)when they shall see the smoke of her burning:*

    a.   I.e. the princes of the world*, or those who have governed their worldly matters well, and have at some time or other fornicated with her, shall be grieved that they were ever similar to her**.
    b.   I.e. they shall suffer pain in their minds.
    c.   I.e. they shall show the pain of their bodies.
    d.   Because they were founded upon her.
    e.   I.e. when their riches shall have run out, which is a sign of the burning*, or when they shall see their punishment raised beyond measure.

Shall weep and bewail. These people, on the other hand, do not have eternal joy.[1]

18:9 (a) *"Of the world" not in Codex 24.**Codex 24 and Rusch: "... and yet have fornicated at some time or other, shall be grieved with her that they were never similar to them." I imagine that "them" would represent the good.] (e) *Codex 24: "which is a sign of the eternal burning or judgment"; Rusch: "which is a sign of the eternal burning of the judgment".] 1 Not in Latin 588. Rusch has: "These people, on the other hand, have eternal joy". This lacks clarity, but I imagine that the good would be implied somehow in both versions: "These people (= the good), on the other hand, have eternal joy" and "These people (= the wicked), on the other hand (= unlike the good), do not have eternal joy".

18:10 *(a)standing afar off (b)for the fear of her torments, saying, (c)Woe, woe, (d)that great city Babylon, that strong city: because in one hour is your* judgment come.*

    a.   In will.
    b.   Sc. because they would like to flee if they could.*
    c.   In soul and in body.*
    d.   The collection of the wicked.*

18:10 In the verse: *Codex 24: "her".] (b) *Only in Rusch.] (c) *Not in Latin 588.] (d) *Not in Latin 588.

18:11 *And (a)the merchants of the earth shall weep, and (b)mourn upon her: (c)because no man shall buy their merchandise anymore,*

    a.   Either literally or those who give their souls for earthly things.
    b.   Because they shall be grieved that those things perish in which they considered that their prosperity was.
    c.   They shall be grieved that the things pertaining to the senses of the body perish.*

18:11 (c) *Not in Latin 588.

18:12 *merchandise of gold and silver and precious stone, and of pearl, and fine linen, and purple, and silk, and scarlet, and all (a)(b)thyine wood*, and all vessels of ivory, and all vessels of precious stone and of brass and iron** and marble,*

    a.   Sc. no one shall buy.
    b.   Precious.*

Merchandise of gold. By gold is signified wisdom, by silver divine words, Christ by precious stone, the apostles by pearls, by fine linen[1] the justifications of the saints, by purple martyrdom, by silk virginity, by scarlet[2] love, by thyine wood[3] unfailing steadfastness, by ivory the beauty of virtues, by brass strength and forbearance, by iron intelligence of sublimity, by marble unconquered humility: these things the reprobates pretend to have, and they grieve when what is understood by them fails: by gold worldly wisdom, by silver eloquence, by precious stone and pearls pseudo-Christians[4] and heresiarchs, by fine linen feigned piety[5], by purple the martyrs of the heretics, by silk integrity of the flesh as a covering to a corrupt mind, by scarlet cruelty dressed in a simulation of love, by thyine wood stubbornness of mind simulating steadfastness, by ivory feigned beauty of virtues, by brass a firm preaching of perfidy instead of the right faith, by iron intelligence of deceiving, by marble the strength of feigned submission.

18:12 In the verse: *Codex 24 and Rusch have "thyine or cedar wood", and Rusch has a gloss above "or cedar" saying "absent from most versions". **Codex 24 and Rusch have "and glass" in addition here.] (b) *Only in Latin 588.] 1 Codex 24 and Rusch: "white fine linen".] 2 Codex 24 and Rusch: "red scarlet".] 3 Codex 24 and Rusch: "incorruptible thyine wood".] 4 Codex 24 and Rusch: "pseudo-prophets".] 5 Codex 24 and Rusch: "feigned justice".

18:13 ^(a)*and cinnamon*, and* ^(b)*of odors, and ointment, and frankincense, and* ^(c)*wine, and* ^(d)*oil, and* ^(e)*flour, and wheat, and* ^(f)*beasts, and sheep, and horses,* ^(g)*and chariots, and* ^(h)*slaves, and souls of men.*

a. And no man shall buy.*
b. I.e. merchandise.*
c. I.e. the New Testament, which inebriates.
d. I.e. in the unction of the Holy Spirit.*
e. I.e. Christ's flesh, by which the faithful are satiated*, the reprobates irritated.
f. And no man shall buy sorrow.*
g. Because they receive the same sacraments.*
h. He makes a distinction because some become slaves only in their bodies, like Joseph (Gen. 39), and some also in their spirits, like if someone* sold to a Jew gets circumcised in their manner, or if someone sold to a pagan worships idols.

By the odors of pigments and by frankincense are symbolized the prayers of the saints, which the vain zeal of the heretics imitates in their prayers[1]. By ointment is symbolized the divinity incarnate, which the roughness of pseudo-Christians imitates under a false gentleness. And when these things are taken away, the reprobates mourn their loss, as the heretics mourned the death of Arius, whom the earth swallowed[2].

They pretend that they have lost flour and wheat, when they have lost darnel and chaff. The beasts signify the elect, who say with the psalmist, *"I am become as a beast before you"* (Ps. 72:23). The sheep signify the saints, to whom it is said, *"Behold I send you as sheep in the midst of wolves"* (Matt. 10:16). By the horses and chariots, understand the preachers, the one saying next to Eliseus[3], *"My father, the chariot of Israel and the guider thereof"* (4 Kings 13:14).

By the slaves are signified the elect, who submit to God's service. The reprobates are grieved that they have lost the beasts, the horses and the chariots, i.e. those whom they consider strong to carry the burdens of others, while they have lost those who are weak for all good[4].

Cinnamon. In cinnamon is the odor of the virtues which they simulate.[5]

18:13 In the verse: *The three books have "amomum" in addition here. It is "an aromatic shrub, from which the Romans prepared a costly, fragrant balsam" (Lewis & Short). Latin 588 has a gloss above it saying "I.e. balsam".] (a) *Not in Latin 588.] (b) *Only in Latin 588.] (d) *Codex 24: "The unction of the saints by the Holy Spirit"; Rusch: "The unction of the Holy Spirit".] (e) *Codex 24 and Rusch: "truly satiated".] (f) *Or possibly: "And no man shall buy the sorrow of...". Not in Latin 588.] (g) *Not in Latin 588.] (h) *Codex 24 and Rusch: "an Egyptian."] 1 Latin 588: "... are symbolized the prayers or orders which the vain zeal of the heretics imitates in their orders.] 2 "Whom the earth swallowed" only in Latin 588.] 3 The Latin here lacks clarity. At first sight it seems to mean "according to Eliseus saying..."; but it is the king Joas visiting Eliseus who says those words in 4 Kings, not Eliseus himself. So the best possible other interpretation I could find was that the glossator meant "understand the preachers (and) the one saying next to Eliseus...", or "understand the preachers, the one saying next to Eliseus..." as if "the one saying (i.e. Joas)" represented somehow the preachers. Either the glossator thus expressed his thought in an unclear way, or all three books have here a mistranscription (perhaps for "... the preachers, saying next to Eliseus...", the preachers being in this case too assimilated to Joas?) — or again, but I think it less likely, the glossator misinterpreted or misremembered the Scripture and thought that those were indeed Eliseus' words. The same Latin word can mean "next to" and "according to".] 4 Codex 24 and Rusch: "for all good work".] 5 Not in Latin 588.

18:14 And ^(a)*the apples of the desire of your soul are departed from you, and all* ^(b)*fat and good things are perished from you, and they shall no more find them.**

a. Because they shall be damned even for very small things if they possess them without moderation.
b. By fat things is understood the food of the soul.

The apples are the virtues of the saints; and the party of the beast pretend that it has everything.

18:14 *Latin 588 and Rusch divide this verse and the following one differently; they have: "(v. 14) .... and the merchants of these things shall no more find them. (v.15) Those who are made rich shall stand....". If you look at the Latin passage without punctuation, it is possible to interpret it either way. Codex 24 lacks punctuation here.

18:15 The merchants of these ^(a)*things which are made rich, shall* ^(b)*stand afar from her for fear of her torments, weeping and mourning,*

a. Men.*
b. In will.*

18:15 (a) *Not in Latin 588. Codex 24 has "men again" in the other ink.] (b) *Only in Latin 588.

18:16 ^(a)*and saying, Woe, woe, that great city, which was* ^(b)*clothed with silk, and* ^(c)*purple, and scarlet, and was gilt with* ^(d)*gold, and* ^(e)*precious stone, and pearls:*

a. And they shall be moved by sympathy for her.
b. The justification of saints with heavenly desire.
c. By pretending to be king.
d. Divine wisdom.
e. I.e. love.*

18:16 *All the glosses of this verse are only in Latin 588.

18:17 *because in one hour are so great riches made desolate*: and every governor, and (a)every one that sails into the lake**, and the shipmen, and they that work in the sea, stood afar off,*

    a.   Those who desire something specific, as some desire the episcopate.*

18:17 In the verse: *Latin 588: "... are so great riches destroyed". **Latin 588 and Codex 24: "into a place". Only one letter differs between the words "lake" and "place" in Latin.] *Maybe the interpretation is "those who sail to a specific place" ---> "those who have a specific aim".

18:18 *and cried seeing the place of her burning, saying, (a)What other is like to this great city?*

    a.   I.e. who has been so exalted as these people flourishing in the world?*

18:18 (a) *Only in Latin 588.

18:19 *And they threw (a)dust upon their heads, and cried weeping and mourning, saying: Woe, woe, that great city, in which (b)all were made (c)rich that had ships in the sea, (d)of her prices: because in one hour she is desolate.*

    a.   I.e. concupiscence of earthly things upon their minds, or like a penitent.
    b.   All these things concerning the riches* may have been seen literally.**
    c.   Sc. in temporal things.*
    d.   I.e. of her sin.*

18:19 (b) *Codex 24: "concerning the judgments". **Not in Latin 588.] (c) *Only in Latin 588.] (d) *Only in Latin 588.

18:20 *Rejoice over her, (a)(b)heaven, (c)and you holy apostles and prophets because God (d)has judged (e)your judgment of her.*

    a.   I.e. angels or the highest patriarchs.*
    b.   I.e. those who are privy to God's secrets.*
    c.   Partially.*
    d.   Sc. you.*
    e.   She shall be condemned justly as she has condemned* unjustly.

After saying[1] that this damnation will happen to the wicked, he tells the good to rejoice, so that it[2] should harmonize with the divine judgment, or because once these are damned, their reward will follow.

18:20 (a) *Only in Latin 588.] (b) *Not in Latin 588.] (c) *Not in Latin 588.] (d) *Only in Latin 588.] (e) *Codex 24: "as she has condemned us"; Rusch: "as she has condemned you".] 1 Codex 24 and Rusch: "foretelling".] 2 Codex 24 and Rusch: "they".

18:21 *And one (a)strong (b)angel (c)took up as it were a great (d)(e)millstone, and threw it (f)into the sea, saying, (g)With this violence shall Babylon the (h)great city (i)be thrown, (j)and shall now be found no more.*

    a.   Because he has subdued the aerial powers.*
    b.   I.e. Christ.
    c.   God lifts up the wicked to punish them more heavily*.
    d.   I.e. people having hard hearts.
    e.   Because they roll in worldly things.
    f.   I.e. into hell.
    g.   I.e. as you see in this image; or the more they have been exalted, the more heavily they shall fall.
    h.   Because many people are assembled into one.*
    i.   Into hell.*
    j.   Sc. as some heretics think that they must be freed after a thousand years have passed.*

All these things were also seen literally.[1]

After every one of the punishments has been described, he is shown the manner of damnation. As if he were saying: What I saw foretold, I also saw fulfilled.

18:21 (a) *Not in Latin 588.] (c) *Codex 24 and Rusch add: "or for them to fall down more heavily".] (h) *Only in Latin 588.] (i) *Not in Latin 588.] (j) *Codex 24 and Rusch have only "As some heretics think".] 1 Not in Latin 588.

18:22 And the voice of harpers, and of musicians, ^(a)and of them that sing on shalm and trumpet, ^(b)shall no more be heard in you*, and ^(c)every ^(d)artificer of every ^(e)art** shall be found no more in you***, and ^{(f)(g)}the noise of the mill shall no more be heard in you****,

a. I.e. there shall be no enjoyment for them anymore, but mourning and pain.*
b. Is no more found.*
c. Here is an argument that the damned forget the knowledge acquired.*
d. For what concerns practice.*
e. For what concerns theory.*
f. The most delicate breads shall not* be sought for there.
g. And by this, what is delightful in taste is removed.*

18:22 In the verse: *Latin 588 and Codex 24: "in her". **Codex 24 and Rusch: "every artificer and every art". ***Latin 588 and Codex 24: "in her". ****Latin 588: "in her".] (a) *Only in Latin 588.] (b) *Only in Latin 588.] (c) *Only in Rusch.] (d) *Only in Rusch.] (e) *Only in Rusch.] (f) *No "not" in Codex 24.] (g) *Only in Rusch.

18:23 ^(a)and the light of the lamp shall no more shine in you*, and ^(b)the voice of the bridegroom and the bride shall no more ^(c)be heard ^(d)in you: ^(e)because ^(f)your merchants were the princes of the earth, ^{(g)(h)}because ⁽ⁱ⁾all nations have erred in ^{(j)(k)}your enchantments.

a. For what concerns sight.*
b. I.e. the joy of nuptials.
c. For what concerns hearing.*
d. O Babylon.*
e. Because, giving their souls in exchange for earthly things, they exercised an excessive power, and I* can no longer tolerate this.
f. This concerning the lustful man.*
g. And for this reason.*
h. This concerning the rational man.*
i. Some people of all nations.
j. Either literally or poisonous persuasions.
k. I.e. evil deeds, i.e. evil persuasions by which you made others err.*

He sometimes talks to Babylon herself about her fall as though pitying her misery, sometimes turns to the listeners to exhort the faithful.

18:23 In the verse: *Latin 588: "in her"; Codex 24: "for you".] (a) *Only in Rusch.] (c) *Only in Rusch.] (d) *Only in Latin 588 - remember that, in Latin 588, this follows a series of "in her", so this gloss is here to clarify what is this sudden "you".] (e) *Codex 24 and Rusch: "they".] (f) *Only in Rusch. It is unclear which word(s) it exactly refers to.] (g) *In Codex 24 and Rusch, this is found above the first "because", but it seems better to belong here, where Latin 588 has it.] (h) *Only in Rusch.] (k) *Only in Rusch.

18:24 ^(a)And in her is found ^(b)the blood of the ^(c)prophets and saints, ^(d)and of all that were slain in the earth.

a. And again because.*
b. I.e. the vengeance of the blood.
c. Lesser ones or greater ones.*
d. If a wicked man kills a wicked man, the killed man's wickedness does not excuse the killer.

18:24 (a) *Latin 588: "And therefore in the meantime". The words look somewhat similar in Latin.] (c) *Only in Latin 588. Its Vulgate reads "of the just and prophets", with this gloss above "prophets"

CHAPTER 19

19:1 AFTER these things I heard as it were [(a)]**the voice** [(b)(c)]**of many multitudes* in** [(d)]**heaven saying,** [(e)]**Alleluia.** [(f)]**Praise, and** [(g)]**glory, and** [(h)]**power** [(i)]**is to our God:**

He sees the damnation of the wicked fulfilled as he had heard from Christ that it was to be fulfilled; now he adds that the saints rejoice at this damnation, as they had been told to rejoice in that verse, *"Rejoice over her, heaven"*; by which the punishment of the wicked is understood to be much more severe.

a.   I.e. the rejoicing.*
b.   I.e. of those who were the trumpets.*
c.   Of the preachers.*
d.   The Church of the saints.*
e.   I.e. praise impossible to set out in human words.
f.   Or "salvation".*
g.   I.e. immortality.
h.   I.e. impassibility.
i.   Because he has overcome the Devil.

We say "alleluia" because praise is our God's, i.e. who made those things for us[1], whence we must praise him antonomasically.

19:1 In the verse: *Latin 588 and Rusch: "the great voice of many trumpets"; Codex 24: "the great voice of trumpets". The Latin words used here for "multitudes" and "trumpets" differ only in one letter.] (a) *Only in Latin 588.] (b) *Only in Latin 588.] (c) *Only in Rusch.] (d) *Only in Rusch.] (f) *Only in Latin 588. The Latin words are very similar.] 1 Codex 24 and Rusch: "We say "alleluia" because praise is to our God, and because he made those things for us..."

19:2 [(a)]**because** [(b)]**true and** [(c)]**just are his judgments which** [(d)]**has judged** [(e)]**of the great harlot, that has corrupted** [(f)]**the earth in her whoredom, and has revenged*** [(g)]**the blood of his servants,** [(h)]**of her hands.**

a.   And praise is to him for this reason.
b.   By giving what he has promised.
c.   By giving back to each person according to their merits.
d.   With the judgment of condemnation.*
e.   Of the congregation of the wicked.*
f.   I.e. they have corrupted themselves, or one another.
g.   Which the wicked multitude has shed.*
h.   Sc. asking it.

19:2 In the verse: *Latin 588: "vintaged". Similar-looking words.] (d) *Only in Rusch.] (e) *Only in Rusch.] (g) *Only in Rusch.

19:3 [(a)]**And again they said, Alleluia. And** [(b)]**her** [(c)]**smoke** [(d)]**ascends** [(e)]**forever and ever.**

a.   By this repetition, we must understand eternal praise.
b.   The judgment's.*
c.   I.e. tearful mourning.*
d.   It does not diminish but increases.*
e.   He judged and they were damned* eternally.

19:3 (b) *Or "of her judgment"; either interpretation is in theory possible. The Latin word in the verse can mean "its" as well as "his" or "her". This gloss is only in Latin 588, in a different ink from the rest.] (c) *Only in Latin 588.] (d) *Only in Latin 588.] (e) *Codex 24 and Rusch: "punished".

19:4 [(a)]**And** [(b)]**the four and twenty seniors fell down, and the four beasts, and adored God sitting upon the throne, saying:** [(c)]**Amen, Alleluia.**

Alleluia. He is really to be praised for having thus punished our enemies.

a.   And the lesser saints were not the only ones to praise God for this damnation, but those greater ones who were the judges and teachers of the others in the Church also did.
b.   All the holy judges, the twelve patriarchs and the twelve apostles.*
c.   It is true that God is so glorious.

19:4 (b) *Only in Rusch.

19:5 And (a)a voice (b)came out (c)from the throne, saying: (d)Say praise to our God all you his servants*: and you that (e)fear him, (f)little and great.

- a. I.e. advice.
- b. To the hearing of all.
- c. I.e. from those in whom God sits.
- d. Saying praise is doing good works.*
- e. With a pure love*.
- f. Sc. those who are unable to penetrate the higher mysteries, and cannot fulfill God's counsel, i.e. "Sell what you have and follow me" (ref. Matt. 19:21; Mark 10:21; Luke 18:22).*

The damnation of the wicked and the rejoicing of the saints having been said, he adds a warning to the present people, as if he were saying: You have seen the damnation, and you have seen the rejoicing: now see to your salvation.[1]

Little. Littleness detracts nothing from the natural quality of the one whose heart and tongue are filled by praising God.[2]

19:5 In the verse: *Codex 24 and Rusch have "saints" instead of "servants", and both mention the variant "servants" in a gloss.] (d) *Only in Latin 588.] (e) *Rusch adds: "and a filial fear".] (f) *In the other ink in Codex 24.] 1 In Latin 588, this is to the next verse.] 2 Only in Latin 588.

19:6 And I heard (a)as it were the voice of a great (b)multitude*, and as the voice (c)of many waters, and as the voice (d)of great thunders, saying, Alleluia: (e)because our Lord God the Omnipotent has reigned.

- a. I.e. the rejoicing of the Son, "Sell everything and seek me" (see Matt. 19:21).*
- b. Exhorting the good and terrifying the wicked.*
- c. Because they are gathered from many peoples.
- d. Because the saints' rejoicing will terrify the wicked.
- e. As if saying, "Previously the wicked reigned".

19:6 In the verse: *The three books have "trumpet" instead of "multitude".] (a) *Only in Latin 588. "Seek" might be a mistake for "follow"; cf. 19:5 (f).] (b) *Only in Latin 588, of course actually referring to "trumpet".

19:7 (a)Let us be glad and (b)rejoice, and (c)give glory to him: because (d)the marriage of the Lamb is come, (e)and (f)his wife has prepared herself.

- a. Having happiness.*
- b. Glorified in our bodies.
- c. Let us consider that everything comes from him*.
- d. Because the Church has been united to Christ.
- e. And it was right for her* to be united, because the Church made herself suitable to be received.
- f. The Church of the saints, which was previously his bride in hope, now is in fact.*

After the joy that the saints will have from the perdition of the wicked has been shown, he[1] mentions another joy they will have from their own salvation, which he is about to speak of.

Those who were trumpets in the world now rejoice in heaven.[2]

19:7 (a) *Codex 24 and Rusch: "Having the happiness of the soul".] (c) *Codex 24: "... that we have all good things from God"; Rusch: "... that we have everything from God".] (e) *Codex 24 and Rusch: "them".] (f) *Only in Rusch.] 1 Codex 24 and Rusch: "the Church".] 2 In Codex 24 and Rusch, this is found as an interlinear above "trumpet" in the previous verse.

19:8 And (a)it was given to her that she (b)clothe herself with (c)silk (d)glittering and white. For the silk are the justifications of saints.*

- a. That she might be able to prepare herself.*
- b. Against the heats of the world.*
- c. I.e. justifications.
- d. Because their consciences are darkened by no stains.*

Another version: "There was given to her fine linen[1] glittering, white with white tooth[2]".[3]

19:8 In the verse: *The second sentence, "For the silk, etc." is absent from Latin 588.] (a) *Codex 24 and Rusch: "In this life that she might be able to prepare herself".] (b) *Only in Latin 588.] (d) *Codex 24: "Because the consciences of the saints are darkened by no stains"; Rusch "Because the knowledge of the saints is darkened by no stains"; "knowledge" certainly being a simple mistranscription for "conscience", as only an abbreviation at the beginning of the word makes the difference, the rest of the word being the same.] 1 Fine linen: what is called "silk" in the verse; but "fine linen" (as the revised Douay-Rheims has it) is a more accurate translation. Cf. the big gloss to 18:12.] 2 Instead of "with white tooth", Codex 24 has "as the white one was giving", the difference in Latin standing in one letter.] 3 Not in Latin 588.

19:9 [a]*And he said to me, Write, Blessed be they that are called to the supper of the marriage of the Lamb. And he said to me, These words* [b]*of God, be true.*

    a.   Having spoken of the marriage to come, he invites the present people to it.

    b.   Not mine, but God's, and therefore true.

19:10 And [a]*I fell before his feet, to adore him. And he said to me, See you do not:* [b]*I am your fellow servant, and of your brethren that have the testimony of Jesus. Adore God.* [c]*For the testimony of Jesus, is the spirit of prophecy.*

    a.   Because I understood that he was greater than I*, and I was ready to obey, likewise, obey me.

    b.   I, you, and all your brethren have one God*.

    c.   That is, everything the prophets said gives testimony to Christ.

See you do not. In the old law he did not forbid himself to be adored; but after the Lord's ascension, seeing a man exalted above him, he was afraid to be adored by a man.

19:10 (a) *This is Codex 24 and Rusch's reading. Latin 588's is a little doubtful, but it could have been meant to be "Because I understood things that were greater than I", though the reading of Codex 24 and Rusch looks more likely.] (b) *Codex 24 and Rusch add: "and one Lord".

19:11 And I saw heaven opened, [a]*and behold* [b]*a white horse: and* [c]*he that sat upon him, was called* [d]*Faithful and* [e]*True, and* [f]*with justice he judges and* [g]*fights.*

    a.   And who opened it? This one.

    b.   Christ's flesh carrying the Word of God to the war against the Devil.

    c.   The divinity.

    d.   Because he fulfills his promises.

    e.   Because he himself is the truth and he makes people truthful.

    f.   Because he gives back to each person according to their works.

    g.   Sc. in his people against the Devil.

saw heaven opened. I.e. mysteries revealed through which man may climb to heaven and know God.

Having said the damnation of Babylon and the rejoicing that the saints will have from it, he follows with the damnation of the Antichrist and his apostles, which is there: *"And the beast was apprehended"*. Why shall these be damned? Because they will fight against Christ as much as they can[1], and Christ will be well able to win because he has such great power according to his divinity and to his humanity that no one can resist him; and therefore we should imitate him, whence he interposes a warning, *"And I saw[2]"*.

I saw people called to the marriage, and I also saw who could come, for they have a good helper and good admonishers.[3]

19:11 1 Codex 24 and Rusch: "Because they have fought against Christ as much as they could".] 2 Codex 24 and Rusch: "And I saw one angel, etc.".] 3 Not in Latin 588.

19:12 And his [a]*eyes* [b]*as a flame of fire, and* [c]*on his head* [d]*many diadems. Having* [e]*a name written, which no* [f]*man knows* [g]*but himself.*

    a.   I.e. the gifts of the Holy Spirit, or love.

    b.   Because they burn up vices, kindle to love and illuminate.*

    c.   I.e. on his divinity.

    d.   Because he and his people are crowned* by them**.

    e.   Unutterable.*

    f.   Unfaithful.

    g.   And his people through him.

All this without regard for any particular time[1], yet in such a way that we may notice how he is and how much he is capable of.

19:12 (b) *Codex 24: "Because he burns up, kindles and illuminates"; Rusch: "Because he burns up vices, kindles and illuminates".] (d) *Codex 24: "renewed". **Rusch: "by it".] (e) *Codex 24 and Rusch have "Man God or Jesus", Codex 24 adding in the other ink, "or the Word of God".] 1 Codex 24 and Rusch: "for anyone". This is just due to a word being left out.

19:13 And he was clothed with ^(a)a garment sprinkled with blood: ^(b)and his name is called, The Word of God.

a.   I.e. the flesh that suffered, or the Church, which is slain in its martyrs.
b.   He said, and things were made; i.e. he through whom the Father made everything, and through whom he announced himself to the world.

19:14 And ^(a)the hosts that are ^(b)in heaven ^(c)followed him ^(d)on white horses clothed in ^(e)white and ^(f)pure ^(g)silk.

a.   I.e. the faithful fighting against the Devil.
b.   In the Church.
c.   I.e. imitated.
d.   I.e. in clean bodies that are bridled from forbidden things and spurred* towards good things** with the goad of love.
e.   By the perfection of virtues.
f.   From criminal sin.
g.   I.e. justice.*

19:14 (d) *Latin 588 has "strive" here, but I decided to follow the two other books because "spurred" does seem better to fit the horse and goad metaphor. **Codex 24 and Rusch add: "i.e. towards justice".] (e), (f) and (g) *(f) Is only in Latin 588; Codex 24 has (e) instead of (f) and, instead of (g), it has "I.e. the Church" referring to all the part "white and pure silk"; Rusch also has (e) instead of (f), but it has (g) in the same way as Latin 588. In the verse, again (cf. 19:8 note 1), "fine linen" would have been a more accurate translation than "silk".

19:15 And ^(a)out of his mouth proceeds ^(b)a sharp sword*: that in it he may ^(c)strike the Gentiles. And ^(d)he shall rule them with ^(e)a rod of iron: and he treads ^(f)the wine press of the ^(g)fury of the wrath of God Omnipotent.

a.   I.e. out of his preaching.
b.   I.e. a divine sentence cutting up perverse thoughts of the mind and forbidden movements of the body; or the Old and the New Testament.
c.   Some to life, some to death.
d.   The saints* from virtue to virtue, the wicked from vice to vice.**
e.   I.e. inflexible justice.
f.   I.e. the wicked.*
g.   Fury is the continuation of wrath.*

The wine press. I.e. death, which was inflicted by God angry on the first sinning man, was destroyed by him when he rose again. Or the wine press is tribulation, in which he treads the saints while he increases [...]¹; which the Lord inflicted on Adam when he sinned, and he extended his fury to his offspring²; but they become wine to be put in God's cellar, and when they are put in it, they shall not be a wine of fury.

19:15 In the verse: *Codex 24 and Rusch have "sharp two-edged sword" — or more literally "sword sharp on either edge" — as in 1:16.] (d) *"The saints" not in Latin 588. **The same Latin verb means both "to guide" and "to rule".] (f) *Only in Latin 588.] (g) *Codex 24, in the other ink: "Fury is the threat of wrath"; Rusch: "Fury with the continuation of wrath".] 1 The interpretation of this passage is very doubtful. It could be "while he increases the saints" or "while he increases the tribulation which..."; or perhaps "while he delays the judgment" — or something else that I could not think of. The Latin is unclear to me (the verb used is polysemic and the glossator failed to express clearly its object) and all this is conjectural.] 2 Codex 24 and Rusch: "which God angry inflicted on Adam when he sinned, and extended, furious, to his offspring".

19:16 And he has ^(a)in his garment ^(b)and in his thigh ^(c)written, ^(d)KING OF KINGS, AND ^(e)LORD OF LORDS.

a.   I.e. in his humanity.*
b.   To denote that he was of the true offspring of the first fathers.
c.   Indelibly.
d.   I.e. Lord* of the saints who rule** themselves and others.
e.   He who exercises lordship over the subjects.

In his garment. Or in the hearts of the faithful, who are the garment of the Son¹, it is written "King of kings, etc.".

19:16 (a) *Latin 588: "I.e. in his humility".] (d) *"Lord" only in Latin 588. **Here again this word could also be interpreted as "guide". See note to 17:9 (d).] 1 Latin 588: "who are his garment and his sons", or possibly "who are his garments and the Son's" — the Latin is ambiguous.

19:17 And I saw ⁽ᵃ⁾one angel standing ⁽ᵇ⁾in the sun, and he cried with a loud ⁽ᶜ⁾voice saying ⁽ᵈ⁾to all ⁽ᵉ⁾the birds that did ⁽ᶠ⁾fly ⁽ᵍ⁾by the midst of heaven, ⁽ʰ⁾Come and ⁽ⁱ⁾assemble together ⁽ʲ⁾to the great supper of God:

a. Preachers standing in the open*.
b. I.e. in Christ.*
c. I.e. purpose.
d. To the faithful who are swift and light in the advancement of good works.
e. Whose conversation is in heaven.*
f. I.e. contemplate heavenly things.
g. I.e. by the Catholic faith*.
h. By doing good works.*
i. In the same faith, not following various heresies like the wicked; or from various parts of the world.
j. I.e. to God himself, who will be your nourishment.

After showing Christ's dignity, by which he will be able to overcome the Devil, he adds an admonition concerning the present, as if he were saying: You must cling to him, since he is such.

19:17 (a) *Codex 24: "In the air".] (b) *Rusch: "In the light of the understanding of the scriptures and in fervor". Codex 24 has no gloss here.] (e) *Not in Latin 588.] (g) *Codex 24 and Rusch add: "which is common".] (h) *In Codex 24 and Rusch, this is in the beginning of (i) (which is found as a marginal gloss in those books), while Codex 24 has here "I.e. do good works", and Rusch has the same but above "assemble".

19:18 ⁽ᵃ⁾that you may eat the flesh of kings, and the flesh of ⁽ᵇ⁾tribunes, and the flesh of ⁽ᶜ⁾valiants, and the flesh of ⁽ᵈ⁾horses and of ⁽ᵉ⁾them that sit on them, and the flesh of all ⁽ᶠ⁾freemen and ⁽ᵍ⁾bondmen, and of little and great.

a. I.e. that you may delight in the torture of the wicked, of the greater ones as well as of the lesser ones.
b. The judges of the others.*
c. In their bodies.
d. Those placed under others.
e. I.e. the superiors.
f. Those who are free from justice or from carnal remorse.*
g. Sc. of iniquity or of the bond of the flesh.*

19:18 (b) *Only in Rusch.] (f) *Codex 24 and Rusch have only "Free from justice".] (g) *Codex 24 and Rusch: "Of sin".

19:19 And I saw ⁽ᵃ⁾the beast and ⁽ᵇ⁾the kings of the earth, and ⁽ᶜ⁾their armies gathered to make war ⁽ᵈ⁾with him that sat upon the horse and with his army.

a. I.e. the Antichrist.
b. I.e. his apostles.
c. I.e. all those who serve them*.
d. I.e. against him, i.e.* Christ and his people, with blasphemies, tribulation and miracles.

As if he were saying: You ought to be very anxious to be able to come to this supper, because if you do not fight well, you shall succumb to the Devil, who is ready to do you a lot of harm; you shall however be able to overcome him with Christ's[1] help.

19:19 (c) *Codex 24 and Rusch: "him" instead of "them".] (d) *"Him, i.e." only in Latin 588.] 1 Codex 24 and Rusch: "God's".

19:20 And the beast was ⁽ᵃ⁾apprehended, and with him ⁽ᵇ⁾the false prophet*: which wrought signs before him, wherewith he seduced them ⁽ᶜ⁾that took the character of the beast, and ⁽ᵈ⁾that adored his ⁽ᵉ⁾image. ⁽ᶠ⁾These two were cast alive into the pool of fire ⁽ᵍ⁾burning also with brimstone***.**

a. I.e. punished eternally.
b. I.e. his disciples.*
c. I.e. that believe* in him.
d. I.e. that receive him with joy, like the Jews.*
e. Resemblance.*
f. The Antichrist and his people* shall suffer greater punishments than the others, similarly to one who is burned alive.
g. Because of the darkness.

19:20 In the verse: *Codex 24: "prophets". **Codex 24 and Rusch: "and he which". ***Latin 588: "into the pool of fire burning with brimstone"; Codex 24 and Rusch: "into the pool of burning fire and brimstone".] (b) *Only in Latin 588.] (c) *Codex 24 and Rusch: "believed".] (d) *Codex 24 and Rusch: "Like the Jews, who will receive him with joy".] (e) *Not in Latin 588.] (f) *Codex 24 and Rusch: "his apostles".

110

19:21 [a]*And the rest were slain by the sword of him that sits upon the horse, which proceeds out of his mouth:* [b]*and all the birds were filled with their flesh.*

- a.   I.e. their followers shall be punished with a lesser punishment. Or those who are the rest (i.e. converted to God), slain to the world, will live to God.
- b.   I.e. all the saints delighted in their punishment, or* in the success of the brethren.

19:21 (b) *Codex 24 and Rusch: "and".

CHAPTER 20

20:1 AND I saw (a)an angel (b)descending from (c)heaven, (d)having (e)the key of the bottomless depth, and (f)a great chain in his hand.

    a.   I.e. Christ.
    b.   I.e. humbling himself in the flesh.
    c.   The secret of the Father.*
    d.   Here is the inevitable power.*
    e.   Power over the Devil.*
    f.   I.e. an inevitable chain that binds everything.*

Having said the damnation of Babylon and of the Antichrist and the pseudo-apostles, he follows with the damnation of the Devil himself, and gives the reason why and the time when he shall be damned, and says who will be able to overcome him; that is, he who was able at his humble coming to bind him as much as he wished, was able, once glorified, to destroy him completely.[1]

The bottomless depth is the dark hearts of the wicked, or the Devil himself. He restrains those whom the Lord will permit to vent their rage.[2]

20:1 (c) *Only in Rusch.] (d) *Only in Rusch.] (e) *Only in Rusch.] (f) *Codex 24 and Rusch: "An inevitable power with which he binds everything".] 1 Not in Latin 588.] 2 Codex 24 and Rusch: "The bottomless depth is the dark hearts of the wicked, or the Devil himself, those whom the Lord permits to vent their rage and restrains".

20:2 And he (a)(b)apprehended the (c)dragon the (d)old (e)serpent, which is the (f)Devil and (g)Satan, and (h)bound him (i)for a thousand years.

    a.   Sc. by the working of the passion and of the resurrection.*
    b.   I.e. he showed that he had sinned when he showed that he was free from sin.*
    c.   Because of his violence in doing harm.*
    d.   Because he has done harm from the beginning of the world.
    e.   Because of his deceptiveness.
    f.   Flowing apart.*
    g.   Adversary.
    h.   I.e. deprived him of his former power.
    i.   From the time of Christ to the Antichrist, within which time men can become perfect.*

Bound him. One should know that the Devil was similarly bound in Abraham and in the other faithful as in these present people; but in the former it was the hope of Christ to come that bound him, in the latter Christ himself bound him when he arrived.[1]

20:2 (a) *In Codex 24 and Rusch, this gloss, modified to "I.e. in the working of the passion and of the resurrection", is above "in his hand" in the previous verse.] (b) *Codex 24 and Rusch: "I.e. he showed that he had sinned when that Devil killed him, who was free from sin".] (c) *Not in Latin 588.] (f) *See note to 12:9] (e). Codex 24 and Rusch have "Flowing downwards", the difference in Latin standing in one letter.] (i) *Rusch: "I.e. all the time from the incarnation to the end of the world". Codex 24 has no gloss here.] 1 In Latin 588, this gloss is found to the next verse, continuing the gloss "He who is shut up, etc.".

20:3 And he threw him into (a)the depth, and (b)shut him up, and sealed over him, that he seduce no more the nations, (c)till the thousand years be consummate, and (d)after these things (e)he must be loosed (f)a little time.

    a.   The hearts of the reprobates.*
    b.   I.e. he forbade him the freedom to go out except by secret judgment of God.
    c.   I.e. till the Antichrist come.
    d.   Because God has so decided.
    e.   So that he shall recover the power he had before Christ's coming.
    f.   And therefore he should not be feared.

And he threw him into the depth. Because, rejected from the faithful, he started to rule more fiercely among the wicked. Hence we read in the Gospel that he entered into the swine (ref. Matt. 8:28-32; Mark 5:1-13; Luke 8:26-33).

Shut him up. He who is shut up never sees outside and does not know whether he shall go out; so does the Devil not know whether he can make any of the just fall except what is permitted to him by the secret judgment of God, nor is it known to him whether he shall lose some of the wicked in whom he is.[1]

Sealed. I.e. he put a seal, that is, the sign of the cross, which overcomes him in such a way as to drive him away from the faithful.

20:3 (a) *Only in Rusch.] 1 Only in Latin 588.

20:4 And I saw (a)*seats: and* (b)*they sat upon them,* (c)*and* (d)*judgment was given* (e)*them, and* (f)*the souls of the* (g)*beheaded for the testimony* (h)*of Jesus, and for* (i)*the word of God, and that adored not* (j)*the beast, nor* (k)*his image, nor received* (l)*his character* (m)*in their foreheads or* (n)*in their hands,* (o)*and* (p)*have lived, and reigned with Christ a thousand years.*

a. The inferior faithful.*
b. The greater ones, by reigning well.*
c. And this because judgment was given them.
d. I.e. God charged them with it.*
e. The superiors.*
f. I saw.*
g. Martyrs.*
h. I.e. of his humanity.
i. I.e. his divinity.
j. I.e. the Antichrist.
k. I.e. his apostles*.
l. I.e. his sign.
m. I.e. in manifest confession.
n. I.e. in work.
o. I do not say "shall live and shall reign" in the future, but in this present age*; that is, they have reigned** with Christ since they were killed.
p. In the present by grace and in the future by glory.*

20:4 (a) *Only in Rusch.] (b) *Only in Rusch.] (c) and (d) *In Codex 24 and Rusch, these are fused into one: "And this because God charged them with this judgment".] (e) *Only in Rusch.] (f) *Not in Latin 588.] (g) *Only in Rusch.] (k) *Rusch: "pseudo-apostles".] (o) *Codex 24 and Rusch: "in the present". **Codex 24 and Rusch: "lived and reigned".] (p) *Only in Rusch.] 1 Not in Latin 588.

After the Devil was bound, I saw the faithful freed, and the lesser ones ready to obey their superiors, and the superiors ready to pass judgment on the inferiors.

I saw at the time of this binding the Church thus free to do good works, and at this same time I saw those who die for Christ enter glory at once and never go down to hell as Abraham and the other prophets did even though they were just. (see Luke 16:22-26, Acts 2:27, Ephesians 4:9, 1 Peter 3:18-20)

And the souls of the beheaded, etc. And I saw the souls of those who did not adore.[1]

20:5 (a)(b)*The rest of the dead* (c)*lived not, until the thousand years be consummate.* (d)*This is the first resurrection.*

a. Different from them.*
b. I.e. those who are dead in the soul.
c. I.e. they shall suffer eternal punishments, and this in the present, sc. as soon as they die.
d. To differentiate it from the one that will be* both in the body and in the soul.

20:5 (a) *Only in Latin 588.] (d) *Codex 24: "that burns".] 1 Not in Latin 588.

This is the first resurrection. That is, the fact that the Devil is thus bound, that men are rising again from sins, and that when they are dead their souls enjoy eternal rest at once.[1]

20:6 (a)*Blessed and* (b)*holy is he that has* (c)*part in the first resurrection,* (d)*in these* (e)*the second death* (f)*has not power*: but* (g)*they shall be priests of God and of Christ: and* (h)(i)*shall reign* (j)*with him* (k)*a thousand years.*

a. Because he has attained blessedness.
b. Because he will be firm in it.*
c. Even though everyone cannot be perfect and shall not be in the same splendor.
d. He is really blessed.
e. I.e. eternal damnation, which will be in the body and in the soul.
f. Because they shall be worried by nothing.*
g. Here and in the future*. Offering eternal praises to the Trinity** and to the humanity.
h. In the present.*
i. I.e. they will always* direct themselves to the better.
j. I.e. with the Trinity and the humanity.
k. Not only in the future, about which it is well agreed.*

20:6 In the verse: *Latin 588: "has not part".] (b) *See note to 11:18 (f).] (f) *Codex 24 and Rusch have another version, probably a mistranscription, which I cannot make sense of.] (g) *This part only in Latin 588. **Codex 24 and Rusch: "divinity".] (h) *Not in Latin 588.] (i) *"Always" only in Latin 588.] (k) *It is a little unsure what this refers to. In Latin 588, it is placed as if it referred to the beginning of the next verse, but it might be there only because there was no place left behind. In Codex 24, it starts above "a thousand years". I Rusch, it is to "and shall reign".] 1 Rusch: "about the beheaded".] 2 Not in Latin 588.

He here says about the other and lesser ones what he had said about the perfect ones[1]. [2]

20:7 And when the thousand years shall be consummate, Satan [(a)]**shall be loosed** [(b)]**out of his prison, and** [(c)]**shall go forth, and** [(d)]**seduce the nations that are upon the four corners of the earth,** [(e)]**Gog, and** [(f)(g)]**Magog, and shall** [(h)]**gather** [(i)]**them into battle, the number** [(j)]**of whom is** [(k)]**as the sand of the sea.**

a.   I.e. he shall recover his former power.
b.   I.e. out of the hearts of the reprobates, in which he is now bound so that he may not vent his rage at will.
c.   I.e. shall exercise his power.
d.   I.e. gather them not locally.*
e.   I.e. "covered".*
f.   I.e. "uncovered".*
g.   I.e. he will persecute secretly and manifestly.*
h.   Not locally but in mind.
i.   Through whom he will fight openly.*
j.   Of Gog and Magog.
k.   They are as innumerable and as barren.

20:7 (d) *Codex 24 and Rusch: "Lead them away from Christ to himself". The Latin verb *seducere*, "to seduce", is compounded of the prefix *se* - meaning "apart", "aside", and *ducere*, "to lead".] (f) *Rusch: "uncovering". Codex 24 has no gloss here.] (g) *Only in Rusch.] (i) *Only in Rusch.] 1 Codex 24 and Rusch: "*Magog*. I.e. the uncovered ones".

Gog and Magog.[1] Which is to say, all the persecutors covering the Devil in themselves, and finally proceeding to open persecution. Or literally, he will seduce these two nations first, and through them will proceed to the others.

20:8 And [(a)]**they ascended** [(b)]**upon the breadth of the earth, and** [(c)]**compassed** [(d)]**the camp of the saints, and** [(e)(f)]**the** [(g)]**beloved city.**

a.   I.e. they will take pride.
b.   I.e. in all the globe.
c.   I.e. as if invading it, they were not able to enter.
d.   I.e. the saints always ready for war.*
e.   The same saints, fortified with virtues and unanimous in this war.
f.   The Church of the saints.*
g.   By God.*

20:8 (c) and (d): in Codex 24, these are fused into one gloss saying: "Because when they invade it, they shall not be able to drag out those who are ready for war". Rusch has the same as Latin 588 in (c), but in (d) it has just "Those who are ready for war".] (f) *Only in Rusch.] (g) *Not in Latin 588. Codex 24 has "by David". The abbreviations look similar enough.

20:9 [(a)]**And there came down** [(b)]**fire from God* out of heaven, and** [(c)]**devoured them:**

a.   But they should not be feared, because they shall perish quickly.
b.   I.e. sudden destruction.
c.   So that they shall not return.*

20:9 In the verse: *Latin 588 does not have "from God" in the verse, but has two interlinear glosses, one above "came down" and one above "out of heaven", saying respectively "from God" and "i.e. from God".] (c) *Only in Rusch.

20:10 and the Devil which seduced them, was cast into [(a)]**the pool of** [(b)]**fire and** [(c)]**brimstone,** [(d)]**where both the beast and the false prophet** [(e)]**shall be tormented** [(f)]**day and night forever and ever.***

a.   The deep punishment of hell.*
b.   Burning.*
c.   Stinking.*
d.   He likens the Devil and his people in punishments so as to dissuade very strongly by this.
e.   With regards to the glory of the just, which is the day, and to their own punishments, which are the night.
f.   I.e. continually.*

20:11 *And I saw (a)a (b)great (c)white throne, and (d)one sitting upon it, from whose (e)sight earth and (f)heaven (g)fled, and (h)there was no place (i)found for (j)them*.*

    a.   I.e. the Church.
    b.   Because of its multitude.
    c.   By immortality and impassibility.
    d.   I.e. Christ resting* in them, he who will make this destruction.
    e.   I.e. presence.
    f.   I.e. the air.
    g.   From this appearance, or literally*.
    h.   Because fire will reach fifteen cubits above the highest mountain.*
    i.   Sc. according to their previous state.
    j.   Heaven and earth.*

Having said the destruction of the Devil and his limbs, he follows with the destruction of the world for the greater punishment of the wicked. For it is appropriate, once the wicked are destroyed, for the world to be destroyed, since it was corrupted by them. Or, having often spoken of the glorification of the saints and of the punishments of the wicked, he had made no mention of the bodies, whether they should be glorified or punished; which he clearly shows here.

20:11 In the verse: *The three books have "by them".] (d) *The word "resting" not in Codex 24; Rusch has "sitting" instead.] (g) *"Or literally" only in Latin 588.] (h) *Only in Latin 588.] (j) *Not in Latin 588.

20:12 *And I saw the (a)dead, (b)great and little, (c)standing in the sight of the throne, and (d)books were opened: and another (e)(f)book was opened, which is of life: and (g)the dead were judged of those things which were written in the books (h)according to their works.*

    a.   Sc. physically.*
    b.   The greater as well as the lesser wicked.
    c.   Because the saints will thoroughly see* the merits of each one.
    d.   Consciences.*
    e.   I.e. Christ.*
    f.   I.e. God's prescience, which is now hidden.*
    g.   The wicked by comparison with the saints. The wicked shall be damned, who shall read in them the things they refused to do.*
    h.   Because a greater punishment will be given to some and a lesser one to others.

Books. I.e. the divine commandments; because they have forsaken them, they will know that they are punished according to their merit. Or the books are the consciences of each person, which will be open to everyone.

Another book. I.e. Christ, who will then appear to all, mighty, and give life to his people. Or the book is God's prescience[1], because the wicked shall then clearly know that they were not predestined to life, which they promised themselves when they existed in the world.

20:12 (a) *In Codex 24 and Rusch, this is above "standing".] (c) *Codex 24: "the saints thoroughly see"; Rusch: "the saints see".] (d) Only in Rusch.] (e) *Only in Latin 588.] (f) *Only in Rusch.] (g) *In Codex 24 and Rusch, this is split into two glosses; an interlinear "I.e. the wicked" above "the dead", and a marginal gloss *Of those things*. I.e. the wicked shall be damned by comparison with the saints. They will read in them the things they refused to do".] 1 Codex 24: "presence"; Latin 588: "presence" corrected to "prescience" in the other ink. These words resemble as much in Latin (whence these English words come) as they do in English.

20:13 *And (a)the sea gave (b)the dead that were in it, and (c)death and (d)hell gave (e)their dead that were in them, and it was judged (f)of everyone according to their works.*

    a.   I.e. the world.*
    b.   I.e. the bodies of the dead.
    c.   I.e. the Devil.
    d.   The place of darkness or the depth of vices*.
    e.   I.e. the souls of the dead.
    f.   Without respect of persons.*

He wants to show clearly that the bodies of the dead, however torn apart, will be restored to life at that judgment; which some people do not believe.

20:13 (a) *Only in Rusch.] (d) *"Or the depth of vices" only in Latin 588.] (f) *Only in Rusch.

20:14 *And (a)hell and (b)death were cast into the pool of fire. (c)This is the second death.*

    a.   I.e. those who are deep in vices.*
    b.   I.e. the Devil.
    c.   As if he were saying, "Beware of the first death, because from that first one follows this second one".

20:14 (a) *Codex 24 does not have this, but instead repeats the same gloss as in the previous verse, "I.e. the place of darkness". Rusch has both.

20:15 And he that was not found [a]written in the book of life, was cast into the pool of fire.

a.   I.e. predestined to life.*

20:15 (a) *Rusch: "I.e. not predestined to faith".

CHAPTER 21

21:1 AND I saw [(a)]*a new heaven and a* [(b)]*new earth,* [(c)]*for the first heaven, and the first earth was gone, and the sea* [(d)][(e)]*now is not.*

    a.   I.e. the air renewed.*
    b.   Renewed.*
    c.   I.e. that state in which they were before is no longer necessary.
    d.   According to the former state.
    e.   Because coarseness and bitterness is taken away.*

In this seventh vision, he treats the subject of the renewing of the elements and of the glorification of the saints, describing the merits by which the saints have been thus glorified.

And the sea now is not. It is not doubtful that the change of the air and of the earth will be made through fire, but concerning water there is doubt, for it is believed that it has cleansing in itself.

21:1 (a) *Codex 24: "I.e. the air in remote places".] (b) *Only in Rusch.] (e) *Only in Rusch.

21:2 And I John saw [(a)]*the* [(b)]*holy city* [(c)]*New* [(d)]*Jerusalem descending from heaven, prepared* [(e)]*of God,* [(f)]*as a bride* [(g)]*adorned for her husband.*

    a.   I.e. the Church now placed in total rest.*
    b.   Destined to keep securely what it has.*
    c.   Immortal, impassible.
    d.   Fully seeing God, who is peace.
    e.   Because she* understands that that Church has received whatever good it has by the sole grace of God.
    f.   As a bridegroom sends gifts to his bride before marrying her, so did Christ send faith, virtues and good works to the Church before receiving her in glory.
    g.   Arranged with virtues.*

21:2 (a) *Not in Codex 24.] (b) *Not in Codex 24. This gloss too is based on the primitive meaning of the Latin word for "holy" (cf. 11:18 (f) and 20:6 (b)).] (e) *I am not completely sure whether it is "she", "Jerusalem/the Church", or "he", John. The Latin could mean either.] (g) *Only in Rusch.

21:3 And I heard a [(a)]*loud* [(b)]*voice* [(c)]*from the throne saying:* [(d)]*Behold* [(e)]*the tabernacle of God with men,* [(f)][(g)]*and he* will dwell with them.* [(h)]*And they shall be his people: and* [(i)]*he God with them shall be their God.*

    a.   Because it is speaking of secret things.*
    b.   I.e. annunciation.*
    c.   I.e. from those in whom God principally* sits.
    d.   I.e. I saw myself that* Christ's humanity in which he fought and the men who have imitated him and made a good use of reason will be in the same glory**.
    e.   Christ's humanity in which he fought against the Devil.*
    f.   As he will have eternal glory, so will his people.*
    g.   Because he will never be driven away from them, because they will never sin.*
    h.   Committing offense in nothing, which is impossible as long as they are in the flesh.
    i.   Present for them also according to his divinity.*

After saying that he saw the renewing of the elements and the glorification of the saints, because it was something unknown and seemed incredible, he mentions the authority of the holy fathers, who foretold this.

21:3 In the verse: *Codex 24 has "the Holy Spirit" instead of "he".] (a) *Remember that in Latin it is literally "great voice". In Rusch, this gloss is to "the throne".] (b) *Rusch: "I.e. prophetic annunciation".] (c) *In Codex 24 and Rusch, this word, "principally", is found not here but in (a), "Because it is speaking principally of secret things".] (d) *Codex 24 and Rusch: "It is manifest that...". **Codex 24: "in the same Church".] (e) *Only in Rusch.] (f) *Codex 24: "As that glory will be eternal there, so will it be in his people".] (g) *In Codex 24 and Rusch, this is above "with them shall be their God".] (i) *Rusch: "According to his divinity and present for them". The difference stands in a small abbreviation.

21:4 ^(a)*And God shall wipe away all tears from their eyes: and* ^(b)*death shall be no more, nor* ^(c)*mourning, nor* ^(d)*crying, neither shall there be* ^(e)*sorrow anymore,* ^(f)*which first things are gone.*

    a.   As if saying, "There will be glory and no sorrow, because both, being of a different nature of things*, could not* be there at the same time".

    b.   Therefore there will be no tears, because there will be no cause for tears, i.e. dissolution of soul and body, or separation from God's presence, whatever separates one from God.*

    c.   I.e. continual weeping.*

    d.   Any agitation or disturbance.*

    e.   Sudden and transitory.*

    f.   I.e. because there is no longer a place for them since there is no sin, which is what these things proceed from.

21:4 (a) *The part "being of a different nature of things" is a little doubtful, but it is the best sense I can make of what Latin 588 has, which seems somewhat flawed grammatically. In Codex 24 and Rusch, this part is found, modified, as a separate gloss above "all tears", saying "which are for the nature of different things". **"Not" is missing in Latin 588, but it does not seem to make sense without it.] (b) *Codex 24 and Rusch have "There will really be no tears there, because there will be no cause for tears" as a marginal gloss, and "dissolution of soul and body" as an interlinear above "death". They do not have the part concerning separation from God's presence.] (c) *Codex 24: "Continual mourning or weeping".] (d) *Codex 24 and Rusch have only "any disturbance".] (e) *The Latin word in the verse basically means "pain", whether physical or mental.

21:5 *And* ^(a)*he that sat in the throne, said:* ^(b)*Behold I make* ^(c)*all things new. And he said to me:* ^(d)*Write, because these words be* ^(e)*most faithful and* ^(f)*true.*

    a.   After citing the authority of the saints concerning this renewing, he cites the authority of God himself.

    b.   As if he were saying, "Manifestly and straight away".*

    c.   The things mentioned above.

    d.   In the hearts of your people, or of others.*

    e.   Fit for one to have faith in.

    f.   Because they will be fulfilled.

21:5 (b) *Only in Rusch.] (d) *Codex 24 and Rusch: "Sc. in you heart and in those of others".

21:6 *And he said to me:* ^(a)*It is done,* ^(b)*I am Alpha and Omega: the beginning and the end.* ^(c)*To him that thirsts I will give of* ^(d)^(e)*the fountain of the water* ^(f)*of life*, gratis.*

    a.   I.e. the things are fulfilled that had to be fulfilled.

    b.   As if he were saying, "I shall be able to do this renewing, because I created all things, and in me shall all things be finished".

    c.   I.e. to him who desires it and is not satiated with earthly things*.

    d.   I.e. myself, who am the beginning of all happiness.*

    e.   Which is Christ himself.*

    f.   Because it makes you live by grace alone.*

It is done. As if he were saying: Whatever was shown to me concerning this renewing, it was done for the benefit of the present people, for whom I was ordered to do this[1]. [2]

It is done. So that he should not ask[3] what is to come after that renewing, he is told that nothing remains to be done, because things will remain in that state[4].

I am, etc. Ordering him to write and announce to others, he adds an encouragement for everyone to strive to attain this renewing.

21:6 In the verse: *Codex 24 and Rusch: "the fountain of living water". Only one letter differs in Latin.] (c) *"And is not satiated with earthly things" only in Latin 588.] (d) *Rusch has here only "I.e. myself" and Codex 24 "I.e. through myself", but both have the entire gloss as a marginal gloss to "these things" in the next verse.] (e) *Only in Rusch.] (f) *Gratis, which is a Latin word — meaning literally "for thanks (sc. and nothing more)" — is the ablative plural of *gratia* meaning among other thinks "gratitude" or "grace".] 1 Rusch: "to whom I was ordered to write this"; Codex 24: "to whom I seemed to write this", which is most certainly just a mistranscription due to the fact that the Latin for "I was ordered" and "I seemed" differ only in one letter.] 2 In Codex 24 and Rusch, this gloss is to the previous verse.] 3 Codex 24 and Rusch: "So that no one should ask".] 4 "Because things will remain in that state" only in Latin 588.

21:7 ^(a)*He that shall overcome, shall* ^(b)*possess* ^(c)*these things, and I will be his* ^(d)*God: and he* ^(e)*shall be my* ^(f)*son.*

    a.   I will not give it to him who thirsts for an hour, but to him that perseveres.

    b.   I.e. obtain securely.

    c.   The immortal God.*

    d.   Immortal, i.e. eternal satiety.*

    e.   In the present by grace and in the future by glory.*

    f.   Which is called "people" above.

21:7 (c) *Not in Latin 588.] (d) *Codex 24 and Rusch have only "eternal satiety".] (e) *Only in Rusch.

21:8 But to [(a)]*the fearful, and* [(b)]*incredulous, and* [(c)]*execrable, and murderers, and fornicators, and sorcerers, and idolaters, and all* [(d)]*liars,* [(e)(f)]*their part shall be in the pool burning with fire and brimstone, which is* [(g)]*the second death.*

a. I.e. those who, for fear of sufferings, avoid to receive faith or receive it and then forsake it.
b. I.e. those who despair of this renewing.
c. I.e. excommunicated.*
d. Those for whom lie is a habit.*
e. I.e. partaking either more or less.
f. According to the nature of their fault.*
g. Of body and soul.*

21:8 (c) *Codex 24: "I.e. eradicated".] (d) *Not in Latin 588.] (f) *Not in Latin 588.] (g) *Only in Rusch.

21:9 And there came one of the seven angels that had the vials full of [(a)]*the seven last plagues, and spoke with me, saying:* [(b)]*Come, and I will show you the* [(c)(d)]*Bride, the* [(e)]*Wife of the Lamb.*

a. For what concerns the wicked.*
b. Extend your intellect.
c. Previously.*
d. Now through faith.*
e. To be glorified and married in the future.*

After describing the glory the saints will have, he says by what merit, or by what help, they will receive it.

21:9 (a) *Only in Rusch.] (c) *Only in Latin 588.] (d) *Only in Rusch.] (e) *Only in Rusch.

21:10 And he took me up in spirit unto [(a)]*a mountain* [(b)(c)]*great and* [(d)(e)]*high: and he* [(f)]*showed me* [(g)(h)]*the* [(i)]*holy city Jerusalem* [(j)(k)]*descending out of heaven from God*,*

a. I.e. Christ, who is the bulwark of his people.
b. Great because he fills all the world.
c. For what concerns his humanity.*
d. High because he is unconquerable.*
e. For what concerns his divinity.*
f. On that mountain.
g. I.e. the Church.*
h. In which God dwells through grace.*
i. Making people holy and making them see God, who is peace.*
j. If the Church deserves to be called Jerusalem, it does not have it from itself, but from those above, i.e. the grace of God.*
k. Through the infusion of grace.*

21:10 In the verse: *"From God" not in Latin 588.] (c) *Only in Rusch.] (d) *If we look at the root meaning of the Latin word *insuperabilis*, "unconquerable", it means literally "that cannot be climbed over", from the privative prefix *in* - and the verb *superare*, "to climb over", and hence "to overcome".] (e) *Only in Rusch.] (f) and (g) *Instead of these, Codex 24 and Rusch have a marginal gloss saying "And on that mountain he showed the foundation of the Church".] (h) *Only in Rusch.] (i) *Only in Latin 588.] (j) *Only in Latin 588.] (k) *Only in Rusch.

21:11 having [(a)]*the glory of God. And* [(b)]*the* [(c)]*light thereof like to a precious stone, as it were to* [(d)(e)]*the jasper stone,* [(f)]*even as crystal.*

a. Knowledge about God.*
b. Itself shining in its own measure, similar to Christ, who was firm in his purpose and shining with virtues.
c. I.e. bright works; it is a figure of hendiadys.*
d. Hard and green; so is the Church green* in faith and firm** in it.
e. There is nothing saddening there, but all is delighting like the greenness of the jasper.*
f. Hiding nothing, because there confession is pure.

21:11 (a) *The Latin noun translated in the verse as "glory", *claritas*, is derived from the adjective *clarus* meaning "clear", "bright" (and figuratively "famous", "renowned") and so it also has a more literal meaning of "clearness", "brightness".] (c) *Not in Latin 588.] (d) *In the sense "vigorous". **Codex 24 and Rusch: "confirmed".] (e) *Only in Rusch.

119

21:12 And it had (a)a wall great and high, having twelve gates, and (b)in the gates (c)twelve angels, (d)and names written thereon, which are (e)the names of the twelve tribes of the children of Israel.

a. I.e. Christ as a defender, who is great in Sion, high with the Father. Or the defenders of others who are great in overcoming some others*.
b. I.e. in the faith and in the footsteps of the patriarchs* and prophets.
c. I.e. the apostles.
d. Because all the faithful are founded and, as it were, inscribed on the prophets, and because all the faithful stand firm in the love of the first fathers.*
e. I.e. the memory of the holy fathers in the old law.*

Twelve angels. That is, the apostles, the prophets, or the angels messengers of the truth.[1]

Twelve gates. I.e. the patriarchs, by whose example others are brought in to faith.

Or the gates are the apostles, who bring others into the Church. The angels are the inferiors who, after having been perfectly instructed, have been substituted in the place of angels.[2]

The number of twelve gates, which are comprised of the four parts of the world under the number three, refers to the mystery of the twelve apostles by whom faith in the Trinity is spread throughout the globe, which is divided into four parts.

The names. That is, the memory of the holy fathers in the old law is in the apostles, because the latter announce as fulfilled what the former foretold as being to come. Or they are all the nations that are in the faith of the apostles and in their love. Whence *"You are our epistle, written in our hearts"* (2 Corint. 3:2).

21:12 (a) *Codex 24 and Rusch: "who are great in overcoming some so that others should not be overcome".] (b) *Codex 24 and Rusch have only "of the prophets".] (d) *Only in Latin 588.] (e) *Not in Latin 588.] 1 Not in Latin 588. In Rusch, this gloss seems to be taken as referring to "twelve gates" (or perhaps, but it is less likely, to "wall"; it is placed between (a), which is found as a marginal gloss in Rusch, and the gloss on "twelve gates" that comes after it here), while Codex 24 does not indicate in any way what it refers to; but it seemed to me a little more likely to refer to the angels.] 2 Not in Latin 588.

21:13 On the east, three gates: and (a)on the north, three gates: and on the south, three gates: and on the west, three gates.

a. Like in Job (ref. maybe to Job 37:22?).*

The east is the Jews, from whom the Sun of justice rose (see Mal. 4:2); in these are three gates because they were the first ones to whom the faith of the Holy Trinity was announced by the prophets[1]. The north is the cold nations who believed after the Jews. On[2] the south: i.e. from[2] the splendor of faith, which is from Christ's advent. On[2] the west: i.e. from[2] the last age of the world, which will receive the faith of the Trinity through Elijah and Enoch (see Rev. 11:1-14).

21:13 (a) *Only in Latin 588.] 1 Codex 24 and Rusch: "by the apostles and by the prophets".] 2 "On" and "from" translate the same Latin word in this context.

21:14 And (a)the wall of the city having twelve foundations: and (b)in them, (c)(d)twelve names, of the twelve Apostles of (e)the Lamb*.

a. I.e. faith in Christ, which fortifies the town, has the twelve patriarchs, by whom it is founded; because they were the first ones to keep this faith, and all those who come to faith rely on them.
b. I.e. in their memory and preaching.
c. They understood and foretold as being to come the faith that these keep.*
d. Because the faith and teaching of the apostles was founded on the faith of the patriarchs.
e. Who they said was to come.

21:14 In the verse: *The three books have "of the twelve Apostles and of the Lamb".] (c) *This is Codex 24 and Rusch's reading. Latin 588 has here something that does not make sense as it stands, but might be a mistranscription for the same as Codex 24 and Rusch's version but with "the just" instead of "these", unless this is a mistranscription too, since the Latin words for "the just" and "these" differ only in one letter.] (d) *Only in Rusch.

21:15 And (a)he that spoke (b)with me, had (c)a measure of a reed, of gold, (d)to measure the city and (e)the gates thereof, and (f)the wall.

    a.   Sc. the angel in the role of Christ.
    b.   To my pleasure.
    c.   The divine Scripture composed by God's wisdom, with which he touches and illuminates the hearts of the faithful.
    d.   To give, according to the measure, understanding of the same Scriptures even to the lesser people.
    e.   I.e. those who bring others in to faith.
    f.   I.e. the defenders of others.

21:15 1 Not in Latin 588.

And he that spoke, etc. I saw this city fortified and adorned, and I saw that not all there were equal between themselves, but that yet each one was perfect in their own measure.[1]

21:16 (a)And the city is situated quadrangle-wise, and the (b)length thereof is as great as also the (c)breadth: and he measured (d)the city with the reed for (e)twelve thousand (f)furlongs, and the (g)length and (h)height and (i)breadth thereof be (j)equal.

    a.   Exposition of the square.
    b.   I.e. faith or long-suffering*.
    c.   I.e. love, because it loves as much as it believes.*
    d.   I.e. the minor Church.
    e.   For what concerns those who are beginning, those who are progressing, and those who are perfect.*
    f.   A stadium* is a place of race, and it denotes those who are directing their course to the prize of victory.
    g.   I.e. faith or long-suffering.*
    h.   Hope and* contemplation.
    i.   I.e. love.
    j.   With regards to their way of provoking action, not with regards to merit.*

21:16 (b) *"Or long-suffering" only in Latin 588.] (c) *Codex 24 and Rusch: "I.e. love by which it loves as much as it believes".] (e) *Only in Rusch.] (f) *In Latin "furlong" = *stadium*.] (g) *Not in Latin 588.] (h) *Codex 24 and Rusch: "or".] (j) *Only in Rusch.] 1 Codex 24 and Rusch: "exceed".] 2 In Latin 588, this is an interlinear gloss placed above "the length and height, etc."; whether it was initially meant to refer to this or the glossator put it there because there was no place left above the preceding words, I do not know. Codex 24, as often, does not make it clear what it refers to. In referring it to "twelve thousand furlongs", I have followed Rusch. It seems possible because of the number twelve = 3X4.

Situated quadrangle-wise. The four sides are faith, hope, love, and work, which are equal because one hopes as much as one believes, loves as much as one hopes, and works as much as one loves. So it is situated quadrangle-wise because it is strong in faith, long-suffering in hope, large in love, and efficient in work. Or the four sides are the four principal virtues, one of which must not dispense with[1] another in a man: good sense to seek the good and avoid evil; which is followed by temperance, so that a man should draw back from pleasures; then courage to do what he understands; then justice, so that he should moderate his actions without looking too just or too wise to himself.

Twelve thousand furlongs. That is, those who are perfect in faith in the Trinity from the four parts of the world.[2]

21:17 And he measured (a)the wall* thereof of a hundred forty four (b)cubits, the measure of a man (c)which is of an angel.

    a.   I.e. the defenders of others.*
    b.   The forearm*, in which is the hand, signifies work.
    c.   Either because they are equal to angels or because they are of as great a number.*

21:17 In the verse: *The three books have "walls".] (a) *Rusch: "I.e. their defenders".] (b) *The Latin word *cubitum*, whence "cubit", means "elbow", "forearm", "cubit".] (c) *Only in Rusch.] 1 Not in Latin 588.

The measure of a man which is of an angel. According to the letter, he shows that an angel appeared to him in the appearance of a man, so as to denote clearly that the one who was signified was true angel, i.e. son of God, and true man.[1]

21:18 (a)And the building of the wall thereof was of (b)jasper stone: but (c)the city itself (d)(e)(f)pure gold, like to (g)(h)pure glass.

    a.   And if someone is instructed to be a defender of others, he has this from the faith that he firmly keeps and preaches, which is what the green jasper signifies.
    b.   The stone which is Christ, or men strong in faith.*
    c.   I.e. the minor Church.
    d.   Because the saints shall shine, etc. (ref. Matt. 13:43).*
    e.   Gold denotes wisdom, glass the purity of faith that promises with the mouth and believes with the heart*.
    f.   For what concerns the soul.*
    g.   Because the hearts of the saints will also let light through.*
    h.   For what concerns the body.*

21:18 (b) *Only in Rusch.] (d) *Only in Rusch.] (e) *Codex 24 and Rusch: "that promises with the mouth what it believes with the heart".] (f) *Only in Rusch.] (g) *Only in Rusch.] (h) *Only in Rusch.

He had said that in this city there were walls, gates and foundations, and that among them some were greater and others lesser; here he describes what that same wall is like, and what the city, the foundations and the gates are like.

21:19 And ^(a)the foundations of the wall of the city were adorned with ^(b)all precious stone. The first foundation, the jasper: the second, the sapphire: the third, the chalcedony: the fourth, the emerald:

a. I.e. the prophets.*
b. I.e. all kind of virtues, or imitators who adorn the Church by their lives*.

The green *jasper* signifies the unfading greenness of faith; or the jasper is the saints' faith not fading, but always persevering in the greenness of work.[1]

The sapphire, similar to a serene sky which, hit by the rays of the sun, emits a burning brightness, signifies the highness of the hope of the saints, whose conversation is in heaven; who, renewed by the true sun, seek eternal things the more ardently and teach others to seek them, saying, *"Our conversation is in heaven"* (Philippians 3:20).[1]

The chalcedony has the color of a pale lamp; it glitters in the open air, while inside a house it is dark; it withstands the arguments of all sculptors; touched by a sunbeam or rubbed by fingers, it gleams and attracts chaff to itself; it signifies the flame of the inner love of the saints who, being despised outside, shine in hiddenness. This love does good things in secret, and in the secret of its conscience, with regards to the fact that it conceals itself and is hidden from others in its work, it does not shine; but when it is ordered to help others, then it appears what brightness it has within itself. It withstands sculptors because, in the midst of the adversity of the world, it is strong and indivisible: it can be conquered by no one; or if someone wants to carve[2] and paint it with adulatory praise, it withstands, it does not allow them to do so, because it despises vainglory. And such people, warmed by the rays of the true sun, i.e. Christ, or, as it were, touched by a finger, i.e. the Holy Spirit, attract chaff, i.e. sinners and weak people, and unite them to themselves.[1]

The emerald, the fourth one, is of an extreme greenness, above every herb and foliage, so that it even makes the air around it green. There are many kinds of it, but the precious one is found in Scythia[3], a desert country. They are guarded by griffins, animals having the body of a lion and the feet, head and wings like those of an eagle (see Herodotus, Histories 4. 27. 1). They have four feet with which they run on the ground like lions, and they fly through the air like birds. They that keep the aforesaid stones do not take them away for their own benefit, but to the detriment of men. An Arimaspus comes and fights against them and takes the stones away from them. Griffins are the Devil, who tries to take Christ or the gem of faith away from the faithful. But against him fights that people having one eye, i.e. having Christ, they who do not walk on two ways and do not have twofold hearts, and snatch Christ or faith[4] away, which is called the fourth because of the four Gospels.[1]

21:19 (a) *Not in Latin 588.] (b) *Codex 24 and Rusch "by their lives and glory".] 1 In Codex 24, all these glosses, as well as those on the next verse, are found grouped at the end of the book of Revelation, doubtless for lack of room to write them at the place where they belonged. They are not found in Latin 588 in this form, but it has a poem on the stones (a prose translation of which I give after verse 20, as well as the English poetic adaptation by Cristalle Watson), found between the prefaces and the beginning of the book, and next to it, it has interpretations in prose (on the whole saying the same things as Rusch and Codex 24, but differently) in a different hand from all the rest. A translation of this is also given after verse 20.] 2 Codex 24: "to take it".] 3 Codex 24: "in Sicily". A mistake without a shadow of a doubt.] 4 Rusch: "his faith".

21:20 the fifth, the sardonyx: the sixth, the sardius: the seventh, the chrysolite: the eighth, the beryllus: the ninth, the topazius: the tenth, the chrysoprasus: the eleventh, the hyacinth: the twelfth, the amethyst.

The fifth, *the sardonyx,* is tricolor: black in the bottom, white in the middle, red on the top; i.e. the saints red[2] in their passion, white inside, but despised because of their humility. Because humility descends from weakness of the body, which is driven by the five senses, it is called the fifth.[1]

The sixth, *the sardius,* of a blood-red color, unicolor, symbolizes the glory of martyrdom. Sixth, because Christ was crucified on the sixth day of the week. Or the sardius, having the appearance of red earth, symbolizes the saints who, even if they are high in mental understanding, nonetheless remember their weakness, keeping in mind that they are the sons of Adam, who is said to be red earth. He was made on the sixth day of the week, whence the sardius is also introduced sixth.[1]

The chrysolite has a golden splendor, and seems to be emitting burning sparks: it is spiritual preaching among miracles; by gold is

122

symbolized the wisdom of above, and by the sparks it emits, exhortations or miracles by which they inflame people to the love of God and neighbor. Because this is done by the Holy Spirit, it is put in seventh position. Chrysolite is also called so because it glitters like gold[3]. [1]

The eighth, the beryllus, is the work of those who preach. It shines like water hit by the sun. It also burns the hand of the one who holds it, because he who unites himself to a saint is kindled by his company. Some also say that it is bicolor, green and pale-colored. It symbolizes the saints who are green in contemplation, but return to the pallor of active life because of the care of earthly management.[1]

The ninth, the topazius, is the more precious as it is rarer, and it has two colors, of gold and ethereal brightness; shining most when touched by the splendor of the sun, surpassing the brightnesses of all gems, singularly provoking those who see it to look at it. If you polish it too much, you darken it; if you leave it to nature, it is brighter; and nothing else among riches is dearer to kings. It symbolizes contemplative life, which holy kings prefer to all riches of works and gems of virtues, and to which they direct their looks most; and this is the more so, the more frequently they are illuminated by divine grace. The golden color is from inner love; the ethereal one is from the sweetness of contemplation, which always grows dark at the rubbing of the world, for one can hardly at the same time be touched by sufferings and observe the joys of heaven with a tranquil mind. Or "if you polish it" means, as it were, that if you honor and adorn them with the honors of the world, you darken them, because then they have less leisure for contemplation or are of lesser merit. And as active life was symbolized by the eighth, so by the ninth is contemplative life symbolized, which is that of angels, of whom there are nine orders. Some say that it has the color of every stone, whence it also has its name, because "pan"[4] means "every", and it is found in an island of Egypt called Topazon. It symbolizes the saints shining with all colors of virtues.[1]

The tenth is the chrysoprasus, which, while it is of a purple color, is colored at intervals with small golden specks. It signifies those who lead their lives in sufferings, tribulations and labors and eventually end them by martyrdom.

The eleventh, *the hyacinth*, changes with the air. Conspicuous in fair weather, dark in cloudy weather, it symbolizes the wisest teachers who adapt to all natures, manners, ages and intellects, like Paul who said, *"We speak wisdom among the perfect"* (1 Corinthians 2:6), *"I, brethren, could not speak to you, etc."* (1 Corinthians 3:1), *"Who is weak, etc."* (2 Corinthians 11:29), and *"I became all things to all men, that I might save all"* (1 Corinthians 9:22).[1]

The twelfth, *the amethyst*, is purple, with a mix of the colors of the violet and of the rose, shedding some little flames out of itself. The purple color symbolizes the condition of the heavenly kingdom, and the dominion of the society of angels which the saints are to join. The violet symbolizes the humble modesty of the saints with a smell of good works. The rose symbolizes the precious death of the martyrs, who emit flames of love not only between themselves, but also towards their enemies and persecutors. So, the amethyst symbolizes the memory of the heavenly kingdom always in the hearts of the humble, as well as that outstanding virtue, that they pray even for their enemies and care about their salvation, which is the virtue of virtues. The diversity of colors is multiplicity of virtues.[1]

21:20 1 see note 1 to previous verse.] 2 Rusch adds "on the outside".] 3 The name is from Greek χρυσόλιθος (chrysolithos), which means literally "gold-stone", from χρυσός (chrysos), "gold", and λίθος (lithos), "stone".] 4 In Greek.] 5 Codex 24: "dew". The difference between the two words is two letters in the beginning.] 6 In Greek again. ""Prason" means "leek"" not in Codex 24.

Latin 588's poetic version (translated in prose).

O citizens of the heavenly fatherland, sing together for the King of kings, who is the supernal builder of the celestial city, in whose structure is found the following foundation:

The green jasper displays the greenness of faith, which in the more perfect people never completely fades; by the powerful assistance of which one resists the Devil.

The sapphire has an appearance similar to the heavenly throne; it signifies the hearts of the simple who wait with a sure hope, by whose life and manners the most High is delighted.

The chalcedony *has a pale*[1] likeness of fire; it glows reddish in public, gives splendor in cloudy weather; it represents the virtue of the faithful who serve in secret.

The emerald is extremely green, it gives an olive-colored light; it is the most spotless faith open to all good, which could not cease from the work of piety.

The sardonyx is tricolor; it is said to signify the inner man whom humility blackens, in whom chastity whitens; in addition to this honorable sum is also red martyrdom.

The sardius is purple-colored, whose blood-red color shows the glory of the martyrs who agonize in right manner. It is sixth in the list; it *is connected with*[1] the mystery of the cross.

With its color, the chrysolite glows like a furnace; it represents the manners of perfectly wise men who shine with the sacred splendor of the sevenfold grace.

The beryllus is watery, like limpid sun in water; it designates the wishes of the sagacious minds that prefer to live in the exercise of beautiful rest[2].

The topazius is the more precious for being rarer; it is red with a golden *sheen*[1] and an ethereal aspect; it shows the sound function of contemplative life.

The chrysoprasus imitates the purple shell-fish; with a certain mix, it is colored at intervals with small golden specks; this is the perfect love which savageness does not pretend to.

The hyacinth holds the middle place between blue and green; its elegant face changes *like the weather*[1]; it designates the angelic life endowed with discernment.

The amethyst is the foremost, with a violet-colored grace; it emits golden flames and purple sparks; it represents the hearts of the humble who die with Christ.

These precious stones designate men of flesh. The diversity of colors is multiplicity of virtues; whoever blooms with these shall be allowed to be a fellow-citizen.

O pacific Jerusalem, these are your foundations; blessed and closest to God is the soul that *deserves*[1] you! The guardian of

Translation of the stones in Latin 588

The diversities of the twelve stones that the foundations and walls of the city are made of are the diversities of the elect and perfect people in the holy Church, because all the faithful are neither of only one merit nor of only one virtue, but *every one has his proper gift from God*, as the apostle says, *one after this manner, and another after that* (1 Corinthians 7:7); and elsewhere, *to one is given the word of wisdom* (ibid. 12:8), *to another, diverse kinds of tongues* (ibid. 12:10), etc. These diversities and varieties of God's gifts, the Holy Spirit distributes like various colors to every one of his faithful as he wants, faithful by means of whom he every day founds, builds and adorns his city, i.e. the holy Church, as though with some kinds of various stones; and the faithful of God are truly living stones, who shine, built in God's house and laid as Christ's foundation. Whence the apostle Peter calls the faithful « stones » because they are firm and stable in God's faith, and he calls them « living » because they are not senseless[1] but live for God (ref. 1 Peter 2:5).

The first stone is the green jasper: he who has it above him fears no spectres; it signifies those who are green in faith and do not fear the tricks of the Devil, who is *as a roaring lion*, etc. (1 Peter 5:8), and such people resist him.

The second is the sapphire, of an indigo color like the sky when it is cloudless; it signifies those who, while still being on earth, apply themselves to heavenly things and despise earthly ones as though they were not on earth, so that they can say with the apostle, "our conversation is in heaven" (Philippians 3:20).

The third is the chalcedony: as long as it is in a house, it does not glitter; outside it does. It withstands those who want to carve it. When warmed by a sunbeam or the rubbing of fingers, it attracts chaff to itself. It signifies those who hide their goodness, do their good works in secret and do not want to be seen by people, according to that: "when you fast, etc." (Matt. 6:17), "when you do an alms deed, etc." (Matt. 6:2), "when you shall pray, enter into your chamber, etc." (Matt. 6:6), but when a master, bishop or abbot orders them to go out, then does their goodness appear, and they shine willy nilly; and if anyone wants to adulate or praise them, as if they wanted to carve and paint them, they do not accept their praise and vainglory, but harshly withstand; they do as Solomon says, "My son, if sinners shall entice you, consent not to them" (Proverbs 1:10). And when such people are touched by the rays of the true sun, i.e. Christ, or, as it were, touched and revealed by fingers, i.e. the gifts of the Holy Spirit, they attract chaff, i.e. sinners, by the word of their preaching and the example of their goodness, and bring them into association with them.

The fourth is the emerald, which surpasses in greenness grass, tree leaves and all gems. It is produced in Scythia, which is uninhabitable due to cold, where no one lives but griffins, which are beasts and birds: they resemble lions because they have four feet, while by their body, head, feet and other limbs they resemble eagles[2]. That country abounds in gems of this kind, and these griffins guard those gems so that no people can take them but the Arimaspians, who have only one eye; they fight against the griffins for these gems, for the griffins want to take them away from them when they receive them; and it is thanks to the Arimaspians that we have those gems, by which are symbolized those who surpass in greenness of faith the unfaithful, who are always cold due to the love and goodness they do not have. The griffins signify devils who envy faithful men the gem of faith and want to take it away, not

your chariots[3] is forever sleepless.

Grant us, O holy King of the heavenly city, after the course of this fleeting life, society in the upper world; among the hosts of the saints, let us sing you canticles.

1 All the words in italics are parts that are corrupt in Latin 588 (either unreadable or nonsensical), and for which I have followed another, printed, version of the poem. I have chosen not to mention the other differences between the two versions, apart from note 3, because it seemed to me that the other version might be more likely.] 2 The part from "it symbolizes" is in the other ink; two words of it, but not the first, had already been written at the end of the previous line in a nonsensical manner.] 3 The printed version has "of your towers". Similar-looking words.

English poetic adaptation by Cristalle Watson of 588's poem on the precious stones

Dwellers of the holy land,
Make your music, hand in hand;
For the King of Kings unite,
Builder of your city bright --
Who, beneath the realm he's made,
Thus has twelve foundations laid.

1. Jasper first, with verdant sheen,
Holds a faith that's evergreen:
Rooted in the perfect soul,
Never withering, always whole;
For its shielding powers great
Can resist the Devil's hate.

2. Blue sapphire, like the high
Throne of God, the archèd sky,
Shows those hearts, sincere and pure,
Waiting in a hope that's sure;
And their honest lives and ways,
Pleasing to the Highest's gaze.

3. Dull chalcedony, within,
Glows like fire's paler twin.
Ruddy splendor, never proud,
Lightning flash concealed in cloud --
Tell the virtue of all those
Who faithful serve, though no-one knows.

4. Leaf-green emerald, ever-bright,
Floods the air with olive light;
So a faith complete, alive,
Eager for all good to strive,
Cannot fade, nor cease to flower
Forth its works of fruitful power.

5. Onyx now, in triple hue,
Paints the inward life of -- you;
Humble black is deepest placed;
By the purest white embraced;
Last a red ring wraps around:
Martyrdom, with honor crowned.

6. Sardius, your crimson tone
Sings to us a martyr's groan:
Tortured grace that freely bled,
Ransom paid in ruby red --
In your sixth-placed history
Hangs the cross's mystery.

7. Chrysolite, of golden name,

because it would be of use to them, but they want man not to have it. These are rightly called griffins, being like terrestrial beasts; those who go down into hell for their bad merits are, as it were, terrestrial, and those who fly by pride are like birds. Against these fight the one-eyed people, i.e. those who do not walk on two ways and do not have twofold hearts or a twofold will and do not serve two lords, but have one will always and one devotion towards God, and firmly keep faith and defend the gem of faith, which devils, i.e. griffins, want to take away from them, but they overcome them with God's help.

The fifth is the sardonyx: it is three-colored: it is black below, white in the middle, red on the top. It signifies those who endure whips and the pains of passion in their bodies for the name of Christ, and within their minds are white and pure, without pretense or trickery, but yet despise themselves and seem to themselves as if they were black, i.e. as if they were sinners, and say with the prophet David, "I am a worm and not a man"(Psalm 21:7).

The sixth is the sardius, which is unicolor, i.e. blood-colored, and signifies the martyrs who have shed their blood for the love of God, about whom David said, "Precious in the sight, etc." (Psalm 115:15).

The seventh is the chrysolite, which glitters like gold and emits burning sparks out of itself. It signifies those who know and understand the divine Scripture and the wisdom in it, and show to others, both in work and in speech, what they know concerning what is good, and utter, like sparks of good work, good words by which they illuminate and kindle others, and do not hide the talent of their lord (ref. Matt. 25:14 etc.), and do not put their candle under a bushel, but in view, that it may shine to all that are in the house (ref. Matt. 5:15), and do what the Lord told them, «Let your light shine before all, etc. » (Matt. 5:16).

The eighth is the beryllus, which shines like water hit by the sun, and is said to heat the hand of the one who holds it; it signifies people who are intelligent and set apart from the world, etc.[3] Thanks to their caution regarding this world, they are illuminated by heavenly grace and heat those who live with them by the fire and example of good way of life, as the beryllus does with the hand of the one who holds it.

The ninth is the topazius: it is rarely found, and for this reason it is costlier and more precious. It has two colors: one very pure like gold, and the other like the sky when it is cloudless; and it surpasses the brightness of all gems, nor is there anything more beautiful to see; and if someone wants to polish it, they darken it ; if it is left alone, it will be more beautiful. Kings love it more than all gems and riches [...][4] and it signifies those who, after having been tested and cleansed of desires and filth, like pure gold, direct their attention to the brightness of the heavenly fatherland and heavenly life. Those who have this virtue and love this life are brighter than all other men, and the kings themselves admire and glorify them. The Lord praised this life[5] when he spoke to Martha, Mary's sister, « Mary has chosen the best part, etc. » (Luke 10:42).

The tenth is the chrysoprasus, which, while it is of a purple color, is colored at intervals with small golden specks. It signifies those who lead their lives in sufferings, tribulations and labors and eventually end them by martyrdom.

The eleventh is the hyacinth: it changes its color with the face of the sky: if the sky is clear, it shines ; if the sky is dark, it is dark. It signifies those who control themselves in such a way that, although they are wise, perfect and strong, they descend to the level of the unwise, imperfect and weak and make themselves equal and similar to them, so that, according to the kind of

Shoots forth sparks like furnace flame;
Thus bright words and actions rise
From those souls perfected, wise,
Sevenfold of grace, that shine
With a dazzling light divine.

8. Beryl blue, like sun's pure light
Beaming back from waters bright:
See the prayers of minds who know
Intellect's sagacious glow
Nor desire once to cease
From their fairest work of peace.

9. Topaz, precious as it's rare,
Shines once freed from worldly care.
Inward love shines golden-bright,
Lifted face beams Heaven's light:
So the contemplative's eyes,
Ever fixed upon the skies.

10. Chrysoprase, like purple shells,
Tale of humble dying tells.
Mingled colors blur and run,
Flecked with gold like rising sun:
Perfect love, which fiercest hate
Cannot kill, nor imitate.

11. Jacinth -- sky-blue when it's clear --
Dims to green when clouds appear.
Shifting hues, like heaven's face,
Tempered by discretion's grace;
Heed, then, its angelic call --
"All in one, and light to all!"

12. Amethyst, those gems supreme,
Glint with purple's royal gleam,
Blushing violet, golden glow --
Flames of caritas that flow
To their enemies in love;
Die with Christ -- and reign above.

Epilogue:

Thus we see that every stone
Holds a virtue all its own;
Rainbow formed of prismed light,
Telling forth twelve natures bright:
Who displays these merits well
There a citizen can dwell --

Peaceful New Jerusalem,
Founded on each precious gem;
Every soul to pass your gate
Knows God in its blessèd state;
He who guards your holy keep
Slumbers not, nor shall He sleep.

Grant us, O Eternal One,
Once this fleeting life has run,
Fellowship with all who shine
In your highest realms divine;
Mingled in this company
Let us sing our songs to Thee.

21:21 (a)And (b)the twelve gates: there are twelve pearls, one to every one: and (c)every gate was of one several pearl. And (d)(e)the street* of the city (f)pure gold, as it were transparent glass.

listeners, they can speak either wisely, or humbly if they are talking to less wise and weak people, like Paul did, who changed according to the quality of those he was talking to, saying, « We speak wisdom among the perfect »(1 Corinthians 2:6), and to less wise people he said, « I could not speak to you as unto spiritual, but as unto carnal ; I gave you milk to drink, not meat » (ibid. 3:1-2). He devoted himself to everyone in such a way that he was all things to all men, as he says, « I became all things to all men, that I might gain them to God » (ibid. 9:22).

The twelfth is the amethyst: it is red like a rose, shedding some little flames out of itself. It signifies those who endure for God the torments of passion. They emit, as it were, sparks of love when they pray for those who kill them, and are more grieved at the sin those people commit than at the pain they themselves endure. And this stone is placed last in the city of God for this is the greatest virtue, above which there is none : to pray for one's enemies ; and we find only a few people who do this, but yet two in the Old Law : Moses and Samuel, and two in the New : Christ and the blessed Stephen. And it is with these twelve stones, i.e. the twelve virtues of the elect, that the city of God is built, i.e. the heavenly Jerusalem in which God dwells and reigns, and in which no other stone shall be placed, i.e. which no other man shall enter, but those who have these virtues which these stones designate.

1 "Senseless" doubtful reading, but likely.] 2 This is not quite accurate, since griffins are supposed to have the head and wings of an eagle and the body of a lion, but my translation is what is written in the manuscript.] 3 I was unable to find what this is making reference to.] 4 Here are a few words that I cannot make head or tail of.] 5 Or « ... the kings themselves admire them and glorify this life. The Lord praised it when... ». Either interpretation is possible due to lack of punctuation in the Latin, which would be the only means to make it clear what belonged with what in the sentence as it stands.

And every gate was of one several pearl. I said that there were twelve gates, and since those twelve gates are so, i.e. bringing people in to faith from the four parts of the world[1], through[2] every one of them, i.e. through the teaching of every one of them, there are pearls; i.e. their

a. As if here were saying, "For there to be gates, there had to be pearls".
b. Since there are...*
c. Because they are similarly shining with virtues.*
d. I.e. married people.*
e. I.e. simple people who use the world more freely.
f. Full of wisdom or love*, clean from criminal stain.*

imitators who are called to faith in the Trinity from whatever part of the world, are shining with virtues.

Transparent glass. I.e. hiding no filth in themselves; or because the wicked can perceive their own wickedness in the works of those people as in a mirror.

21:21 In the verse: *The three books have "streets".] (b) *Not in Latin 588.] (c) *Codex 24: "Because the prophets themselves are also similarly shining with virtues".] (d) *Not in Latin 588.] (f) *Codex 24 and Rusch have "brightness" instead of "love". The Latin words differ only in one letter.] 1 Codex 24 and Rusch: "the prophets bringing people in to faith from the four parts of the world".] 2 The same Latin word that is translated as "to" in the verse, but requires the translation "through" (its primary meaning) in the context of the gloss.

21:22 *(a)*And temple I saw not therein, for our Lord the God Omnipotent is the (b)temple thereof, and *(c)*the Lamb.

a. It is a place of prayer and offering, and these things will have no place there.
b. I.e. total rest.*
c. Is similarly the temple thereof.*

21:22 (b) *Perhaps this gloss was inspired by the word "omnipotent" — *omnipotens* in Latin, "almighty" — since it reads in Latin *omnimoda requies*, omni- meaning literally "all".] (c) *Not in Latin 588.

21:23 *(a)*And the city needs not *(b)*sun nor *(c)*moon, *(d)*to shine in it. For *(e)*the glory of God has illuminated* it, and *(f)*the Lamb is *(g)*the lamp thereof.

It *needs not sun nor moon*, i.e. greater or lesser preachers.[1]

a. Here it needs* sun and moon for God's service; not there, for God will illuminate them fully.
b. The light of faith.*
c. Acquired knowledge.*
d. For this purpose.*
e. I.e. the Trinity.
f. I.e. his humanity to the illumination of others*.
g. I.e. containing light, i.e. divinity.

21:23 In the verse: *The three books have "will illuminate".] (a) *Codex 24 and Rusch: "they need".] (b) *Only in Rusch.] (c) *Only in Rusch.] (d) *Only in Rusch.] (f) *Rusch has the part "to the illumination of others" to "shall walk" in the next verse.] 1 Not in Latin 588.

21:24 *(a)*And *(b)*the Gentiles shall walk in the light of it*: and *(c)*the kings of the earth shall bring their *(d)*glory and *(e)*honor *(f)*into it**.

In the light. I.e. in the hope of his[1] light, or through the rays of the knowledge of him[1,2].

a. And that light will be so great in the future that until the end of the world the Gentiles shall walk, i.e. move forward from good to better.
b. The lesser people and the inferiors.*
c. The greater ones.*
d. I.e. the people they have won, for whom they shall be crowned.
e. I.e. purity of conscience.
f. In order to have it.

And the kings. I.e. those greater ones who control their earthliness[3].

Shall bring. Similarly to the conquerors who bring booty into their cities.[4]

21:24 In the verse: *Latin 588: "in your light". **Latin 588: "into the way".] (b) *Only in Rusch.] (c) *Only in Rusch.] 1 The translations "its" and "of it" are also possible, because the Latin word used here does not change with gender; it is difficult for me to tell for sure whether the glossator understood it as "of the city" or "of God", though the latter may seem a little more plausible. See the first note on the verse.] 2 Codex 24 and Rusch: "In the hope of this light, or through the light, or through the rays of the knowledge of him (or "of it")".] 3 Codex 24 and Rusch add: "and that of others".] 4 Codex 24 and Rusch have this gloss to "they shall bring the glory and honor of nations into it" in verse 26. Codex 24 has "those who..." instead of "the conquerors who...".

21:25 [a]And [b]the gates thereof shall not be shut by day*: for there shall be no night [c]there.

a. This about the future. In the present, preaching is sometimes taken away so that thieves should not enter and tread it underfoot* while there is night, i.e. an occasion for treacherous attack; but since there it will be perpetual day, all fear will be dispelled.
b. The understanding and disposition of mind to see and praise God.*
c. I.e. in that same future.*

21:25 In the verse: *Rusch has "by night" instead of "by day", and there is a gloss above it saying "by any adversity". Codex 24 has "by night or day", but "night or" has been crossed through.] (a) *Codex 24: "and hide it". Similar Latin words.] (b) *Only in Rusch.] (c) *Codex 24 and Rusch have this to "shall bring" in the next verse.

21:26 And [a]they shall bring the [b]glory and [c]honor of nations into it.

a. I.e. they shall bring the glorified nations before God the Father.
b. I.e. the people they have won, for whom they shall be crowned.*
c. I.e. the purity of the consciences of nations.

21:26 (b) *Same as interlinear (d) of verse 24. Repeated in this place only in Codex 24.

21:27 There shall not enter into it any [a]polluted thing, nor that [b]does [c]abomination [d][e]and makes lie, but they that are written in the book of life of the Lamb.

a. Polluted with others* through consent.**
b. For what concerns sin in work.*
c. I.e. something criminal.
d. He makes lie who takes pleasure in inventing lies.
e. Or for what concerns sin of the mouth.*

Having said the honorableness of the city, so that no false brother should imagine he belongs to one of these ranks, he defines who shall enter and who shall not.

But they that are written. As if he were saying, "Why enumerate in detail? No one shall enter but they...".

In the book. I.e. in the presence of the divinity, or in the imitation of the life of the Lamb, who offered in himself an example of humanity, through which it will be given.[1]

21:27 (a) *The Latin word used in the verse for "polluted" is *coinquinatum*, compounded of *inquinatum*, "polluted", and the prefix *co(n)-*, whose basic meaning is "together", although it also sometimes does nothing else but intensify the meaning of a verb. The glossator based his interpretation on its first basic meaning. **Rusch adds: "for what concerns sin of the heart".] (b) *Only in Rusch.] (e) *Only in Rusch.] 1 In Codex 24 and Rusch, this gloss is split in two: one marginal gloss saying "In the presence of the divinity, or in the imitation of the life of the Lamb, who offered us an example in himslef" and an interlinear above "of life", saying "I.e. of humanity, through which it will be given". In both of those books, the marginal gloss is placed as if it referred to the next verse, but it seems better to belong in the place it is in in Latin 588. The thing that "will be given" is probably life.

CHAPTER 22

22:1 AND he showed me ^{(a)(b)}a river ^(c)of living water*, clear ^(d)as ^(e)crystal, proceeding ^{(f)(g)}from the seat of God and of the Lamb.

a. I.e. abundant water, sc. eternal happiness, which, in the appearance of water, is signified to have reached this through the cleansing of baptism.*
b. Eternal happiness.*
c. Because it refreshes you after labor and vivifies you eternally.*
d. Because they will shine eternally.
e. Because of the transparency of their hearts and bodies.*
f. I.e. from those in whom God will principally sit, because he is in them most, and the lesser ones will be crowned through their teaching.
g. From the greater ones, who are the seat of God, to the lesser ones.*

After showing the layout of the city, its dignity, and its walls and foundations, he describes the refection God grants to the city, in the present and especially in the future.

22:1 In the verse: *Codex 24 has only "of water"; Rusch has "of the water of life".] (a) *Codex 24 and Rusch: "That is, flowing water, i.e. eternal happiness. In the appearance of water, it is signified that it has reached this through the cleansing of baptism".] (b) *Only in Rusch.] (c) *Only in Rusch.] (e) *Only in Rusch.] (g) *Not in Latin 588.

22:2 ^(a)In the midst of the street thereof, and ^(b)on both sides of the river, ^{(c)(d)}the tree of life*, yielding ^{(e)(f)(g)}twelve fruits, rendering his ^(h)fruit every month, and ⁽ⁱ⁾the leaves of the tree ^(j)for the curing of the Gentiles.

a. I.e. in the common of those who have walked on a broader way.*
b. On the way and in the country of happiness.*
c. Christ.*
d. Because if he himself gives refection, he also gives people who must prepare those to whom he will render it.*
e. I.e. the prophets and apostles bearing fruit in faith in the Trinity throughout the four parts of the world, in every age or continually.
f. The reward of immortality.*
g. Eternally.*
h. I.e. refection.
i. I.e. Christ's precepts, which cover* and adorn the fruits.
j. If they are fulfilled.

On both sides of the river, the tree. On this side of the river, i.e. in this life, we have the tree of life, i.e. the body and blood of Christ, with which we nourish ourselves. Across the river, i.e. in the future, we shall have him present in person. Or by "on this side of the river", let us understand the time before baptism, by "across", the one after baptism, so as to denote the faithful saved by Christ both in the old and in the new law. This was prefigured[1] by Moses, who led the children of Israel all the way to the river Jordan, and by Jesus son of Nave, who led them from the river Jordan into the Promised Land (see Joshua 1:2).

The tree of life, yielding twelve fruits. Another version has "the tree of life, rendering its fruit through the twelve months", i.e. through the twelve apostles, because Christ is the day or the year, and the apostles are the hours or the months, as it is said there: *"Are there not twelve hours of the day?"* (John 11:9). As if he were saying: You are placed under my authority, and I have to take care, not you. There are also other trees there that render their fruit, i.e. the saints who render[2] rewards to those placed under their authority according to their merits.

And the leaves. As if he were saying: As to the fact that Christ will render fruit, this will be so in such a way that the apostles and others after them will scatter the leaves of that same Christ.

22:2 In the verse: *"Of life" is missing in Latin 588.] (a) *Codex 24 has, above "street": "of those who walk on a broader way".] (b) *Only in Rusch.] (c) *Only in Rusch.] (d) *Codex 24 and Rusch: "As if he were saying: "He himself gives refection, and he also gives people who must prepare those to whom he will render it", and this is what is meant by "yielding twelve fruits"".] (f) *Only in Rusch.] (g) *Only in Rusch.] (i) *Codex 24: "direct". On the first letter of the word differs.] 1 Codex 24 and Rusch: "signified".] 2 Codex 24 and Rusch: "will render".

22:3 And ^(a)no ^(b)curse shall be anymore: and ^(c)the seat of God and of the Lamb shall be in it, and his ^(d)servants ^(e)shall serve him.

a. I.e. removal of grace shall not happen anymore.
b. Sin for which curse is deserved.*
c. I.e. the God Trinity and the man Christ will rest eternally in them.
d. Not of fear but of love.
e. Shall disquiet him in no way.

22:3 (b) *Only in Rusch.

22:4 And (a)***they shall see his face: and*** (b)***his name*** (c)***in their foreheads.***

    a.   Not in a dark manner as now but as it is (ref. 1 Corinthians 13:12).
    b.   They shall be called gods*.
    c.   I.e. where it is openly visible, just as they have confessed him openly.

22:4 (b) *Codex 24 and Rusch add: "and lambs".

22:5 And (a)***night shall be no more: and they shall not need*** (b)***the light of lamp, nor the light*** (c)***of the sun, because*** (d)***our Lord God does illuminate* them, and they shall*** (e)***reign forever and ever.***

    a.   I.e. any ignorance.
    b.   I.e. the teaching of the old law or of an ordinary preacher.
    c.   I.e. of the new law or of a topmost preacher.*
    d.   Which is incompatible with needing the light of others.
    e.   With God.

22:5 In the verse: *The three books have "will illuminate".] (c) *Only in Latin 588.

22:6 And (a)***he said to me,*** (b)***These words are*** (c)***most faithful and*** (d)***true.*** (e)***And our Lord the God of the spirits of the prophets, sent*** (f)***his angel to show his*** (g)(h)***servants those things which*** (i)***must be done quickly.***

    a.   The same angel who showed all the rest.
    b.   I.e. all the things that are shown by the words and images.*
    c.   I.e. fit for one to have faith in.*
    d.   Sc. because they will be fulfilled.
    e.   As if he were saying, "You ought well to believe, because he who has in his power the gifts of the Holy Spirit through which the prophets spoke..."
    f.   I.e. me.*
    g.   Not kings, not philosophers.
    h.   Not by fear.*
    i.   Because they cannot remain unfulfilled.

Just as he put a recommendation of the vision in the beginning, so does he also put one now in the end.[1]

22:6 (b) *Codex 24 and Rusch: "I.e. all the things that he showed me by words and images".] (c) *Not in Latin 588.] (f) *Only in Latin 588.] (g) *In Latin 588, this is above "must be done".] 1 Not in Latin 588.

22:7 And (a)***behold I come quickly.*** (b)***Blessed is he that*** (c)***keeps the words of the prophecy of this book.***

    a.   I.e. they will really be done quickly because he himself says so.
    b.   He also said this.*
    c.   I.e. fulfills in deed.

22:7 Codex 24: "For he said this: Blessed, etc.".

22:8 And (a)(b)**I John which* have** (c)**heard, and** (d)**seen these things. And after I had heard and seen, I** (e)**fell down to adore before the feet of the angel** (f)**which showed me these things:**

a. Who am not wont to announce you anything false.
b. Am.*
c. Sc. the words or voices*.
d. The images.*
e. I.e. humbled myself.
f. As if he were saying, "For this reason".

And I John. As the angel recommends the vision to John, so does John recommend it to his disciples, as if he were saying: It is not for me that this admonition was given[1], but so that you may believe me.

22:8 In the verse: *"Which" not in Codex 24 and Rusch.] (b) *Only in 588.] (c) *"Or voices" only in Latin 588. The gloss is not at all in Codex 24.] (d) *Not in Codex 24.] 1 Codex 24 and Rusch: "that this announcement was made to me".

22:9 and (a)**he said to me,** (b)**See** (c)**you do not, for I am your** (d)**fellow-servant, and of your brethren** (e)**the prophets*, and of** (f)**them that keep the words of this book. Adore God.**

a. These things.*
b. Beware.*
c. Because of human nature exalted in Christ.*
d. Because we are the servants of one and the same God.*
e. I.e. those who preach.
f. I.e. those who obey the preachings.

Here he gives us to understand that we must hold him in reverence for these things, but not, however, adore him, but adore God, and attain the purification of angels through observance of the words of the book.

And of your brethren the prophets, etc. Those who have the grace of interpreting, like Augustine, Jerome, Ambrose and Gregory, are not to be thought strangers to the gift of prophecy.[1]

22:9 In the verse: *Latin 588: "of your brethren and of the prophets".] (a) *Only in Latin 588. The only way I can perhaps find a point to this gloss is by supposing that, at some point, the beginning of this verse was taken as belonging to the previous one: "which showed me these things, and said (them) to me"; it is not altogether impossible to interpret it like this if you look at the Latin without punctuation, although "And he said to me, See you do not" is much more likely, and Latin 588's punctuation does not even suggest the former interpretation...] (b) *Only in Rusch.] (c) *Only in Rusch.] (d) *Only in Rusch.] 1 Not in Latin 588.

22:10 And he said to me, (a)**Seal not the words of the prophecy of this book: for** (b)**the time is near.**

a. I.e. do not seal them, but make them known to everyone.
b. Within which brethren* should be acquired.

Because one might have objected that it was wrong to prophesy to the wicked since they were to be quite severely punished[1], he was told not to stop for that, because it is right.

22:10 (b) *Codex 24: "fruit".] 1 Or perhaps "since they were to be more severely punished as a result".

22:11 (a)**He that hurts, let him hurt** (b)**yet: and he that is** (c)**in filth,** (d)**let him be filthy yet: and** (e)**he that is just, let him be justified yet: and let the** (f)**holy** (g)**be sanctified yet.**

a. Let the wicked inflict on you* what they inflict on you*.
b. I.e. after the manifestation of the book.*
c. I.e. in his own wickedness.
d. The mood is permissive, not imperative, by the just judgment of God.*
e. I.e. let him who bestows good on others bestow it more lavishly.
f. In himself.
g. Or "do justice" in another version.*

He that is in filth. Another version has "he that is in filth, let him be filthy yet, and let the just one be justified yet".[1]

22:11 (a) *Codex 24 and Rusch: "on the good".] (b) *Not in Latin 588.] (d) *Only in Rusch.] (g) *Not in Latin 588. This should probably have been above "be justified yet", as the Greek version I consulted has there "let the just one (or less literally "he that is just") do justice yet".] 1 Not in Latin 588.

22:12 [a]*Behold I come quickly, and my reward is with me,* [b]*to render to every man* [c]*according to his works,*

    a.   It is really a short time, because...
    b.   Namely.*
    c.   More to one, less to another.

22:12 (b) *Not in Latin 588.

22:13 [a]*I am* [b]*Alpha and Omega,* [c]*the first and the last,* [d]*the beginning and* [e]*the end.*

    a.   And I shall be able to do so, because I, etc.*
    b.   I.e. of all things.
    c.   Of all creatures.*
    d.   He from whom all things began.
    e.   He in whom all things are finished.*

22:13 (a) *Latin 588 has one gloss saying "because" at the very beginning of the verse, and a second one with the part "and I shall be able to do so" just next to it. It could be either simply that the glossator first forgot to write what was supposed to be the first part ("And I shall be able, etc.") and then added it afterwards, or (perhaps less likely) that his interpretation was "I am (and shall be able to make) Alpha and Omega". The same Latin verb can mean "to do" or "to make", and "so" is not literally expressed in the Latin.] (c) *Codex 24 and Rusch have (b) to "the first" and (c) to "the last".] *Latin 588 just has "He in whom". Understand "he in whom (the end is)".

22:14 Blessed are they that wash [a]*their stoles*:* [b][c]*that their power may be in the tree of life, and they may enter* [d]*by the gates into the city**.*

    a.   I.e. their bodies and souls.*
    b.   I mean they that wash in such a way that...*
    c.   I.e. that they may be able to eat of the tree of life.
    d.   I.e. by the faith of the teachers.

Since he had said, "Let him that hurts hurt, let him that is filthy be filthy", so that no wicked man should say, "Since I am wicked, why would I repent?", he says, "Not only those who receive greater perfection[1] are blessed, but also those who stained their stoles that they received in baptism, if yet they have washed them and regret that they have sinned".

22:14 In the verse: *Codex 24 and Rusch add "in the blood of the Lamb". **Latin 588: "into the holy city".] (a) *Only in Latin 588.] (b) *Latin 588 has "I mean they that wash in such a way" above "blessed".] 1 Codex 24 and Rusch: "persecution".

22:15 [a]*Without are* [b][c]*dogs and* [d]*sorcerers, and* [e]*the unchaste, and murderers, and servers of idols, and everyone that* [f]*loves and* [g]*makes a lie.*

    a.   Sc. but.
    b.   These are wretched and those are blessed.*
    c.   I.e. the barking ones.
    d.   I.e. the unclean.
    e.   Literally.*
    f.   By listening to it.
    g.   I.e. invents.

22:15 (b) *Not in Latin 588.] Rusch has "I.e. the barking and unclean" above "dogs", and "literally" above "sorcerers" (the Latin word here used for this, *venefici*, literally means "poison-making"). Codex 24 also has these in two glosses as Rusch, but seeing the way they are placed, there is still a possibility for "I.e. barking and unclean" to refer to "dogs and sorcerers" and "literally" to "unchaste" (the Latin word, *impudici*, means more or less literally "shameless", although it is used much more commonly in the sense "unchaste", "lewd") because they are placed just above these words respectively. However, there is no absolute certainty, for Codex 24 is often a bit inexact in its placement of glosses, and it is not rare for a gloss referring to a word not to be placed right above it.

22:16 *(a)I Jesus have sent my angel, to testify to you these things in the churches. (b)I am the (c)root and (d)stock of David, the (e)(f)bright and morning star.*

a. And I should be believed in this, because...*
b. And I should be believed*, because...
c. Support.
d. Begotten of him.*
e. I.e. great.*
f. I.e. illuminating the night of this world.*

He has recommended the book through the angel and through his own dignity; now he does also through the authority of Christ himself, as if he were saying: Let all those who hear know that I Jesus have sent...

The bright and morning star. I.e. the great brightness announcing the day[1], i.e. the future happiness through my resurrection, which happened in the morning.

22:16 (a) *Not in Latin 588.] (b) *Codex 24 and Rusch add "in this".] (d) *Codex 24: "And yet begotten of him"; Rusch: "While I was also begotten of him".] (e) *Only in Latin 588.] (f) *Not in Latin 588.] 1 Latin 588: "And yet the brightness announcing the day"; Codex 24: "I.e. the great love announcing the day" — the Latin words corresponding to "brightness" and "love" differ only in one letter.

22:17 *And (a)(b)the Spirit and (c)the Bride say, (d)Come. And he that (e)hears, let him (f)say, (g)Come*. (h)And he that (i)thirsts**, let him (j)come: (k)and he that will, let him (l)take the water of life (m)gratis.*

a. I.e. the Trinity, which is called Spirit for the excellence of its purity.
b. Or "the Bridegroom".
c. I.e. the faithful.*
d. To the knowledge of the book.*
e. I.e. understands.*
f. To the others.*
g. To the knowledge of the things that are in this book.*
h. And not just* anyone, but let him only who thirsts**, i.e. desires to believe, come.
i. Desires to believe in Christ.*
j. Through true faith.*
k. And it is no hard work, because will alone suffices.
l. By preparing himself and willing.*
m. Without price of merits.

And the Spirit and the Bride. Here he even adds the testimony of the Trinity and of the faithful, as if he were saying: You must accept it, because the Spirit and the Bride, etc.

22:17 In the verse: *Latin 588: "let him say: He will come". **Codex 24: "knows" corrected to "thirsts" in the other ink. The two words differ in two letters.] (c) *Only in Latin 588.] (d) *In Codex 24, "of the book" was struck through and replaced by "of the Trinity", in the other ink.] (e) *Not in Codex 24. Rusch has "understands the book".] (f) *Not in Codex 24.] (g) *Only in Rusch.] (h) *Codex 24 and Rusch: "however" instead of "just". Very similar words when abbreviated. **Codex 24: "knows".] (i) *Only in Rusch.] (j) *Only in Rusch.] (l) *Only in Rusch.

22:18 *For (a)I testify to everyone hearing the words of the prophecy of this book, (b)If any man shall (c)add to these things, God shall add upon him (d)the plagues written in this book.*

a. As if he were saying, "Because the angel has testified to me, similarly...".
b. This is what I testify.*
c. In order to support error by that means.*
d. Above about the vials and the trumpets.*

After having put a recommendation by himself, by the angel, by Christ, by the Trinity, and by the faithful, since he knew that there were some people in Asia who would add or remove something in order to support their errors, he adds an excommunication.

22:18 (b) *Not in Latin 588.] (c) *Not in Latin 588.] (d) *Not in Latin 588.

22:19 And if any man shall diminish of the words of the book of this prophecy: God shall take away his part ^(a)out of the book of life, and out of the holy city, and of these things that be written in this book.

a.   Or "out of the tree".*

22:19 (a) *Latin 588 has "the tree" instead of "the book" in the verse, and no gloss.

22:20 ^(a)Says he that gives testimony of these things. ^{(b)(c)}Yes I come quickly: ^(d)Amen. ^{(e)(f)(g)}Come Lord Jesus.

a.   As if he were saying, "I excommunicate, and Christ excommunicates with me".*
b.   Beware, because I come.*
c.   As if he were saying, "All these things are true, and he that changes them is excommunicated".
d.   Turning to God.*
e.   The apostle's confirmation to Christ's words.*
f.   To reward.*
g.   Come, Lord, and do not delay.*

22:20 (a) *Instead of this, Codex 24 and Rusch have "As if he were saying, "of the excommunication"", referring to "testimony".] (b) *Not in Latin 588.] (d) *Not in Latin 588.] (e) *Codex 24 has this gloss to "Amen" and Rusch to "the grace of our Lord" in the next verse. To me, both Latin 588's and Codex 24's interpretations can make sense, but that of Rusch, hardly.] (f) *Not in Latin 588.] (g) *Not in Latin 588.

22:21 ^(a)The grace of our Lord Jesus Christ be with you all. Amen.

John's vision ends: it will last in the years.
John's vision ends but it will remain for the years.[1]

a.   Just as he started with grace above, so does he conclude.*

22:21 (a) *Only in Rusch.] 1 Only in Latin 588.

Bibliography

Allen, William, "Holy Bible faithfully translated into English: out of the authentical Latin, diligently conferred with the Hebrew, Greek, and other editions in divers languages: Vol. 2 Rheims New Testament (1582), Printed by John Cousturier, 1635.

Frans van Liere, 'An Introduction to the Medieval Bible,' Cambridge University Press, Mar 31, 2014 p. 155.

Lobrichon, Guy, "Une nouveaute: les gloses de la Bible", in Le Moyen Age et la Bible, ed. P. Riche and G. Lobrichon, Bible de tous les temps 4 (Paris 1984), p. 109.

Matter, Ann, 'The Reception of the Church Fathers in the West, From the Carolingians to the Maurists; Article: The Church Fathers and the Glossa Ordinaria,' BRILL, Nov 30, 1996. p. 85

Smith, Lesley, 'Medieval Exegesis in Translation: Commentaries on the Book of Ruth,' TEAMS (the Consortium for the Teaching of the Middle Ages), 1996, p. xiv.

Smith, Lesley, 'The Glossa Ordinaria: The Making of a Medieval Bible Commentary'. BRILL, 2009. p.26, 32.

www.ingramcontent.com/pod-product-compliance
Lightning Source LLC
LaVergne TN
LVHW081333060426
835513LV00014B/1270